Sources of Power

Sources of Power

How People Make Decisions

20th Anniversary Edition

Gary Klein

The MIT Press
Cambridge, Massachusetts
London, England

First MIT Press paperback edition, 1999

This book was set in Sabon LT Std by Toppan Best-set Premedia Limited. Printed and bound in the United States of America.

Printed and bound in the United States of America.

Library of Congress Cataloging-in-Publication Data

Names: Klein, Gary A., author.
Title: Sources of power : how people make decisions / Gary Klein.
Description: 20th Anniversary Edition. | Cambridge, MA : MIT Press, [2017] |
    Revised edition of the author's Sources of power, c1998. | Includes
    bibliographical references and index.
Identifiers: LCCN 2017006485 | ISBN 9780262534291 (pbk. : alk. paper)
Subjects: LCSH: Decision making.
Classification: LCC HD30.23 .K456 2017 | DDC 658.4/03--dc23 LC record available at
https://lccn.loc.gov/2017006485

10   9   8   7   6   5   4   3   2   1

For

Helen Gail

Devorah

Rebecca

Contents

Examples

Figures

Tables

Acknowledgments

I have been fortunate in working with good people on good projects. I thank the friends and colleagues who helped me shape the content of this book. In a class by himself is Buzz Reed, the chief executive officer of my company. He had the patience to scrutinize several drafts, searching for inconsistencies, weak arguments, and ways of improving the overall quality of the chapters. He also provided important encouragement for me throughout the writing process, including his support for a sabbatical in Jerusalem, where I wrote the first draft of the manuscript.

Barbara Law deserves special thanks for her careful editing of each draft. She worked at both the microlevel to make sure the details were accurate and the macrolevel to prevent implications of text changes in one place from contradicting statements made elsewhere. Mary Alexander showed great patience in weaving together edits and modifications in producing one draft after another.

A number of people helped review and improve the technical content. I appreciate the feedback I received from Rebecca Pliske, Julia Pounds, Lee Beach, Jens Rasmussen, Mike Doherty, Caroline Zsambok, Beth Crandall, Marvin Thordsen, Steve Wolf, Leon Segal, Stuart Dreyfus, Bill Irving, and Dave Klinger.

I am also thankful for the help in editing provided by Devorah Klein, Rebecca Klein, Karen Getchell-Reiter, Diane Chiddester, Ken Clark, Michael Ames, Paula John, and Rose Olszewski. Debbie Goessl, Teresa Laney, Tom Scruggs, Betsy Knight, Jason Chrenka, and Sharon Murray also helped with manuscript production.

I must also acknowledge the impact of Hubert Dreyfus on the naturalistic decision making approach to research that I have taken. In 1976 I read Dreyfus's book *What Computers Can't Do* and realized that his critique of the Artificial Intelligence position was also a critique of the information-processing account of cognition and expertise. My decision to start a research company in 1978 was largely stimulated by my desire to work out the implications of his views. I have benefited from his ideas and friendship for over twenty years.

In addition, I appreciate all the contract monitors who funded the research projects described in this book and helped drive the different aspects of the framework. Those deserving special mention are Judith Orasanu, Michael Drillings, Michael Kaplan, Milt Katz, Jeff Grossman, Dennis Leedom, Owen Jacobs, Ken Boff, Steve Snyder, Ed King, Susan Ede, Ellen Martz, Dave Artman, Paul Van Riper, Bill Vaughan, Gerry Malecki, Mike McFarren, Marie Gomes, Josephine Randel, Steve LeClair, Ray Perez, Angelo Mirabella, Jack Thorpe, Jim Banks, Stan Halpin, Jon Fallesen, Rex Michel, Ed Salas, Jan Cannon-Bowers, Ev Palmer, George Brander, Larry Miller, Hugh Wood, Carol Bouma, Bob Eggleston, John Lemmer, Fumiya Tanabe, and Ron Lofaro.

Finally, I would like to thank my wife Helen for all the usual reasons, and for some unusual ones as well.

Gary Klein
gary@macrocognition.com
http://www.gary-klein.com

Introduction

An anniversary edition offers an opportunity to reflect on how a book came into being and the impact it has made.

I did not expect *Sources of Power: How People Make Decisions* to be deemed successful enough for the MIT Press to publish a 20th anniversary edition. Yet MIT Press editors Amy Brand and Phil Laughlin tell me that *Sources of Power* regularly appears on the MIT Press's list of best sellers even after two decades, and that it still sells between 1,500 and 2,000 copies a year. Since its publication, the book has sold over 50,000 copies and has been translated into six languages. A number of people have described the book as a classic, required reading for anyone who wants to study—or better understand—decision making. Twenty years later, it is worth explaining how I came to write the book and the impact it has made.

How *Sources of Power* Came to Be Written

I wasn't part of the decision research community and I never took a single course in decision making in graduate school. Maybe that worked to my advantage. My specialty was how to develop expertise, a real problem for the research team I belonged to in 1974 as we set guidelines for Air Force flight simulators. After the Arab oil embargo, jet fuel had become much more expensive and pilots had to do more training in simulators. Our team searched for ways to help them.

Thus, when I started to investigate decision making in the early 1980s, my perspective was on developing expertise—not on calculating probabilities or determining which of several options was optimal.

I had left my job with the Air Force in 1978 to start my research and development company, Klein Associates, and to conduct studies of decision making. Starting in 1985, my colleagues and I published descriptions of the recognition-primed decision (RPD) model which is described in detail in *Sources of Power*. Our research method was to study critical incidents in which people made difficult decisions under time pressure and uncertainty. The incidents were stories; many of them seemed exciting, at least to us. We never had a chance to tell these stories, however, because articles in professional journals have to be short and their format discourages stories. The only way to present these stories would be in a book, but who had the time to write a book?

Sources of Power got started because of a broken ankle. In 1992, my wife Helen took a six-month sabbatical in Jerusalem to continue her research on cultural differences in cognition. I accompanied her along with our younger daughter, who enrolled in high school. I didn't have any consulting work lined up, but I didn't mind because I was busy visiting friends and relatives. I also stayed in shape by running. It seemed suicidal to run on the roads so I used a path along a ravine next to our apartment. It wasn't a proper running path—it was pretty rocky, and one morning I judged that it was just a matter of time until I sprained an ankle. Prophetically, I did just that about ten minutes later, breaking a bone in my ankle. Somehow I limped back to the apartment. I was pretty well immobilized and would be stuck in the apartment for the next month, after which I was scheduled to fly back to the United States for some lectures.

It seemed like a good time to work on that book idea. I had a 30-day window to churn out a first draft. I had a laptop computer with me (although I had never turned it on until then). I spent a few days outlining the book, mapping out the chapters, deciding which stories went into which chapters.

And then I started. I would read over my notes for the next day's quota before I went to sleep, and then as soon as I woke up I'd be at it, at least six pages a day, sometimes ten or more, finishing by late afternoon, and then in the evening reviewing the topics for the following day. That's how I wrote about 250 pages—most of the first draft—in a month.

After I returned to the United States with the draft manuscript, Buzz Reed, the CEO of Klein Associates, marshaled the resources of our company to edit it, track down references, fact check it, set aside my time for rewrites, and produce it. Five years and many drafts later, I submitted the manuscript to the MIT Press. It was published in 1998.

What Happened after *Sources of Power* Was Published?

Thanks to the MIT Press marketing director, the book was reviewed in several different outlets, including *Nature*. I think what attracted readers was that the book described a new model of decision making. The RPD model was different from the existing accounts, focusing on how we use prior experience. It explained the mystery of how people were able to make tough decisions under time pressure and uncertainty. Previous research studies had usually ignored expertise and eliminated its influence. The RPD model demystified intuition.

All of these features made the RPD story fairly compelling. After one of our researchers wrote Tom Petzinger, the *Wall Street Journal* columnist featured *Sources of Power* in two columns, bringing it widespread attention. Then Malcolm Gladwell gave the book some prominence in *Blink*, which came out in 2005.

I think what is happening now is that each new citation the book receives keeps the momentum going, either bringing it to the attention of readers who haven't heard of it, or encouraging readers who have heard of it to finally get a copy. Google Scholar finds more than 3,000 citations to *Sources of Power* from a wide range of professional journals including *The Bulletin of the American Meteorological Society*, *Journal of Sport and Exercise*, *Personnel Journal*, *Journal of Marketing Research*, *Review of Policy Research*, *Journal of Nursing*, *Journal of Macromarketing, and Computer Methods and Programs in Biomedicine.*

Sources of Power has reached a diverse audience. My colleagues and I continually hear from readers in a variety of fields working on topics such as railway safety, special operations, and avalanche avoidance decision making. We also hear about how training departments are replacing old models of decision making with the RPD model in different professional fields. Because of all the interest in applying the RPD model to training, several colleagues and I designed a ShadowBox® training program to foster effective decision making. We have been using it with child protective services caseworkers, petrochemical plant operators, law enforcement training developers, and military units.

The success of *Sources of Power* created lots of different kinds of opportunities, including very enjoyable collaborations with the Nobel prize winner Daniel Kahneman and the chance to serve on a team redesigning the White House Situation Room so that it could support more effective decision making.

The book described a different way of conducting research, a naturalistic decision-making (NDM) approach that investigated experienced decision makers performing realistic tasks, rather than novices performing artificial tasks in a laboratory. Researchers have subsequently applied this naturalistic strategy to other processes besides decision making—to sensemaking, problem detection and planning. Now there are hundreds of researchers around the world engaging in naturalistic decision-making projects and participating in regular meetings in the U.S. and in Europe.

Inevitably, the success of *Sources of Power* also encouraged caricatures and oversimplifications. One of the most common, and most annoying, is that the RPD model is just about using intuition and gut instinct, as opposed to more systematic decision strategies. Actually, the RPD model posits a two-stage process, starting with intuition, as decision makers recognize how they need to respond, followed by deliberate evaluation as they mentally simulate a possible response to see if it will work. A blend of intuition and analysis, not just gut feelings.

In reflecting on the impression that *Sources of Power* has made, I am struck by the primacy of stories over data. Certainly, my colleagues and I had to collect data to make a convincing case for the RPD model, yet when I read any extended citation of the work it is rare to come across any discussion of the numbers. Instead, people cite the stories, and go into detail about the firefighter who thought he had ESP (probably the most popular of the stories) and several others. Data are necessary to convince people, but stories are what they carry with them. Even in an era of Big Data, stories have a unique potential for conveying understanding. I decided to write *Sources of Power* because I wanted a home for the stories, so it is satisfying to see how strongly readers resonate with them. As you prepare to read or reread the book, I hope you will enjoy the stories as well.

1

Chronicling the Strengths Used in Making Difficult Decisions

During the past twenty-five years, the field of decision making has concentrated on showing the limitations of decision makers—that is, that they are not very rational or competent. Books have been written documenting human limitations and suggesting remedies: training methods to help us think clearly, decision support systems to monitor and guide us, and expert systems that enable computers to make the decisions and avoid altogether the fallible humans.

This book was written to balance the others and takes a different perspective. Here I document human strengths and capabilities that typically have been downplayed or even ignored.

In 1985, I did my first study of how firefighters make life-and-death decisions under extreme time pressure. That project led to others—with pilots, nurses, military leaders, nuclear power plant operators, chess masters, and experts in a range of other domains. A growing number of researchers have moved out of the laboratory, to work in the area of naturalistic decision making—that is, the study of how people use their experience to make decisions in field settings. We try to understand how people handle all of the typical confusions and pressures of their environments, such as missing information, time constraints, vague goals, and changing conditions.[1] In doing these studies, my research team and I have slept in fire stations, observed intensive care units, and ridden in M-1 tanks, U.S. Navy AEGIS cruisers, Blackhawk helicopters, and AWACS aircraft. We have learned a lot about doing field research.

Instead of trying to show how people do not measure up to ideal strategies for performing tasks, we have been motivated by curiosity about how people do so well under difficult conditions. We all have areas in which we can use our experience to make rapid and effective decisions, from the mundane level of shopping to the high-stakes level of firefighting. Shopping in a supermarket does not seem like an impressive skill until you contrast an experienced American shopper to a recent immigrant from Russia. Moving to the other extreme of high-stakes decisions, an example is a fireground commander working under severe time pressure while in charge of a crew at a multiple-alarm fire at a four-story apartment building. Our research concentrated on this high-stakes world. The fireground commanders seemed to be making effective decisions.

Example 1.1
The Torn Artery

My research assistant, Chris Brezovic, and I are sitting in a fire station in Cleveland on a Saturday afternoon in the summer of 1985. We slept only a few hours in the station the night before since we had been up late interviewing the commander during that shift. He was going to stay up all night catching up on his work. We were assigned beds on the second floor. I was told to be ready to get down the stairs and onto the truck no more than twenty-five seconds after an alarm sounded. (No, we did not slide down the pole, although the station still had one. Too many firefighters had broken ankles that way, so they no longer used the pole.) I even slept with my eyeglasses on, not wanting to waste precious seconds fumbling with them. There was only one call, at around 3:00 in the morning. The horn suddenly began blaring, we all jumped out of bed, ran down the flight of stairs, pulled on our coats and boots, and climbed onto the trucks within the time limit. The fire was pretty small—a blaze in a one-car garage.

Chris and I are feeling a little sleepy that next afternoon when the alarm comes in at 3:21 P.M. for the emergency rescue team. Three minutes later, the truck is driving up to a typical house in a residential neighborhood. It is summer, and young women in bikinis who had been tanning themselves on their lawns are running over to their neighbor's yard.

When we pull to a stop, we see a man lying facedown in a pool of blood, his wife crouching over him. As the emergency rescue team goes to work, the woman quickly explains that her husband had been standing on a ladder doing some home repair. He slipped, and his arm went through a pane of glass. He reacted foolishly by pulling his arm out and, in doing so, sliced open an artery. The head of the rescue team, Lieutenant M, later told us that the man had lost two units of blood. If he lost four units, he would be dead. Watching his life leak out of his arm, the man is going into shock.

The first decision facing Lieutenant M is to diagnose the problem. As he ran to the man, even before listening to the wife, he made his diagnosis. He can see from the amount of blood that the man has cut open an artery,

> **Example 1.1** (continued)
>
> and from the dishcloths held against the man's arm he can tell which artery. Next comes the decision of how to treat the wound. In fact, there is nothing to deliberate over. As quickly as possible, Lieutenant M applies firm pressure. Next, he might examine whether there are other injuries, maybe neck injuries, which might prevent him from moving the victim. But he doesn't bother with any more examination. He can see the man is minutes from death, so there is no time to worry about anything else.
>
> Lieutenant M has stopped the bleeding and directs his crew to move the man on a stretcher and to the truck. He assigns the strongest of his crew to the hardest stretcher work, even though the crew member has relatively little experience. Lieutenant M decides that the man's strength is important for quick movement and thinks the crew member has enough training that he will not drop the stretcher as it is maneuvered in through the back of the rescue truck.
>
> On the way to the hospital, the crew puts inflatable pants on the victim. These exert pressure on the man's legs to stabilize his blood pressure. Had the crew put the pants on the man before driving, they would have wasted valuable time. When we reach the hospital I look down at my watch: 3:31 P.M. Only ten minutes has elapsed since the original alarm.

This example shows decision making at a very high level. Lieutenant M handled many decision points yet spent little time on any one of them. He drew on his experience to know just what to do. Yet merely saying that he used his experience is not an answer. The challenge is to identify how that experience came into play.

We have found that people draw on a large set of abilities that are sources of power.[2] The conventional sources of power include deductive logical thinking, analysis of probabilities, and statistical methods.[3] Yet the sources of power that are needed in natural settings are usually not analytical at all—the power of intuition, mental simulation, metaphor, and storytelling. The power of intuition enables us to size up a situation quickly. The power of mental simulation lets us imagine how a course of action might be carried out. The power of metaphor lets us draw on our experience by suggesting parallels between the current situation and something else we have come across. The power of storytelling helps us consolidate our experiences to make them available in the future, either to ourselves or to others. These areas have not been well studied by decision researchers.[4]

Features of Naturalistic Decision-Making Settings

This book examines some recent findings that have emerged from the field of naturalistic decision making. It also describes how research can be done outside the laboratory setting by studying realistic tasks and experienced people working under typical conditions. Features that help define a naturalistic decision-making setting are time pressure, high stakes, experienced decision makers, inadequate information (information that is missing, ambiguous, or erroneous), ill-defined goals, poorly defined procedures, cue learning, context (e.g., higher-level goals, stress), dynamic conditions, and team coordination (Orasanu & Connolly, 1993).

We like to study people under *time pressure*. We have estimated that fireground commanders make around 80 percent of their decisions in less than one minute.[5] As in the case of the torn artery, most of these decisions take only seconds. We have studied chess players under blitz conditions, where the average move was made in six seconds.

Our results seem to hold even when there is not much time pressure. We get the same findings with design engineers who may have weeks or months to finish a project. They insist that they are working under extreme time pressure relative to their tasks, but in comparison to the fireground commanders and chess players, they are almost on vacation.

Naturalistic decision making is concerned with *high stakes*. When a fireground commander makes a poor decision, lives can be lost. When a design engineer makes a poor decision, hundreds of thousands of dollars can be lost.

We are interested in *experienced decision makers* since only those who know something about the domain would usually be making high-stakes choices. Furthermore, we see experience as a basis for the sources of power we want to understand. The fireground commanders we studied had an average of twenty-three years of experience as firefighters, and the chess masters we studied had played thousands of games. In contrast, in most laboratory studies, experience is considered a complicating factor. Subjects who know something about the task may have preconceived notions that could get in the way, or their strategies could distort the results. Therefore, subjects are given totally novel tasks to make sure all of them start with the same level of experience: zero.

We want to know how people carry on even when faced with uncertainty because of *inadequate information* that may be missing, ambiguous, or unreliable—either because of errors in transmission or deception by an adversary.

We are interested in tasks where the *goals are unclear.* Most of the time when we have to make difficult choices, we do not fully understand what we want to accomplish. For instance, when fireground commanders are called out to a blaze, they do not know what type of outcome they will be trying to reach: a fire needs to be extinguished, or the fire is so big that the best thing to do is to prevent it from spreading further, or they need to begin with search and rescue rather than fighting the fire, or they may have to call in a second or third alarm to get more resources, or the situation does not warrant extra resources and they can let the fire burn itself out. In contrast, laboratory studies concentrate on tasks with well-defined goals, since the achievement of a well-defined goal is easy to measure. With an ill-defined goal, you are never sure if the decision was right.

Naturalistic decision making is concerned with *poorly defined procedures.* Conventional laboratory studies, in contrast, prefer to keep decision making distinct from problem solving and do not require subjects to invent or modify procedures.

Cue learning refers to the need to perceive patterns and make distinctions. In laboratory studies we can present unambiguous stimuli: "If you choose option A, you have a 20 percent chance winning $100,000, whereas option B gives you a 100 percent chance of winning $15,000. Which do you pick?" For a task with ambiguous stimuli, consider a skilled racetrack handicapper, who notices that one of the horses in a race does better in the mud, examines the track that is slightly moist from an early morning drizzle, and tries to judge if the track is sufficiently moist to make a difference.

Most tasks are performed within a larger *context* that includes higher-level goals and different tasks with their own requirements, and this must be taken into consideration. Context also includes background conditions, such as noise, poor lighting, constant interruptions, and stressors.

Dynamic conditions (that is, a changing situation) are an important feature of naturalistic decision making. New information may be received, or old information invalidated, and the goals can become radically transformed. In our research with fireground commanders, we estimated that the situation changed an average of five times per incident. Our work with U.S. Navy commanders showed the same thing. Some changes were minor; they were elaborations on what the commanders already knew. Some were major, requiring a shift in the way the commanders understood the situation.

Finally, we want to know how people working in *teams* make decisions. For most of the domains we have studied, teams are involved: a fireground commander in charge of a fire company, a helicopter pilot working with a navigator or other helicopters, or a three-person airline cockpit crew. Rarely do we find a single decision maker, such as a chess player, who does not have to coordinate with anyone else.

The field of naturalistic decision making tries to understand how these features come into play. This book focuses on what we have learned about the way people think and decide in natural settings, using different sources of power. It explores the sources of power themselves, what they offer us, and where they fall short or get us in trouble. And it describes some ways of using these sources of power, whether for training or for designing better systems. Most of the chapters end with a section entitled Applications. One reason to discuss applications is that many applied researchers believe that there is nothing as practical as a good theory. If the things we learn do not have much practical value, perhaps we are investigating questions that are not important.

Some chapters end with a listing of key points and others do not. Some chapters seemed more straightforward, and the listing of key points seemed unnecessary. I added this listing for chapters that covered a lot of material and needed some summary.

2

Learning from the Firefighters

In our first study of firefighters, my research team and I developed our methods and our basic model of naturalistic decision making. We came to this task in 1984, when the federal government issued a published notice asking for written research proposals to study how people make decisions under time pressure. The request came from the U.S. Army Research Institute for the Behavioral and Social Sciences, which is in charge of studying the human side of the battlefield equation. The notice was sent out through a new program for small research companies such as my own. The entire description of what the army wanted was covered in a single paragraph:

> *Topic Description:* Commanders, intelligence analysts, and others are often required to make decisions under conditions of uncertainty and severe time stress. Uncertainties may be associated with missing, incomplete, or ambiguous information, or with future outcomes that are unknown. Research is needed to: (1) better understand the cognitive processes (e.g., memory, judgment, or problem solving) of the decisionmaker under such conditions, and (2) suggest approaches for supporting the cognitive processes so that the overall quality of timeliness of decisions made under uncertainty and time stress are enhanced.

My research company wrote a short proposal (it was requested to be only twenty-five pages or fewer), and we won the contract. Years later, during discussions with some civilians who administer programs at the Army Research Institute, I got some insight into why our proposal was judged favorably. They explained to me that the U.S. Government had spent millions of dollars in the 1970s and early 1980s finding out how people make decisions, and the army had used these findings to build very expensive decision aids for battle commanders in the field. Unfortunately, most of the aids were disappointing. No one would use them. After ten years of research and considerable expense, they were not much further along than when they had begun.

These civilian program directors were also concerned about how to train people to make better decisions. Turnover in the army is high, with people coming in for two- or four-year stints. Even officers who stay in for a full twenty years are rotated every few years. For example, a new tank commander may spend six months getting trained in the rudiments, then another year coming up to speed. That gives him little more than a year to help train other people before he is moved to his next rotation. How can these officers develop skills faster? Here again, the decision research program had been a disappointment. The experiments did not shed much light on how to train a new lieutenant to make effective decisions in controlling his tank platoon. The army has doctrine about how decisions should be made, but it seemed that soldiers usually did not follow the doctrine.

Recovering from a Research Plan

I am still amazed at how poorly I designed this study of decision making. We developed our recognitional model of decision making from this study and spent the next several years following up leads from our results, but almost every major design feature in my original plan was wrong.

In the following paragraphs, I list all the design features we had planned to use, along with our starting hypotheses. (You can try to guess which were the good ones and which were the bad ones.)

1. *Fireground commanders.* We wanted to study fireground commanders— the people in charge of urban and suburban fires. They decide how to attack the fire and how to use the crews. They are highly experienced and take charge of life-threatening situations. If someone is injured or killed, they are responsible. Commanders work under a great deal of time pressure. In between the fires, they might tolerate a team of scientists asking them questions.

2. *Observers.* We planned to train college undergraduates as observers and put them in firehouses or in radio communication with the fire dispatchers, so they could quickly get to the scene of new fires and observe the decision making on the spot. We planned to observe the

commanders during the fires and then interview them after. If we used our higher-priced and better-trained researchers, we might have wasted a lot of money having them sit idly in station houses waiting for action.

3. *Exceptional cases.* We thought that the most interesting decisions to examine would be the most difficult ones, such as whether to try to extinguish a fire or to give up and make sure it does not spread, rather than the routine ones, such as where to park the trucks.

4. *Two-option hypothesis.* We hypothesized that under time pressure, the commanders could not think of lots and lots of options. Instead, they would have to consider only two options: one that was intuitively the favorite, and the other to serve as a comparison to show why the favorite was better.

5. *Analogies.* We expected to see lots of analogical reasoning. We believed that the commanders could use their experience like a memory bank, to recognize that a fire was just like one they had worked on previously. In this way, they could directly use their memory to make their decisions quickly.

6. *Data analysis.* We believed that all we would need to do to test the two-option hypothesis was to count how often the commanders had compared lots of options versus how often they had compared just two options.

Only two of these six expectations worked out well. The others were wrong.

1. Studying fire department commanders was a good idea—probably the best of the design. I was not always so sure. A friend who was in charge of some research programs for the U.S. Air Force asked, "What do these firefighters have to do with the military?" He argued that I had picked the wrong group to examine, since soldiers fight an intelligent adversary, whereas firefighters do not. "It makes all the difference in the world," he assured me.

My friend was wrong about the value of studying firefighters. These commanders showed us how people function under the stress of having to make choices with high stakes. Our later studies showed that military commanders use the same strategies as the fireground commanders.

2. Place college undergraduates in fire stations? This plan was foolish. The largest cities in Ohio—Cleveland, Cincinnati, and Columbus— do not have enough interesting fires to make this feasible. Our observers would have been sitting around all day, gathering no data. Fortunately, we found all of this out when the study began through preliminary interviews with fire department officials, and we dropped the idea.

Even if there had been enough fires, we should not have used relatively inexperienced undergraduates. For an initial study, we needed to be on the spot ourselves. Only after we knew what was happening could we have turned this task over to others. We can easily train inexperienced research assistants to collect data in a standardized laboratory experiment, but at this first step of observation, we needed researchers with more experience and sophistication.

3. Following exceptional cases was a good idea. If we had asked the commanders about the routine cases, we would have heard tired generalities. By focusing on the nonroutine cases, we were asking them about the most interesting ones—the ones they come back to the station house and tell everybody else about. We were asking for their best stories, and they were happy to oblige.

4. In the two-option hypothesis, we thought that under time pressure, the commanders would be making decisions by reducing the option set down to two: a favorite and a comparison. This is what Peer Soelberg (1967) found in a study of job-seeking behavior.

Soelberg's course on decision making at the MIT Sloan School of Management taught students how to perform the classical decision analysis method we can call the rational choice strategy. The decision maker:

1. Identifies the set of options.
2. Identifies the ways of evaluating these options.
3. Weights each evaluation dimension.
4. Does the rating.
5. Picks the option with the highest score.

For his Ph.D. dissertation, Soelberg studied the decision strategies his students used to perform a natural task: selecting their jobs as they finished their degrees. He assumed that they would rely on the rational choice strategy.

He was wrong. His students showed little inclination toward systematic thinking. Instead they would make a gut choice. By interviewing his students, Soelberg found he could identify their favorite job choice and predict their ultimate choice with 87 percent accuracy—up to three weeks before the students themselves announced their choice.

Soelberg had trained his students to use rational methods, yet when it was time for them to make a rational and important choice, they would not do it. Soelberg was also a good observer, and he tried to capture the students' actual decision strategies.

What did the students do during this time? If asked, they would deny that they had made a decision yet. For them, a decision was just what Soelberg had taught: a deliberated choice between two or more options. To feel that they had made such a decision, they had to go through a systematic process of evaluation. They selected one other candidate as a comparison, and then tried to show that their favorite was as good as or better than the comparison candidate on each evaluation dimension. Once they had shown this to their satisfaction (even if it meant fudging a little or finding ways to beef up their favorite), then they would announce as their decision the gut favorite that Soelberg had identified much earlier. They were not actually making a decision; they were constructing a justification.

We hypothesized that the fireground commanders would behave in the same way. We thought this hypothesis—that instead of considering lots of options they would consider only two—was daring. Actually, it was conservative. The commanders did not consider two. In fact, they did not seem to be comparing any options at all. This was disconcerting, and we discovered it at the first background discussion we had with a fireground commander, even before the real interviews. We asked the commander to tell us about some difficult decisions he had made.

> "I don't make decisions," he announced to his startled listeners. "I don't remember when I've ever made a decision."

For researchers starting a study of decision making, this was unhappy news. Even worse, he insisted that fireground commanders *never* make decisions. We pressed him further. Surely there are decisions during a fire—decisions about whether to call a second alarm, where to send his crews, how to contain the fire.

He agreed that there were options, yet it was usually obvious what to do in any given situation. We soon realized that he was defining the making of a decision in the same way as Soelberg's students—generating a set of options and evaluating them to find the best one. We call this strategy of examining two or more options at the same time, usually by comparing the strengths and weaknesses of each, *comparative evaluation*. He insisted that he never did it. There just was no time. The structure would burn down by the time he finished listing all the options, let alone evaluating them.

Because Soelberg's theory was one of my favorites, we kept asking questions about the two-option hypothesis for much of this study. We never found any evidence for it.

5. Analogies. We expected to see a heavy use of analogous cases. We found very little. Never was there an entire fire that reminded a commander of a previous one. The people we studied had over twenty years of experience, and all of it had blended together in their minds. On the few occasions where they did think of an analogue, it had to do with an aspect of the incident rather than the entire incident. The following example shows how this worked.

Example 2.1
The Falling Billboards

Chief V, a veteran with about twenty-five years of firefighting experience, is in charge of putting out an apartment fire. He looks up and sees some billboards on the roof, then remembers a previous fire where the wooden supports for the billboards were burned through, sending the billboards crashing to the street below. He orders his crew to push the crowds farther back, to make sure no bystanders are injured by a falling billboard.

In this incident, the memory of an earlier experience led the commander to detect a possible danger and make a quick decision by issuing an order that would reduce that danger. The memory was of part of an incident, though, not of a whole fire.

6. Data analysis. We thought the data analysis would be straightforward. We expected that we would count the number of times people used the Soelberg evaluation strategy of favorite versus comparison, as opposed to the number of times they used a more complete decision matrix. In fact, were using a different strategy altogether.

Figuring Out How to Do the Project

Rather than waiting for the tough cases to happen, we asked the commanders to tell us about the big fires they had worked on during the previous few weeks or months. We treated each critical incident as a story and made the interview flow around the storytelling of the commanders. This method enabled us to get at the context of their decision making. It also ensured their interest and participation, because they enjoyed relating their experiences.

We have found the same thing in other studies. People who are good at what they do relish the chance to explain it to an appreciative audience. Once, one of our data collectors was interviewing the command staff of firefighters who worked on forest fires. She was doing the interviews during an actual fire that had spread over six mountains in Idaho and took weeks to bring under control. Even under these circumstances, she got their cooperation. In fact, firefighters who watched what she was doing but were not on her list to be contacted would ask her for permission to be interviewed. They wanted to explain to her and to themselves what had happened at critical times.

The study did not just consist of people telling us stories. It is important to select the right incident to study. To define what we want to learn from the stories, we plan strategy, sometimes with checklists of items to cover so that if they do not emerge during the story, we can ask about them. Usually we send two people on an interview: one to lead the interview and get the story moving, and the other to take notes and review the checklist of probes to make sure everything has been included.

Over the years, we have compiled lists of cognitive probes we use, such as ways that the person's understanding of the situation changed during the episode or ways that someone with less experience might have faltered. We have learned where the expertise comes in during an incident, so we know where to probe more deeply. We have evolved ways of diagraming the incidents during the telling and after. New staff members take a short workshop on interviewing and then assist others for at least six months before they lead any interviews. (I cover some of the details in chapter 11, when I discuss storytelling.)

In this first study with fireground commanders, we needed to build a framework for conducting the interviews and guiding the stories. Roberta Calderwood, one of the research team members, took the lead in preparing interview guides and standardizing them to make it easy to listen to the stories and direct them where needed.

In these first interviews, we asked the participants if they could recall a recent event that had been nonroutine and had demanded special experience. Once we found such an incident, we asked the commanders to go through it, telling it in their own words. After we had a sense of the story, we would go through the incident again to pin down what happened and when. We tried to identify what we call decision points—times when several courses of action were open. We asked whether the commander thought about other courses of action, and if so, how the choice was made. If the commander had not considered other options, we asked why not, and what about the situation made it so obvious. We tape-recorded the interviews and took extensive notes, since we were not sure what we were after or what would be important later.

3

The Recognition-Primed Decision Model

As we conducted our interviews, we heard stories about rescues, fires that went out of control, restaurants and apartment buildings that burned down. We heard stories about bravery, and stories about mistakes. There were stories of teamwork—of young firefighters climbing on roofs to chop open holes for smoke to escape—and stories where teamwork broke down. A sergeant grimly remembered the time he had been in charge of a fire until a more senior official arrived, not his usual boss. The official had issued orders to section (cut a hole in) the roof. The sergeant had to climb off the roof to confront the man face to face to explain that because the roof was too spongy, he was going to pull his men off it. "This was a guy I hadn't worked with before. If it had been my usual commander, he would have trusted my judgment." We asked what a spongy roof is, and he told us that the heat weakens the supports so the surface feels softer just before it collapses, then drops everyone into the fire below. We asked what a spongy roof feels like, and he answered that he couldn't put it into words. To new firefighters, all roofs feel spongy.

This incident was typical of the ones we studied. We asked people to tell us about their hardest cases, thinking that these would show the most decision making. But where were the decisions? The commander sees a vertical fire and knows just what to do. But in an instant, that decision is negated because the fire has spread. He still knows just what to do in this changed situation. He never seems to decide anything. He is not comparing a favorite option to another option, as the two-option hypothesis suggests. He is not comparing anything.[1]

The commander did not seem to be making any decisions at all if a decision results from actively comparing two or more options in a process of

Example 3.1
The Laundry Chute Fire

The initial report is of flames in the basement of a four-story apartment building: a one-alarm fire. The commander arrives quickly and does not see anything. There are no signs of smoke anywhere. He finds the door to the basement, around the side of the building, enters, and sees flames spreading up the laundry chute. That's simple: a vertical fire that will spread straight up. Since there are no external signs of smoke, it must just be starting.

The way to fight a vertical fire is to get above it and spray water down, so he sends one crew up to the first floor and another to the second floor. Both report that the fire has gotten past them. The commander goes outside and walks around to the front of the building. Now he can see smoke coming out from under the eaves of the roof. It is obvious what has happened: the fire has gone straight up to the fourth floor, has hit the ceiling there, and is pushing smoke down the hall. Since there was no smoke when he arrived just a minute earlier, this must have just happened.

It is obvious to him how to proceed now that the chance to put out the fire quickly is gone. He needs to switch to search and rescue, to get everyone out of the building, and he calls in a second alarm. The side staircase near the laundry chute had been the focus of activity before. Now the attention shifts to the front stairway as the evacuation route.

comparative evaluation. We tried using a broader definition: a decision is a choice point where reasonable options exist, and the commander might have selected a different option. In other words, even if no other option was consciously considered, as long as one was available and known to the commander, a decision was made. We labeled these decision points. We did not bother with the trivial choices but rather concentrated on the points where there seemed to be a meaningful choice (e.g., "I wanted to section the roof but someone else might have held off until there was more information").

We developed a standard way of doing the interviews to highlight the decision points and define the types of questions, and we worked out a way to code the interviews to make our work easier. Each interview was tape-recorded. Then the interviewers listened to the tapes to write an account of the incident, giving the background, the time line of events, and the decision points we probed.

Listening to the Data

We still had a problem: the data would not conform to the hypothesis. I wanted the incidents to show how the commanders used the two-option strategy. I wanted the incidents to show analogical reasoning. I wanted the incidents to show us how people wrestled with choices. None of these things had happened. We still had to figure out just what those commanders were doing.

We sought to explain two puzzles: how the commanders could reliably identify good options and how they could evaluate an option without comparing it to any others.

Our results turned out to be fairly clear. It was not that the commanders were *refusing* to compare options; rather, they did not *have* to compare options. I had been so fixated on what they were not doing that I had missed the real finding: that the commanders could come up with a good course of action from the start. That was what the stories were telling us. Even when faced with a complex situation, the commanders could see it as familiar and know how to react.

The commanders' secret was that their experience let them see a situation, even a nonroutine one, as an example of a prototype, so they knew the typical course of action right away. Their experience let them identify a reasonable reaction as the first one they considered, so they did not bother thinking of others. They were not being perverse. They were being skillful. We now call this strategy *recognition-primed decision making*.

We tried classifying all the decision points according to whether the commander showed any evidence of comparing one option to another. We carefully defined the categories. The decision point was considered a comparative evaluation if the decision maker reported considering two or more options at the same time to contrast their relative advantages. Another category was composed of decision points where the decision maker consciously made up a new course of action that he had never tried or seen before. In the recognitional decision category, the decision makers used their experience to know what to do and showed no evidence of comparing options.

It was not easy to classify the decision points. After we identified 156 decision points, we had plenty of discussion about how to categorize each, and these exchanges helped us clarify what each category meant. We wanted to make sure that the classifications were reliable, so we adopted a rule that two people had to judge each decision point, at least one of whom had been at the interview and the other of whom had listened to the tape recording. If they could not agree, a third person was brought in to arbitrate. (In some of our later studies we established the reliability of these category judgments.)[2]

If we had any doubt about what strategy a fireground commander used, we put it in the comparative evaluation category. We did this to make sure we were not biasing the data in favor of recognitional decision making. We also found cases where the commanders were inventing procedures, rather than choosing them.

Example 3.2
The Overpass Rescue

A lieutenant is called out to rescue a woman who either fell or jumped off a highway overpass. She is dunk or on drugs and is probably trying to kill herself. Instead of falling to her death, she lands on the metal supports of a highway and is dangling there when the rescue team arrives.

The lieutenant recognizes the danger of the situation. The woman is semiconscious and lying bent over one of the metal struts. At any moment, she could fall to her death on the pavement below. If he orders any of his team out to help her, they will be endangered because there is no way to get a good brace against the struts, so he issues an order not to climb out to secure her.

Two of his crew ignore his order and climb out anyway. One holds onto her shoulders and the other to her legs.

A hook-and-ladder truck arrives. The lieutenant doesn't need their help in making the rescue, so tells them to drive down to the highway below and block traffic in case the woman does fall. He does not want to chance that the young woman will fall on a moving car.

Now the question is how to pull the woman to safety.

First, the lieutenant considers using a rescue harness, the standard way of raising victims. It snaps onto a person's shoulders and thighs. In imagining its use, he realizes that it requires the person to be in a sitting position or face up. He thinks about how they would shift her to sit up and realizes that she might slide off the support.

Example 3.2 (continued)

Second, he considers attaching the rescue harness from the back. However, he imagines that by lifting the woman, they would create a large pressure on her back, almost bending her double. He does not want to risk hurting her.

Third, the lieutenant considers using a rescue strap—another way to secure victims, but making use of a strap rather than a snap-on harness. However, it creates the same problems as the rescue harness, requiring that she be sitting up or that it be attached from behind. He rejects this too.

Now he comes up with a novel idea: using a ladder belt—a strong belt that firefighters buckle on over their coats when they climb up ladders to rescue people. When they get to the top, they can snap an attachment on the belt to the top rung of the ladder. If they lose their footing during the rescue, they are still attached to the ladder so they won't plunge to their death.

The lieutenant's idea is to get a ladder belt, slide it under the woman, buckle it from behind (it needs only one buckle), tie a rope to the snap, and lift her up to the overpass. He thinks it through again and likes the idea, so he orders one of his crew to fetch the ladder belt and rope, and they tie it onto her.

In the meantime, the hook-and-ladder truck has moved to the highway below the overpass, and the truck's crew members raise the ladder. The firefighter on the platform at the top of the ladder is directly under the woman shouting, "I've got her. I've got her." The lieutenant ignores him and orders his men to lift her up.

At this time, he makes an unwanted discovery: ladder belts are built for sturdy firefighters, to be worn over their coats. This is a slender woman wearing a thin sweater. In addition, she is essentially unconscious. When they lift her up, they realize the problem. As the lieutenant put it, "She slithered through the belt like a slippery strand of spaghetti."

Fortunately, the hook-and-ladder man is right below her. He catches her and makes the rescue. There is a happy ending.

Now the lieutenant and his crew go back to their station to figure out what had gone wrong. They try the rescue harness and find that the lieutenant's instincts were right: neither is usable.

Eventually they discover how they should have made the rescue. They should have used the rope they had tied to the ladder belt. They could have tied it to the woman and lifted her up. With all the technology available to them, they had forgotten that you can use a rope to pull someone up.

This rescue helped us see several important aspects of decision making. First, the lieutenant's deliberations about options took him only about a minute. That may seem too short, but if you imagine going through it in your mind, a minute is about right.

Second, the decision maker looked at several options yet never compared any two of them,[3] He thought of the options one at a time, evaluated in each turn, rejected it, and turned to the next most typical rescue technique. We can call this strategy a *singular evaluation approach,* to distinguish it from comparative evaluation. Singular evaluation means evaluating each option on its own merits, even if we cycle through several possibilities.

Distinguishing between comparative and singular evaluation strategies is not difficult. When you order from a menu, you probably compare the different items to find the one you want the most. You are performing a comparative evaluation because you are trying to see if one item seems tastier than the others. In contrast, if you are in an unfamiliar neighborhood and you notice your car is low on gasoline, you start searching for service stations and stop at the first reasonable place you find. You do not need the best service station in town.

The difference between singular and comparative evaluation is linked to the research of Herbert Simon, who won a Nobel Prize for economics. Simon (1957) identified a decision strategy he calls satisficing: selecting the first option that works. Satisficing is different from optimizing, which means trying to come up with the best strategy. Optimizing is hard, and it takes a long time. Satisficing is more efficient. The singular evaluation strategy is based on satisficing. Simon used the concept of satisficing to describe the decision behavior of businesspeople. The strategy makes even more sense for fireground commanders because of their immense time pressure.[4]

Our model of recognitional decision making was starting to fit together. The experienced fireground commanders could judge a situation as prototypical and know what to do.[5] If their first choice did not work out, they might consider others—not to find the best but to find the first one that works.

But there was still the second puzzle. If they did not compare one course of action to another, how did they evaluate the options? All of the evaluation procedures we knew about required contrast: looking at the degree to which each option satisfies each criterion, weighing the importance of the criteria, tabulating the results, and finding the best option. If the commanders did not compare options, how did they know that a course of action was any good?

The answer lies in the overpass rescue story. To evaluate a single course of action, the lieutenant imagined himself carrying it out. Fireground commanders use the power of mental simulation, running the action through in their minds. If they spot a potential problem, like the rescue harness not working well, they move on to the next option, and the next, until they find one that seems to work. Then they carry it out. As the example shows, this is not a foolproof strategy. The advantage is that it is usually better than anything else they can do.

Before we did this study, we believed that novices impulsively jumped at the first option they could think of, whereas experts carefully deliberated about the merits of different courses of action. Now it seemed that it was the experts who could generate a single course of action, while novices needed to compare different approaches.

In one case we studied commanders who had no experience with the type of incident they faced. This helped us to see better what is required for proficient decision making.

Example 3.3
The Christmas Fire

Dotted around the Midwest are oil tank farms: large complexes of storage tanks filled with oil piped in from the Texas and Oklahoma fields and held at these farms before being pumped to specific points in the Midwest. This incident took place at a tank farm. The pipeline field at this farm had twenty tanks, each forty-five feet high and a hundred feet in diameter and each with a capacity of more than sixty thousand barrels of oil.

On Christmas night in the middle of a bitterly cold winter, one of the tanks bursts open. The oil comes pouring out—a bad enough situation— and then ignites. A large oil tank instantly turns into a giant torch and sets fire to another tank. Most of the big power lines of the tanks are down and burning. The telephone lines are also on fire. Burning oil has spilled into a ditch, and fierce winds push the fire along.

The setting is a rural farm community crisscrossed with underground oil pipes. If the flames spread, they can conceivably set the whole town on fire.

The fire departments of the surrounding townships report to the call. These departments are staffed by volunteer firefighters who are used to

Example 3.3 (continued)

putting out barn fires and garage fires, and maybe a house fire or two in a year. Now they are looking at a wall of flames fifty to one hundred feet high. They have never seen anything like it before in their lives. As one commander described it to us, "Our heads turned to stone."

As they watch, one of the two burning tanks ruptures. A wave of crude oil rides over the highway and engulfs a new tank, number 91, which is filled with oil. A man from the pipeline company tells the fireground commanders that if the fire comes any farther south, it will reach a twenty-inch propane gas line. The oil is following gravity northward, "creepin' like a little monster" toward a large chemical plant.

Because of the cold, everyone is bundled up, many wearing face masks. The crews have trouble recognizing if someone is from their own district. It is hard to tell who the commanders are. Worse, there is no source of water in the area. Foam is needed to put out oil fires, but the commanders can locate only a thousand gallons.

In short, they have no resources for fighting the fire and no understanding of what to do. They are afraid the fire will spread to the other tanks. They wonder if they should evacuate the town. They are bewildered.

For two days, they remain uncertain about how to proceed. A commander of one of the fire departments orders a trench to be built to contain the oil. A different commander's idea is to pipe the oil out of tank 91. But no one can tell if the lines are still working, and no one wants to take a chance of leaking oil into a field where the fire might spread. A third commander calls the power company to turn off the electricity to the downed power lines, but the power company does not comply right away. Each department goes off in a different direction.

Eventually the power company turns off power in the early morning of the second day. Crews can approach tank 91. The plan is to spray foam down onto the fire, if they can get enough foam. It is freezing cold and windy. Where should they position the ladder truck? Should a firefighter, carrying a hose, climb up a ladder to the rim of tank 91? The dikes around the tank make it hard to get close, and the field around the dikes has dangerous ravines. Eventually a ladder truck gets near tank 91, and firefighters spray foam onto the rim of the oil tank. The wind just blows the foam away, and suddenly the origination point fire, in a nearby tank, starts to boil up menacingly. Fearing an eruption, the commander evacuates his men.

Sometime during the second day, one of the chiefs asks a person working at the oil company if all the pipes leading into the complex have been turned off. The reply is that no one knows, since the tangle of pipelines is so confusing. Spurred on by the question, the plant personnel start tracing all the incoming pipelines and find a source of fuel: a large twenty-two-inch pipe that has been pumping new oil directly into one of the burning tanks. During the second day, they get all the pipes turned off.

Example 3.3 (continued)

On the third day, the volunteer fire chiefs finally take organized action: they choose not to try to do anything. They let the fire burn while they devote all their energies to planning. One of the fireground commanders later told us that this was their first effective decision.

Here is how they go about planning. They ask themselves what their options are, and what the advantages and disadvantages are of each. Finally, in the confusion of a runaway oil fire, we find the strongest example of deliberative decision making—by chiefs who are essentially the baffled about what is happening: they try rigging up a tower to get a man above the rim of a tank to spray foam down onto the fire. Near the rim, he sees cracks with crude oil coming through. The pumps start spraying foam, and the command is given to start the water truck cycle. Because of earlier delays, the water truck freezes up before it can be used. Then the foam pump starts to malfunction, so they give up and call the firefighter down.

Next they try rigging up a nozzle to spray the foam down, but the high winds sweep it away, and the heat cooks it off. They order more foam from a nearby U.S. Air Force base, but the different foams that arrive are incompatible. Finally, they give up, abandon their pride, and call in some consultants. They call in the team of "Boots and Coots," former colleagues of Red Adair, a world-famous fighter of oil well fires.

Boots and Coots arrive, look briefly at the scene, and say that they will need a great deal more foam. "We don't have that much foam," the volunteer fireground commanders argue. "Of course not," Boots and Coots answer. "We've already ordered it. It will be here tomorrow."

From that point on, under the direction of the experts, the fire operations go smoothly. The entire fire is extinguished within the next two days. Although no one is seriously injured, the cost of the fire is estimated at $10 to $15 million.

From this episode we learn that there are times for deliberating about options. Usually these are times when experience is inadequate and logical thinking is a substitute for recognizing a situation as typical. Although the commanders in this case study had been firefighters for a long time, they had no experience with a fire this large. Deliberating about options makes a lot of sense for novices, who have to think their way through the decision. It is what I do when I have to buy a house or a car. I have to start from scratch, identifying features I might want, looking at the choices.

Comparing the Categories

Table 3.1 shows how often we found examples of each category. The first category, preselected options, is for cases where the fireground commander was given a set of options by someone else and had to select one. There were no incidents of this nature.

The second category is for cases of comparative evaluation. There were only eighteen decisions of this type, with about half of them coming from the incident with the oil tank farm, where the fireground commanders were essentially novices.

The third category is for cases where new and creative options were initiated, like the overpass rescue. There were eleven decisions of this type.

Finally, there was the category for recognitional decisions. Fully 80 percent of the decisions fit in here. Moreover, these were the findings for nonroutine incidents. The results would have been more extreme with a sample of typical episodes.

Defining the Recognition-Primed Decision Model

The recognition-primed decision (RPD) model fuses two processes: the way decision makers size up the situation to recognize which course of action makes sense, and the way they evaluate that course of action by imagining it.

Figure 3.1 shows the basic strategy as variation 1. Decision makers recognize the situation as typical and familiar—a typical garage fire, or

Table 3.1
Categories of the Decisions Studied

Type of Strategy	Number of Cases
Choosing from preselected options	0
Comparative evaluation	18
Novel option	11
Recognitional decision (singular evaluation)	127
Total decision points classified	156

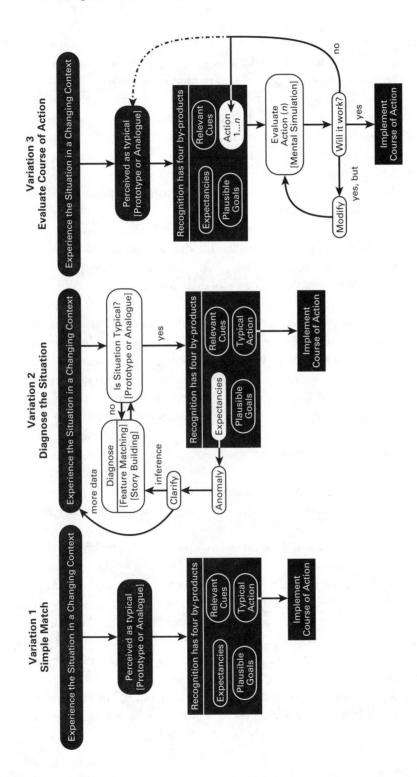

Figure 3.1

Recognition-primed decision model

apartment building fire, or factory fire, or search-and-rescue job—and proceed to take action. They understand what types of *goals* make sense (so the priorities are set), which *cues* are important (so there is not an overload of information), what to *expect* next (so they can prepare themselves and notice surprises), and the *typical ways of responding* in a given situation. By recognizing a situation as typical, they also recognize a *course of action* likely to succeed. The recognition of goals, cues, expectancies, and actions is part of what it means to recognize a situation. That is, the decision makers do not start with the goals or expectancies and figure out the nature of the situation.

Some situations are more complex, as shown by variations 2 and 3 in figure 3.1. Variation 2 occurs when the decision maker may have to devote more attention to *diagnosing* the situation, since the information may not clearly match a typical case or may map onto more than one typical case. The decision maker may need to gather more information in order to make a diagnosis. Another complication is that the decision maker may have misinterpreted the situation but does not realize it until some *expectancies* have been violated. At these times, decision makers will respond to the anomaly or ambiguity by checking which interpretation best matches the features of the situation.[6] They may try to build a story to account for some of the inconsistencies. (See chapters 5 and 6 for examples.)[7]

Variation 3 explains how decision makers evaluate single options by imagining how the course of action will play out. A decision maker who anticipates difficulties may need to *adjust* the course of action, or maybe *reject* it and look for another option. (These aspects are discussed in more detail in chapters 5 and 6.)

One way to think about these three variations is that variation 1 is basically an "if ... then" reaction, an antecedent followed by the rule-based response. The expertise is in being able to recognize when the antecedent condition has been met. Variation 2 takes the form "if (???) ... then," with the decision maker deliberating about the nature of the situation. Variation 3 takes the form "if ... then (???)" as the decision maker ponders the outcome of a reaction. Figure 3.2 shows an integrated version of all three variations.

The RPD model has some elements of other models, but in its integrated form, it has not been proposed before.[8] We have confidence in

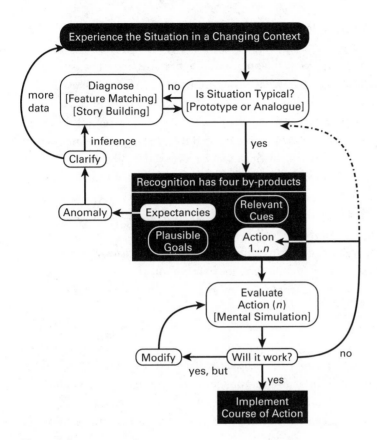

Figure 3.2

Integrated version of recognition-primed decision model

this model for several reasons. First, our results show how frequently this strategy is used.

Second, our coding in this and other studies was conservative. If there was any evidence that a person compared several options, even for an instant, we counted it as a comparative evaluation. We coded a decision point as recognitional only if the options came from experience and were not consciously compared,[9] and the decision maker selected the first action that was acceptable.

Third, our data collection was conservative. We kept asking the fire-ground commanders if they had considered a set of options at each choice point. Even when they said they thought of only one option, we pressed them for others, hoping to find evidence for the two-option model that Soelberg had presented. That approach worked in our favor.

If we had started with the one-option hypothesis and only asked questions to elicit data that would support it, we could have been fooling ourselves. People conducting experiments have a certain power over the people being studied. We refer to this as the demand feature of the experiment. If we made it clear that we wanted data to support the one-option hypothesis, some of the people we interviewed might have given us such data. Therefore, because we probed for evidence of the two-option hypothesis, which included concurrent evaluation, the demand characteristics worked against the recognitional strategy, giving us more confidence in our findings.

Fourth, we had gone after the most difficult decisions, not the easy ones. If the commanders did not contrast options for the toughest cases, then the model should apply even more strongly to all the other decisions they face.

Fifth, the RPD model has been widely accepted by the decision makers themselves. As we began to present our findings at conferences, we got the reactions, "Of course that's how people make decisions." Our findings seemed obviously right to everyone, even though they were so different from earlier decision theories. We began to realize that the force of our findings was in their obviousness. Of course the RPD strategy was the strategy used most frequently.

The Theoretical Importance of the RPD Model

Recognitional decision making can be contrasted with the more classical approaches. Perhaps the most widely known of these models stems from the work of Janis and Mann (1977), who warned that people try to avoid making decisions because of the stress of carrying out the analysis. Janis and Mann offered these prescriptions for making better decisions:

- Thoroughly canvas a wide range of options.
- Survey a full range of objectives.
- Carefully weigh the costs, risk, and benefits of each option.
- Intensively search for new information in evaluating options.

- Assimilate all new information.
- Reexamine the positive and negative consequences of each option.
- Carefully plan to include contingencies if various risks occur.

Janis and Mann probably did not intend this advice for time-pressured situations, but the RPD model predominates even when time is sufficient for comparative evaluations. Yet in one form or another, Janis and Mann's prescriptive advice is held up as an ideal of rationality and finds its way into most courses on cognitive development. The advice is more helpful for beginners than for experienced decision makers. In most applied settings, beginners are not going to be put in a position to make critical decisions.

The prescriptions of Janis and Mann are an example of the rational choice strategy that we had encountered: define the evaluation dimensions, weight each one, rate each option on each dimension, multiply the weightings, total up the scores, and determine the best option—that is, unless you do not have all the data you need, or are not sure how to do the ratings, or disagree with the weights, or run out of time before you have finished.

There are advantages to the rational choice strategy:

- It should result in reliable decisions (that is, the same result each time for the same analysis).
- It is quantitative.
- It helps novices determine what they do not know.
- It is rigorous; it does not leave anything out.
- It is a general strategy, which could apply in all sorts of situations.

The problem is that the assumptions of the rational choice strategy are usually too restrictive. Rarely is there the time or the information needed to make this type of strategy work. Furthermore, if we cannot trust someone to make a big judgment, such as which option is best, why would we trust all of the little judgments that go into the rational choice strategy?[10] Clearly this method is not going to ensure that novices make choices, and it usually is not helpful for experienced decision makers. It can be useful in working with teams, to calibrate everyone's grasp of the strengths and weaknesses of different options.

Applications

One application is to be skeptical of courses in formal methods of decision making. They are teaching methods people seldom use.

A second application is to be sensitive to when you need to compare options and when you do not. For many tasks, we are novices, and the rational choice method helps us when we lack the expertise to recognize situations. Sometimes we may need to use formal methods to look at a wide array of alternatives. Other times we may judge that we should rely on our expertise to look in greater depth at a smaller set of alternatives—maybe the first one considered.

One final application involves training. The ideas set forth in this chapter imply that we do not make someone an expert through training in formal methods of analysis. Quite the contrary is true, in fact: we run the risk of slowing the development of skills. If the purpose is to train people in time-pressured decision making, we might require that the trainee make rapid responses rather than ponder all the implications. If we can present many situations an hour, several hours a day, for days or weeks, we should be able to improve the trainee's ability to detect familiar patterns. The design of the scenarios is critical, since the goal is to show many common cases to facilitate a recognition of typicality along with different types of rare cases so trainees will be prepared for these as well.

Key Points

We can summarize the key features of the RPD model in comparison to the standard advice given to decision makers. The RPD model claims that with experienced decision makers:

- The focus is on the way they assess the situation and judge it familiar, not on comparing options.
- Courses of action can be quickly evaluated by imagining how they will be carried out, not by formal analysis and comparison.
- Decision makers usually look for the first workable option they can find, not the best option.
- Since the first option they consider is usually workable, they do not have to generate a large set of options to be sure they get a good one.

- They generate and evaluate options one at a time and do not bother comparing the advantages and disadvantages of alternatives.

- By imagining the option being carried out, they can spot weaknesses and find ways to avoid these, thereby making the option stronger. Conventional models just select the best, without seeing how it can be improved.

- The emphasis is on being poised to act rather than being paralyzed until all the evaluations have been completed.

4

The Power of Intuition

Intuition depends on the use of experience to recognize key patterns that indicate the dynamics of the situation. Because patterns can be subtle, people often cannot describe what they noticed, or how they judged a situation as typical or atypical. Therefore, intuition has a strange reputation. Skilled decision makers know that they can depend on their intuition, but at the same time they may feel uncomfortable trusting a source of power that seems so accidental.[1]

Bechara, Damasio, Tranel, and Damasio (1997) found that intuition has a basis in biology. They compared patients who were brain damaged to a group of normal subjects. The brain-damaged subjects lacked intuition, an emotional reaction to anticipated consequences of good and bad decisions. In the normal subjects, this system seemed to be activated long before they were consciously aware that they had made a decision.

This chapter will describe the research we have done to understand how intuition is used during decision making. It will describe studies with tank platoon leaders, U.S. Navy officers, and nurses, as well as fireground commanders.

For the first formal interview that I did in our first research project with firefighters, I was trying to find some difficult incident where my interviewee, a fireground commander, had to make a tough decision. He could think of only one case, years ago, where he said his extrasensory perception (ESP) had saved the day. I tried to get him to think of a different incident because the one he had in mind was too old, because he was only a lieutenant then, not a commander, and because I do not have much interest in ESP. But he was determined to describe this case, so I finally gave up and let him tell his story.

Example 4.1
The Sixth Sense

It is a simple house fire in a one-story house in a residential neighborhood. The fire is in the back, in the kitchen area. The lieutenant leads his hose crew into the building, to the back, to spray water on the fire, but the fire just roars back at them.

"Odd," he thinks. The water should have more of an impact. They try dousing it again, and get the same results. They retreat a few steps to regroup.

Then the lieutenant starts to feel as if something is not right. He doesn't have any clues; he just doesn't feel right about being in that house, so he orders his men out of the building—a perfectly standard building with nothing out of the ordinary.

As soon as his men leave the building, the floor where they had been standing collapses. Had they still been inside, they would have plunged into the fire below.

"A sixth sense," he assured us, and part of the makeup of every skilled commander. Some close questioning revealed the following facts:

- He had no suspicion that there was a basement in the house.

- He did not suspect that the seat of the fire was in the basement, directly underneath the living room where he and his men were standing when he gave his order to evacuate.

- But he was already wondering why the fire did not react as expected.

- The living room was hotter than he would have expected for a small fire in the kitchen of a single-family home.

- It was very quiet. Fires are noisy, and for a fire with this much heat, he would have expected a great deal of noise.

The whole pattern did not fit right. His expectations were violated, and he realized he did not quite know what was going on. That was why he ordered his men out of the building. With hindsight, the reasons for the mismatch were clear. Because the fire was under him and not in the kitchen, it was not affected by his crew's attack, the rising heat was much greater than he had expected, and the floor acted like a baffle to muffle the noise, resulting in a hot but quiet environment.

This incident helped us understand how commanders make decisions by recognizing when a typical situation is developing. In this case, the events were *not* typical, and his reaction was to pull back, regroup, and try to get a better sense of what was going on. By showing us what happens when the cues do not fit together, this case clarified how much firefighters rely on a recognition of familiarity and prototypicality. By the end of the interview, the commander could see how he had used the available information to make his judgment. (I think he was proud to realize how his experience had come into play. Even so, he was a little shaken since he had come to depend on his sixth sense to get him through difficult situations, and it was unnerving for him to realize that he might never have had ESP.)

The commander's experience had provided him with a firm set of patterns. He was accustomed to sizing up a situation by having it match one of these patterns. He may not have been able to articulate the patterns or describe their features, but he was relying on the pattern-matching process to let him feel comfortable that he had the situation scoped out. Nevertheless, he did not seem to be aware of how he was using his experience because he was not doing it consciously or deliberately. He did not realize there were other ways he could have sized the situation up. He could see what was going on in front of his eyes but not what was going on behind them, so he attributed his expertise to ESP.

This is one basis for what we call intuition: recognizing things without knowing how we do the recognizing. In the simple version of the RPD model, we size the situation up and immediately know how to proceed: which goals to pursue, what to expect, how to respond. We are drawn to certain cues and not others because of our situation awareness. (This must happen all the time. Try to imagine going through a day without making these automatic responses.)

There may be other aspects of intuition than the one I have been describing. I do know that the firefighters' experience enables them to recognize situations quickly.

Many people think of intuition as an inborn trait—something we are born with. I am not aware of any evidence showing that some people are blessed with intuition, and others are not. My claim in this chapter is that intuition grows out of experience.

We should not be surprised that the commander in this case was not aware of the way he used his experience. Rather than giving him specific facts from memory, the experience affected the way he saw the situation. Another reason that he could not describe his use of experience was that he was reacting to things that were *not* happening rather than to things that were. A third reason that he was unaware of his use of experience was that he was not drawing on his memory for any specific previous experience. A large set of similar incidents had all blended together.

These are reasons why decision makers have trouble describing their intuition. Even researchers have problems with this concept. For example, in 1978, Lee Beach and Terry Mitchell presented a contingency model of decision making, arguing that the type of strategy a person uses will change depending on the context of the decision task. Sometimes people use the rigorous analytical methods; sometimes they rely on nonanalytical methods. Beach and Mitchell had no trouble explaining what they meant by rigorous analytical methods, and they could point to a number of techniques being studied at the time. However, when they wanted to explain what they meant by nonanalytical methods, they came up short. They suggested things like "gut feeling," and tossing a coin, and even going "eeney meeny miney moe."

Now we can say that at least some aspects of intuition come from the ability to use experience to recognize situations and know how to handle them. Described in this way, intuition does not sound very mysterious.[2] In fact, the simple version of the RPD model is a model of intuition.

Intuition is an important source of power for all of us. Nevertheless, we have trouble observing ourselves use experience in this way, and we definitely have trouble explaining the basis of our judgments when someone else asks us to defend them. Therefore, intuition has a bad reputation compared with a judgment that comes from careful analysis of all the relevant factors and shows each inference drawn and traces the conclusion in a clear line to all of the antecedent conditions. In fact, research by Wilson and Schooler (1991) shows that people do worse at some decision tasks when they are asked to perform analyses of the reasons for their preferences or to evaluate all the attributes of the choices.

Intuition is not infallible. Our experience will sometimes mislead us, and we will make mistakes that add to our experience base. Imagine that you are driving around in an unfamiliar city, and you see some landmark, perhaps a gas station, and you say, "Oh, now I know where we are," and (despite the protests of your spouse, who has the map) make a fateful turn and wind up on an unescapable entrance ramp to the highway you had been trying to avoid. As you face the prospect of being sent miles out of your way, you may lamely offer that the gas station you remembered must have been a different one: "I thought I recognized it, but I guess I was wrong."

The fireground commanders we studied were aware that they could misperceive a situation. Even the commander who thought he had ESP did not make a habit of counting on it. The commanders rely on their expectancies as one safeguard. If they read a situation correctly, the expectancies should match the events. If they are wrong, they can quickly use their experience to notice anomalies.[3] In the example of the vertical shaft fire, the commander walked out of the building as soon as he heard that the fire had spread beyond the second floor. He needed to get another reading about what was happening to the building. The commander who thought he had ESP was so discomfited when his expectancies were violated that he pulled his crew out of the building. These decision makers could formulate clear expectancies based on their experience, so that early in the sequence they could detect that they had gotten it wrong.

Firefighters are not the only ones who confuse intuition and experience with ESP. Naval officers also do it.

Example 4.2
The Mystery of the HMS *Gloucester*

In February 1992, I heard about a curious incident in which the HMS *Gloucester*, a British Type 42 destroyer, was attacked by a Silkworm missile near the end of the Persian Gulf War. The officer in charge of air defense believed strongly that the radar contact was a hostile missile, not a friendly aircraft, seconds after first detection and before the identification procedure had been carried out—even though the radar blip was indistinguishable from an aircraft, and the US. Navy had been flying airplanes through the same area. The officer could not explain how he believed this was a Silkworm missile. The experts who looked at the recordings later said there was no way to tell them apart. Nevertheless, he insisted that he knew. And he shot the object down.

At the time, his captain was not so confident. We watched the videotape of the radar scope and listened to the voices. When the radar blip is destroyed, the captain asks hesitantly, "Whose bird was it?" (that is, who

Example 4.2 (continued)

shot the missile that destroyed this unknown track?). The anti–air warfare officer nervously replies, "It was ours, sir." For the next four hours
the HMS *Gloucester* sweats out the possibility that they shot down an
American plane.

The mystery of the HMS *Gloucester* was how the officer knew it was a
Silkworm missile, not an aircraft.

In July and August 1993, I conducted a workshop on cognitive task
analysis interviews for George Brander, a human factors specialist at
the Defense Research Agency in the United Kingdom. (The methods of
using cognitive task analysis for interviewing are discussed in chapter 11.)
Brander arranged to have us practice the methods with actual naval officers. One of them was Lieutenant Commander Michael Riley, the anti-air
warfare officer on the *Gloucester* who spotted the Silkworm.

We expected that Riley would be tired of going over the incident, but we
found just the reverse. He was still puzzling it out, and he suggested to us
that we focus our session around the Silkworm attack.

The facts were simple. The *Gloucester* was stationed around twenty
miles off the coast of Kuwait, near Kuwait City. The Silkworm missile was
fired around 5:00 A.M. As soon as he saw it, Riley believed it was a missile. He watched it closely for around forty seconds until he had gathered
enough information to confirm his intuition. Then he fired the *Gloucester's*
own missiles and brought the Silkworm down. The whole incident lasted
only around ninety seconds, and the *Gloucester* almost did not get its shot
off in time. Riley confessed that when he first saw the radar blip, "I believed
I had one minute left to live." The puzzle was how he knew it was a Silkworm instead of an American A-6 aircraft. The Silkworm travels at around
600 to 650 knots, the same speed as the American A-6s as they return from
bombing runs. Both are around the same size and present the same profile
on the radar scopes. They are the same size because of all the explosive the
Silkworm carries. It is about as large as a single-decker bus, large enough
to devastate a type 42 destroyer like the *Gloucester*.

There are four ways to distinguish an American A-6 airplane from an
Iraqi Silkworm missile.

The first way is *location*. The Allied forces knew the location of the Iraqi
Silkworm sites and the naval ships. Theoretically the airplanes should return to aircraft carriers by preestablished routes, but the American pilots
returning from bombing runs were cutting corners, and flying over the Silkworm site in question. All the previous day they had done so. Even worse,
the British Navy ships had recently moved closer to shore, and the pilots
had not yet taken this changed position into account, so the A-6s were frequently overflying the ships. Riley and others had insisted that the practice
of overflying ships be ended, but he had not seen any change. So the first
cue, location, was useless for identifying the radar blip.

Radar is the second way to distinguish airplanes from missiles. The A-6s
were fitted with identifiable radar, but most of them did not have their radar

Example 4.2 (continued)

on when they were returning (the radar would make them more easily detectable by the enemy). Thus, the absence of radar was not conclusive.

The third way is a special system, *Identify Friend or Foe* (IFF), which allows an aircraft to be electronically interrogated to find out its status. Pilots obviously shut it down as they approach enemy territory, because it would be a homing beacon for hostile missiles. They are supposed to switch it back on when they leave enemy territory so their own forces will know not to shoot them down. Yet after completing a bombing run and avoiding enemy defenses, many A-6 pilots were late in turning their IFF back on. So the absence of IFF did not prove anything either.

Finally is *altitude*. The Silkworm would fly at around 1,000 feet, and the A-6s at around 2,000 to 3,000 feet and climbing. Therefore, altitude was the primary cue for identification (unless an A-6 had damaged flaps and had to fly lower, but none had been seen coming in below 2,000 feet). Unfortunately, the *Gloucester's* 992 and 1022 radars do not give altitude information. In fact, it didn't have any radar that worked over land, so the first time it picked up a track was after the track went "feet wet" (i.e., flew off the coast and over water). The radars sweep vertically, through 360 degrees, until the radar operator spots a possible target. Only then can the *Gloucester* turn on the 909 radar that sweeps in horizontal bands, to determine roughly the altitude of the target. It takes about thirty seconds to get altitude information after the 909 radar is turned on. (Maddeningly, the *Gloucester's* weapons director failed in his first two attempts to type in the track number, first because the track number was changed just before he typed it in, and next, he transposed the digits.) As a result, it was not until around forty-four seconds into the incident that the 909 informed Riley that the target was flying at 1,000 feet. Only then did he issue the order to fire missiles at the track. Yet he had felt it was a Silkworm almost from the instant he saw it, before the 909 radar was even initiated, and long before it gave him altitude information. Because there was no objective basis for his judgment, Riley confessed to us that he had come to believe it had been ESP.

You can see how little information there is here. To make matters worse, clouds of smoke particles from the burning oil fields were adhering to moisture in the air and obscuring the radars. The *Gloucester's* mission was to protect a small battle force, including the USS *Missouri*, whose guns were pounding the Kuwait coast, some minesweepers clearing the way for the ships to get closer, and a few other ships as well. The *Missouri* wanted to get closer to the coast and on the day of the attack was only twenty miles off. And the closer it got, the less time the *Gloucester* had to react to a Silkworm attack.

Riley told us about the background to the incident. The war was ending, with American-led forces driving up the coast toward Kuwait City. Soon they would overrun the Silkworm site. The constant shelling from the *Missouri* was taking its toll. Also, the Allies had just flown a helicopter feint.

Example 4.2 (continued)

Large numbers of helicopters, launched off carriers, staged a mock attack and then flew back. Riley had earlier run a mental simulation, putting himself in the minds of the Iraqi Silkworm operators. If they did not fire their missiles soon, they would lose any chance. There was nothing to save the missiles for. And they had a nice, fat target, the *Missouri*. If Riley was a Silkworm operator, this was when he would fire his missiles.

The *Gloucester's* crew had been working more than a month on a six-hour-on, six-hour-off schedule. That meant six hours of staring at radar screens, then six hours to eat, perform other tasks, and grab some sleep. Fatigue had been building up during that time. Riley's shift had started at midnight, so his crew had been going for five hours. Because of Riley's imagining what he would do if he were running a Silkworm site, he believed they were under greater risk than at any time earlier. Perhaps an hour before the attack, he warned his crew to be on their highest alert, because this was when the Iraqis were likely to fire at them. Riley repeated his warning again, maybe at 4:55 A.M. As a result, the crew was ready when the missile came.

When we pressed Riley about what he was noticing when he first spotted the radar blip, he said that he knew it was a missile within the first five seconds. Since the radar sweep on the 922 is around four seconds, that means he identified it by the second sweep. Riley said he felt it was accelerating, almost imperceptibly. That was the clue. The A-6s flew at a constant speed, but this track seemed to be accelerating as it came off the coast. Fortunately, there were no other air tracks at the time, so he and his crew could give it their full attention. Otherwise, he doubts he would have noticed the acceleration.

That should have wrapped things up—except that after Riley left the interview, we discovered some inconsistencies in his account. First, he had no way to calculate acceleration until he saw at least three radar sweeps. He needed to compare the distance between sweeps 1 and 2 to the distance between 2 and 3, to see which was larger. Even more troubling, there was no difference at all between the distance traveled by the track during its entire course. We could not see any signs of acceleration, nor could the experts who analyzed the tape. So, using objective measures, there was no indication of acceleration.

We also wondered about Riley's sense that he knew it was a missile almost from the first contact. That first blip was recorded a little way off the coast, because the ground clutter had masked the missile until it flew far enough over water. This took one or two sweeps. Then the 992 radar picked up the track. What was there about that track that alerted Riley? We watched the tape again and again, trying to figure it out. Eventually we succeeded. Rob Ellis, from the Defense Research Agency at Farnborough, realized what it was. (Before reading on, you may want to reread the information and see what you come up with. All the relevant information has been presented.)

Example 4.2 (continued)

Ellis tried to figure out why a track would look as if it was accelerating, when it really was not, and before all the necessary information was in. He realized that the one difference between an A-6 and a Silkworm was altitude: 1,000 feet versus around 3,000 feet. Just as the track came off the coast, the track was masked by ground clutter. The *Gloucester* was twenty miles away. Ellis reasoned that the 992 radar would pick up a track flying at 3,000 feet earlier than one flying at 1,000 feet. The lower track would be masked by ground for a longer time. Maybe that meant that the higher tracks, at 3,000 feet, could be spotted on radar on the second radar sweep, after they went feet wet, whereas the Silkworm, flying at 1,000 feet, would not give a radar return until the third radar sweep. Perceptually, the Silkworm would first be spotted farther off the coast than the A-6s had been. The *Gloucester's* crew, and Riley, were accustomed to A-6s. They knew the location of the Silkworm site, and they were looking for a radar blip coming from that direction, at a certain distance off the coast. Instead, Riley saw a blip farther off the coast than usual. That caught his attention and chilled him. The second radar return showed the usual distance for a track flying around 600 to 650 knots. Compared to how far that first track had come, it must have felt as if the track was moving really fast when it came off the coast. Then it seemed to slow down. Riley must have had a sense of great acceleration as he confounded altitude with speed.

We asked Riley if he wanted to hear our hypothesis, and when we explained it, he agreed that we might have solved the riddle. Although the 992 radar does not scan for altitude, a skilled observer was able to infer altitude using the distance from the coast where the blip was first seen when the track went feet wet.

In this example, as in the previous one, it is the mismatch or anomaly that the decision maker noticed. Perhaps such instances are difficult to articulate because they depend on a deviation from a pattern rather than the recognition of a prototype.

We have seen the use of intuition with firefighters and U.S. Navy officers, and each time the decision makers had trouble describing it. The next section illustrates the point using another domain, nursing.

The Infected Babies

In this project, we studied the way nurses could tell when a very premature infant was developing a life-threatening infection. Beth Crandall, one of my coworkers, had gotten funding from the National Institute of Health to study decision making and expertise in nurses. She arranged to work with the nurses in the neonatal intensive care unit (NICU) of a large hospital. These nurses cared for newly born infants who were premature or otherwise at risk.

Beth found that one of the difficult decisions the nurses had to make was to judge when a baby was developing a septic condition—in other words, an infection. These infants weighed only a few pounds—some of them, the microbabies, less than two pounds. When babies this small develop an infection, it can spread through their entire body and kill them before the antibiotics can stop it. Noticing the sepsis as quickly as possible is vital.

Somehow the nurses in the NICU could do this. They could look at a baby, even a microbaby, and tell the physician when it was time to start the antibiotic (Crandall & Getchell-Reiter, 1993). Sometimes the hospital would do tests, and they would come back negative. Nevertheless, the baby went on antibiotics, and usually the next day the test would come back positive.

This is the type of skilled decision making that interests us the most. Beth began by asking the nurses how they were able to make these judgments. "It's intuition," she was told, or else "through experience." And that was that. The nurses had nothing more to say about it. They looked. They knew. End of story.

That was even more interesting: expertise that the person clearly has but cannot describe. Beth geared up the methods we had used with the firefighters. Instead of asking the nurses general questions, such as, "How do you make this judgment?" she probed them on difficult cases where they had to use the judgment skills. She interviewed nurses one at a time and asked each to relate a specific case where she had noticed an infant developing sepsis. The nurses could recall incidents, and in each case they could remember the details of what had caught their attention. The cues varied from one case to the next, and each nurse had experienced a limited number of incidents. Beth compiled a master list of sepsis cues and patterns of cues in infants and validated it with specialists in neonatology.

Some of the cues were the same as those in the medical literature, but almost half were new, and some cues were the *opposite* of sepsis cues in adults. For instance, adults with infections tend to become more irritable. Premature babies, however, become less irritable. If a microbaby cried every time it was lifted up to be weighed and then one day it did not cry, that would be a danger signal to the experienced nurse. Moreover, the nurses were not relying on any single cue. They often reacted to a pattern of cues, each one subtle, that together signaled an infant in distress.

Some of the Costs of Field Research

The project with the NICU nurses was draining for our staff. The problem was not solely the minor shocks of inadvertently witnessing distressing medical procedures or the strain of seeing such tiny babies struggling to survive. It was the strain in the nurses themselves. More than half of the nurses interviewed cried at some point as they recalled infants who had not made it, signs they should have seen but missed, and even babies who had close calls. None of our other studies were as emotionally demanding as this one.

Other studies posed their own challenges. Once we had a chance to observe and interview the command staff of a Forest Service team trying to bring a forest fire under control that had spread over six mountains in Idaho. One member of the research team was Marvin Thordsen.

In Idaho, Marvin was attached to a team in charge of the fire on one of the mountains. He dutifully tagged along, listening and looking agreeable. After a few days of this, Marvin was sitting in on one of their planning meetings. The team got to an issue and realized that they had already made this decision several days ago, but no one could remember what they decided. Marvin could listen only so long before he broke down. Knowing that he was violating the creed of observers just to watch and never to intervene, he flipped back a few pages in his notebook and read to them what their plan had been. Jaws dropped open as the team found out how helpful it is to have someone serving as their official memory. By the end of his stint with the Forest Service, he was included as part of the planning team. Before finishing their meetings, they would ask him if he had anything to add.

Marvin was a witness when another member of our research team, Chris Brezovic, tear-gassed himself during our study of tank platoon leaders being trained at Fort Knox, Kentucky. As their training scenario was winding down, Chris was standing with one of the instructors, a sergeant. Part of the exercise was to train the platoon leaders to don their protective gear quickly in case of chemical weapons. As the sergeant tossed out several canisters of tear gas, the wind shifted. It collected the tear gas and lifted it up in a cloud that began to move slowly toward Chris and the sergeant, neither of them with gas masks or protective gear. Chris knew about tear gas, and his first impulse was to run away while there was still time. But the sergeant was standing firm, and Chris decided that he did not want to be the first one to run. The sergeant decided that he did not want to look like a coward in front of observers.

He would stay until this civilian could not take it anymore, and then he would leave. So they both stayed where they were, while the cloud got closer. As the cloud floated directly overhead, the wind plunged the tear gas down at them. They tried to run, but it was too late. They collapsed, coughing uncontrollably, their faces covered with tears and mucus.

In terms of pure adrenaline rush, I do not think any of our experiences can exceed the time we were studying airport baggage screeners, to understand how they interpreted the X-ray images. Their difficult job is to identify weapons that may be rotated in any direction and may be superimposed on other metal objects. They need to make the judgment in only a few seconds. During this project sponsored by the Federal Aviation Administration, two of our researchers, Steve Wolf and Dave Klinger, traveled to Cleveland to observe and conduct interviews. Approximately ten minutes after they arrived at the checkpoint, a baggage screener saw something suspicious in the bag that a large, expensively dressed man had sent through the machine. The baggage screener did not know it was a gun (if she had, she would have locked it into the machine). She asked the man if she could open the bag. Security guards were summoned and quickly confiscated a gun, then led the man off in handcuffs. Our stunned researchers looked on in amazement. The odd part of the story is that the man had not intended to smuggle the weapon at all. He was carrying drugs and had forgotten to remove his 0.38 when he arrived at the airport.

Applications

The part of intuition that involves pattern matching and recognition of familiar and typical cases can be trained. If you want people to size up situations quickly and accurately, you need to expand their experience base. One way is to arrange for a person to receive more difficult cases. A fireground commander in a small, rural community may get little direct experience. Recall the case of the Christmas fire where the commanders acted like novices compared to the two consultants. In contrast, firefighters in a large city with many old buildings can get a tremendous amount of experience in a short time.

Another approach is to develop a training program, perhaps with exercises and realistic scenarios, so the person has a chance to size up numerous situations very quickly. A good simulation can sometimes provide more training value than direct experience. A good simulation lets you stop the action, back up to see what went on, and cram many trials together so a person can develop a sense of typicality. Another training strategy is to compile stories of difficult cases and make these the training materials.

In the NICU project, when Beth Crandall showed her findings to the nurse manager of the unit, the woman asked if Beth would present the cues to nurses on the unit in a training program. Beth objected that all the items on the list of critical cues had come from the nurses themselves. The head nurse was not deterred. Because this type of perceptual expertise was not getting shared or compiled, it was a particularly hard thing for new nurses on the unit to master. Beth eventually developed training materials to illustrate all of the critical cues that the nurses could use to diagnose when an infant was in the early stages of an infection. There were different ways to present these materials, such as simple lists of cues; Beth embedded the cues in the stories themselves so that the nurses could see how the cue appeared in context.

Another project that Beth performed involved the study of myocardial infarction, commonly known as heart attacks. We had been working in the area of cardiopulmonary resuscitation to investigate how paramedics develop perceptual skills. The paramedics we interviewed said they could judge whether the person was actually having a heart attack or just suffering from indigestion. They also said they could tell when a person was going to have a heart attack, days or even months ahead. At first we did not give this much thought; it sounded like the commanders who insisted they had ESP. After we heard it from more than one source, we paid attention. For instance, a paramedic described a family gathering where she saw her father-in-law for the first time in many months.

"I don't like the way you look," she said.

"Well, you don't look so great yourself," was his answer.

"No, I really don't like the way you look," she continued. "We're going to the hospital."

He grudgingly agreed to go the next day, but she insisted they go right then. An examination showed a blockage to a major artery. By the next day, he was having surgery to clear the blockage.

Many of us view the heart like a balloon. A person is walking along just fine and then, ping, something snags the balloon and the person goes down with a heart attack. This metaphor is not accurate. The heart is a pump, with thick, muscular walls. It does not burst, like a balloon. Instead, it clogs up, like a pump. Sometimes it clogs up quickly, as when a clot lodges somewhere (here the balloon metaphor may come in). When it clogs up slowly, during congestive heart failure, there are signs. Areas of the body that are less important get less blood. By knowing what they are and by being alert to patterns in several of these areas, you can detect a problem in advance. The skin gets less blood and turns grayish. That is one of the best signs. The wrists and ankles show swelling. The mouth can look greenish. Our interviews with physicians, paramedics, and others turned up these indicators and several others. We also scanned the literature and verified our list of critical cues with specialists.

Perceptual cues can be defined. This expertise does not have to remain in the realm of the specialist or in the intuition of the nurse or paramedic who has seen similar cases. It should be possible to train ordinary citizens to look at each other and recognize when a friend or coworker is starting to show the signs of impending heart problems.

Hugh Wood (program chair for emergency incident policy and analysis curriculum) and Carol Bouma (instructional design specialist) at the Federal Emergency Management Agency/National Fire Academy have been using the RPD model to revamp the academy's curriculum in order to supply commanders more training in pattern matching and in recognizing situations. In the U.S. Marine Corps, Lieutenant General Paul Van Riper has guided organizations such as the Marine Corps Combat Development Command at Quantico, Virginia, to support intuitive decision making. The marines are beginning to use rapid pattern-matching exercises developed by Major John Schmitt (U.S. Marine Corps Reserves) and other officers. In both places, the emphasis on pattern matching seemed more useful than lessons on formal analysis of alternate options.

5

The Power of Mental Simulation

During a visit to the National Fire Academy we met with one of the senior developers of training programs. In the middle of the meeting, the man stood up, walked over to the door, and closed it. Then in a hushed voice he said, "To be a good fireground commander, you need to have a rich fantasy life."

He was referring to the ability to use the imagination, to imagine how the fire got started, how it was going to continue spreading, or what would happen using a new procedure. A commander who cannot imagine these things is in trouble.

Why did the developer close the door before he revealed this ability? Because the idea of using fantasy as a source power is as embarrassing as the idea using intuition as a source of power. He was using the term *fantasy* to refer to a heuristic strategy decision researchers call *mental simulation,* that is, the *ability to imagine people and objects consciously and to transform those people and objects through several transitions, finally picturing them in a different way than at the start.* This process is not just building a static snapshot. Rather, it is building a sequence of snapshots to play out and to observe what occurs.

Here is a simple exercise that calls for mental simulation. Figure 5.1 shows two pictures: a truck on the ground—the initial state—and a truck in the air supported by a column of concrete blocks—the target state. Can you think of a way that you, working alone, can get that truck up in the air on a column of blocks? You need to do this all by yourself, using an inexhaustible pile of concrete blocks and a jack, the only machine you are permitted.

One way to imagine the task is shown in figure 5.2. You begin with the initial state. Then you jack up the right rear tire, slip a set of blocks

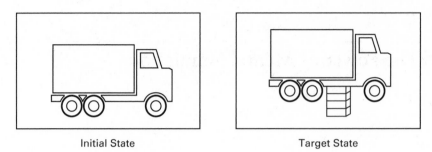

Initial State   Target State

Figure 5.1

Truck levitation

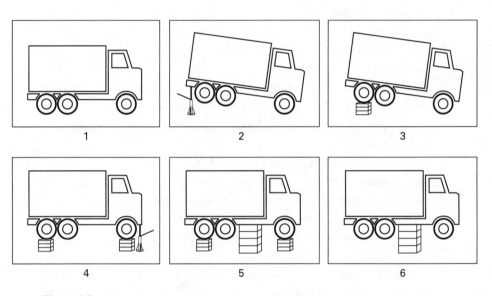

Figure 5.2

Transition sequence

underneath that tire, remove the jack, and use it on the left rear tire. You repeat the process until all the tires have been raised. You build a pile of blocks underneath the center of the truck. Then you (carefully) remove all of the blocks supporting each tire so that you wind up with the target state.

This is an action sequence because you are changing from one state to another, bridging the gap between the initial state and the target state. Some people do this with visual imagery, perhaps what is shown in figure 5.2. Others claim that they figure it out logically without ever using visual images.

Example 5.1
The Car Rescue

The leader of the emergency rescue team is called out to save a person who crashed his car into a concrete pillar supporting an overpass. Other firefighters are already on the scene when he arrives, and they are bringing out the Jaws of Life, a hydraulic machine that can be inserted into a narrow place to exert great force that widens the opening. It is designed to force open things like car doors that have become crumpled in an accident, trapping the victim.

The head of the rescue team goes over to the car to investigate. The driver is the only person in the car, and he is unconscious. The commander walks around the car to test each door, but each is badly damaged and will not open. Using the Jaws of Life to pry open the doors will be difficult.

During his investigation, the commander has noticed that the impact has severed most of the posts holding up the roof of the car. He begins to wonder if they can lift off the roof and then slide the passenger out rather than fighting their way through the doors. He tries to imagine how that might be done. He imagines the roof being removed. Then he visualizes how they will slide the driver, where rescue workers will stand to support the driver's neck, how they will turn the driver to maneuver around the steering column, and how they will lift him out. It seems to work. He runs through the sequence again to try to identify any problems but can't find any. He had heard that rescues could be made this way, but he had never seen it.

He explains to his crew what they need to do, and the rescue works out as he had imagined. The only problem is that the driver's legs become wedged underneath the steering wheel, and additional firefighters have to reach in to unlock his knees.

The car rescue is an example of a mental simulation that worked out well. The earlier example of the harness rescue (example 3.2) showed a case where the mental simulation was incomplete; it neglected the fact that the ladder belt could not be pulled tightly enough.

Mental simulation does not always work, as the next example shows.[1]

Exampie 5.2
The Libyan Airliner

It is almost 2:00 P.M., February 21, 1973, and a Libyan airliner that took off from Bengazi airport is heading toward its destination, Cairo. At least, that is what its crew believes. In fact, the plane is just passing over Port Touafic, at the southern end of the Suez Canal. It is about to cross over to the Sinai Peninsula, occupied by Israel at that time. The plane is seriously off course.

Israeli radar has spotted the plane. The Israeli Defense Forces are on alert because of warnings of a terrorist attack—a plan, it is said, to hijack an airplane and explode it over a populated area. Possible targets include the city of Tel Aviv, the nuclear installation at Dimona, and other civilian or military targets. The Israelis note that this airplane is deviating from the typical air corridors and violating Egyptian airspace. It has flown above the most sensitive spots of the Egyptian war zone, yet no Egyptian MiGs are being scrambled to investigate. No Egyptian ground-to-air missiles are fired, although the Egyptians are supposed to be on full alert. The Egyptian communications do not refer to the intruding plane. The Israelis know that the Egyptians have a very sensitive early warning system. A month earlier, they had shot down an Ethiopian plane that had flown over an Egyptian war zone by mistake.

At 1:54 P.M., the aircraft penetrates into the Israeli war zone in the Sinai Desert, cruising at 20,000 feet. The plane is flying a route referred to by the Israelis as "hostile," one used by Egyptian fighters in their intrusions.

At 1:56 P.M., two Israeli F-4 Phantom fighters are sent to investigate. At 1:59 P.M., the F-4s intercept the plane. They do not see any passengers since all the window shades are down. The F-4 pilots identify the plane as an airliner with Libyan markings. They can see the Libyan crew in the cockpit. They are certain the Libyan crew recognizes them, by the Shield of King David markings on their planes. One of the F-4 pilots reports that the airplane's copilot looked directly into his eyes.

Using the international practice of signaling by radio and rocking their wings, the F-4s signal for the airliner to land at Refidim air base. The intercepted plane is supposed to respond by following the instructions, notifying the appropriate air traffic services unit, and establishing radio communications with the interceptor. The Libyan airplane performs none of these actions. The air crew does seem to convey by hand signals that they understand the request and intend to obey; nevertheless, the airliner continues to head northeast.

At 2:01 P.M., the F-4s fire some tracer shells in front of the airliner's nose. The airliner turns toward Refidim air base and descends to 5,000 feet. The pilot lowers the landing gear. Suddenly he turns back toward the west and increases altitude, as if he is trying to escape. The F-4s fire warning shots in front of him, but he continues. The Israeli generals monitoring the situation decide that the airplane is indeed on a terrorist mission, and

Example 5.2 (continued)

they are determined to prevent its escape. They direct the F-4s to force it to land.

At 2:08 P.M., the F-4s shoot at the airliner's wing tips. Even after its right wing tip is hit, the airliner continues west. The F-4s begin firing at the wing bases, and finally the airliner attempts a crash landing. The pilot is almost successful but slides into a sand dune. Of more than a hundred passengers and crew, only one person survives.

The Israeli Perspective

The airliner is not in direct communication with Cairo airport. It receives no attention as it flies over sensitive Egyptian locations, and for these and other reasons, it is identified as a hostile intrusion.

The Israelis try to imagine how they can be dealing with a legitimate civilian airliner. A captain responsible for the safety of passengers avoids even the slightest risk. That is why pilots obey hijackers so quickly. Given this mind-set, any legitimate crew would land when clear signals are given.

This plane does not land. Here is what Israeli Air Force General "Motti" Hod said: "The captain sees our Israeli insignia on our F-4s. He sees Refidim airfield ahead. He knows we want him to land, since he lowers his landing gear. Then he retracts the landing gear and flies off! At first he doesn't fly directly west but turns to circle the air base. We interpret this as an attempt to make a better approach. Then he turns and starts to fly west. That is when we order our F-4s to start firing tracer bullets, which the crew must see. Still they keep going west. No genuine civilian captain would behave in such a manner. In contrast, a crew on a terrorist mission would show such behavior. Therefore, we must prevent their escape and force them to land.

"Moreover, recent history just confirmed our beliefs. A few months earlier, an Ethiopian airliner had strayed into the Egyptian ground-to-air missile system and was shot down. An American private airplane also was shot down by missiles above the delta. Several other planes were fired on when they penetrated areas that maps warn pilots to avoid. Pilots have learned to become familiar with these free-fire zones and to stay far away from them. Yet here was a plane flying right through them!"

The Israelis try to imagine how a civilian airline captain would behave in the ways they were observing. They cannot fit the pieces together. In contrast, they can fit the pieces together if they imagine that the plane is on a terrorist mission. The Israelis' diagnosis of the situation is not very difficult, given the clear-cut nature of the evidence.

The Airliner Perspective

During the afternoon, a sandstorm covers the sky of Egypt. The airliner is on a routine flight. The captain and the flight engineer are French, the

Example 5.2 (continued)

copilot Libyan. The black box from the airplane is later recovered and shows that the pilot and flight engineer are conversing in French; the copilot is not sufficiently fluent to participate in the discussion. The captain and flight engineer are drinking wine and do not realize they have deviated more than seventy miles from their planned route.

At 1:44 P.M., the captain begins to have his doubts about their course. He talks to the flight engineer, but not the copilot, about these doubts. He does not report his worries to Cairo airport. Instead, at 1:52 he receives permission from Cairo airport to start his descent.

At 1:56 P.M., the captain is still uncertain about his actual position. He tries to receive beacon signals from Cairo airport, and those he receives are contrary to the ones he expects according to his flight plan. Nevertheless, he continues flying as scheduled.

Between 1:59 and 2:02 P.M., the crew achieves radio contact with Cairo airport and explains its difficulties in receiving the radio beacon and their inability to receive the Cairo nondirectional beacon. Cairo airport believes that they are close and directs them to descend to 4,000 feet.

When the Israeli Phantoms come up, the crew identifies them as Egyptian fighters. The Libyan copilot reports, "Four MiGs behind us," The Egyptians fly Soviet MiGs; the Israelis do not.

When the Israeli pilot approaches the airliner and gives hand signals to land, the Libyan copilot reports this to his colleagues. The captain and the flight engineer gesticulate angrily about the rudeness of the MiGs. These may have been the hand signals the pilot reported. The Libyan captain and flight engineer continue to speak in French.

There are two airfields in the Cairo area: Cairo West, an international airport, and Cairo East, a military base. The crew interprets the fighters' actions as warning them that they have overshot Cairo West and are over the military base. The air crew interprets the fighters as a military escort. When they begin to descend at Refidim air base, they see that it is a military base, so they realize they must be at Cairo East. They decide it would be a mistake to land at Cairo East, so they turn toward Cairo West.

At 2:09 P.M., the captain reports to Cairo control: "We are now shot by your fighter." This is unthinkable, since at the time Egypt and Libya were on excellent terms. When they are fired on again, they think the Egyptian fighters are crazy. Why would an Egyptian fighter shoot a Libyan civilian airliner? The fighters were friendly escorts, making sure they did not land in the wrong place. They change course obediently. They are fired on unexpectedly and are unable to build this into their story. Why would Egyptian fighters be firing on them?

They are still trying to figure this out when, just before they crash, the Libyan copilot finally identifies the fighters as Israeli planes. The black box does not reveal how they incorporate that fact into their diagnosis of the situation.

What happened here? The Israeli generals ran into a situation that exceeded their wildest fantasies. Similarly, the crew of the airliner was not able to imagine what was happening to them until the very end. In this example, mental simulation is used differently than in the car rescue. In that case, mental simulation was used to imagine how a course of action would be played out into the future. Here, the Israeli generals were using mental simulation to imagine what could have happened in the past to account for the strange goings-on. Mental simulation about the past can be used to explain the present. It can also be used for predicting the future from the present.

Beth Crandall and I have been interested in mental simulation for several years because the process seems so central to decision making and because we keep finding it in expert performance.

We found that as early as 1946 Adriaan de Groot had studied the mental simulation of chess masters. Two decision researchers, Kahneman and Tversky (1982), had written a paper on the simulation heuristic, based on laboratory studies. They described how a person might build a simulation to explain how something might happen; if the simulation required too many unlikely events, the person would judge it to be implausible.[2]

With funding from the Army Research Institute, Beth and I did an exploratory study on mental simulation to learn more about its nature. Our idea was to gather and examine a set of cases to see if there were any regularities. For the most part, the cases came from our own records (the harness rescue case, the car rescue), and we also included cases from other sources, such as the Libyan airliner incident, as well as examples from a book by Charles Perrow, *Normal Accidents* (1984), which gives the details behind a variety of disasters and breakdowns. In addition, we performed some informal interviews and asked the people in our company to volunteer examples.

After we had collected all the cases, we reviewed them for commonalities and differences. Then we tried to code them for features such as time pressure, experience level of the person, use of visual versus nonvisual simulations, and so on. We dropped about 20 percent of the cases because the description did not clearly show how the mental simulation was being used. We could imagine how the person might have been using mental simulation, but when it was a stretch, we were not sure if we were studying the person's fantasies or our own. That left us with seventy-nine cases.

These cases showed the same patterns (Klein & Crandall, 1995). The people were constructing mental simulations almost the way you build a machine: "Here is the starting point. Then this kicks in, which changes that, and then this other thing happens, and you wind up there." It's like designing a watch or a mousetrap. For the overpass harness rescue, the fireground commander imagined how they would lower the ladder belt down, then lift the woman up by an inch, slide the belt under her, buckle it, then lift it up. For the car rescue, the commander imagined how they would lift off the roof, climb in the car, support the man's neck, slide him away from the steering column, grab hold of his arms and legs, and swivel him up and out of the car.

We noticed something else: the mental simulations were not very elaborate. Each seemed to rely on just a few factors—rarely more than three. It would be like designing a machine that had only three moving parts. Perhaps the limits of our working memory had to be taken into account. Also, there was another regularity: the mental simulations seemed to play out for around six different transition states, usually not much more than that. Perhaps this was also a result of limited working memory. If you cannot keep track of endless transitions, it is better to make sure the mental simulation can be completed in approximately six steps.

This is the "parts requirement" for building a mental simulation: a maximum of three moving parts. The design specification is that the mental simulation has to do its job in six steps. Those are the constraints we work under when we construct mental simulations for solving problems and making decisions. We have to assemble the simulation within these constraints.

Of course, there are ways of avoiding the constraints. If we have a lot of familiarity in the area, we can chunk several transitions into one unit. In addition, we can save memory space by treating a sequence of steps as one unit rather than representing all the steps. We can use our expertise to find the right level of abstraction. For example, in the car rescue, the team leader could count the removal of the car roof as one step without imagining the coordination needed to make sure no one got hurt. If he had included the position where everyone would stand before lifting the roof, how they would step in unison, and so forth, the simulation might have bogged down. If he were worried about this particular step, he might do a separate mental simulation for it, to satisfy himself that the roof could be quickly disposed of. The more of these side trips he had to take, the more he would need to hold in his mind. Another strategy for overcoming memory limits is to write things down and draw diagrams to keep track of the transitions.

If the moving parts interact with each other in each transition, you have to remember a lot more since you have to keep track of the parts themselves at each point. Even diagrams start to fall apart as more and more arrows are drawn to represent interactions. We heard a lot about this from some software programming experts we interviewed. Part of a quality inspection team, they had recently finished inspecting a program with over 900,000 lines of code. Each person on the team inspected around 5,000 lines of code a day. They told us that a software program is like a giant machine, with many different moving parts (all the variables) and fixed parts (the operators that transform the variables). Since the code was written down, they did not have to remember all the moving parts; the variables were listed in front of them. The inspection was to imagine how the machine was going to work when the program started running. If the program was linear, as in the truck example in figures 5.1 and 5.2, the job was not too hard. If the variables interacted with each other, the job of visualizing the program in action became quite difficult. So this is another challenge in building a mental simulation. We search for a way to keep the transitions flowing smoothly by building a simulation that has as few interactions as possible.

Considering all these factors, the job of building a mental simulation no longer seems easy. The person assembling a mental simulation needs to have a lot of familiarity with the task and needs to be able to think at the right level of abstraction. If the simulation is too detailed, it can chew up memory space. If it is too abstract, it does not provide much help.

We came across a few cases where people could not assemble a simulation. For instance, the Israeli generals failed to construct a simulation of how a genuine commercial airline pilot would take so many risks. Because of this failure, the generals concluded that the airplane was not a legitimate airliner. Cases like this gave us some idea about how experience is needed to build a mental simulation.

We wanted to study how people failed to build a mental simulation, so we tried something else. We asked people to generate mental simulations in front of us. This was how we came to study the Polish economy.

The Polish Economy

The Polish economy received little coverage in the news media when it was reformed, yet it is one of the boldest experiments of our time. In 1989 the Polish government, freed from control by the Soviet Union, realized that socialism was leading it nowhere, so the government made preparations to convert to a market economy. On January 1, 1990, the new Polish government decreed the switch to capitalism. From that moment, the government would no longer use state companies to provide meaningless jobs. They allowed zlotys to be traded on the open market. They let inflation and unemployment run uninhibited. It was a dramatic moment in the retreat from communism.

The announcement about Poland's switching to a market economy came as we were gathering cases of mental simulation. I realized that I could find some experts and ask them to simulate mentally what was going to happen in Poland during the coming year. Would the reform succeed, or would the Poles have to back down?

Fortunately I was able to interview a bona fide expert: Andrzej (pronounced Andrei) Bloch, an associate professor of economics at Antioch University. He is Polish and received all his education up through his B.A. in Poland. (He got his Ph.D. in the United States.) He makes regular trips back to Poland.

Before I tell you about Andrzej, think about what you would have if I had interviewed you. Could you have set up a mental simulation for the Polish economy during the year 1990? Could you do it now, for the coming year? Where would you start? What would you include in the simulation? Most people shrug their shoulders. If they give any answer at all, it is to parrot back something they have heard on TV: "I hear there is more expansion in Eastern Europe these days."

Andrzej created wonderful simulations. Without prompting, he boiled it down to three variables: the rate of inflation, the rate of unemployment, and the rate of foreign exchange. I asked Andrzej to imagine how the Polish economy would do on these three variables by quarter for the year 1990. According to Andrzej, since the government was not going to fight inflation artificially, the inflation rate was going to zoom up from its (then) current rate of 80 percent a year to an annual rate of about 1,000 percent for a few months. (This meant prices would increase around 80 percent a month instead of 80 percent a year.) Goods were going to become quite expensive. Prices would rise faster than wages. Quickly, people would not be able to afford to buy very much, so demand would fall, and the prices would stabilize. He estimated that this would take about three months. To put things in perspective for me, he noted that food shortages were the traditional source of unrest in Poland and Russia; people were more likely to protest food shortages than a lack of political freedom. If they could not afford to buy bread, that might cause the government to collapse. Nevertheless, he felt that the euphoria over the Solidarity movement was high enough and that the period of sharp inflation would be short enough so there would not be problems on this score. When I reviewed his predictions with him a year later, we found that this was accurate. He had accurately called the sharp increase up to 1,000 percent for January and February, as well as the downturn to around 20 to 25 percent by April and thereafter.

Next, he considered unemployment. If the government had the courage to drop unproductive industries, many people would lose their jobs. This would start in about six months as the government sorted things out. The unemployment would be small by U.S. standards, rising from less than 1 percent to maybe 10 percent. For Poland, this increase would be shocking. Politically, it might be more than the government could tolerate and might force it to end the experiment with capitalism. When we reviewed his estimates, we found that unemployment had not risen as quickly as he expected, probably, Andrzej believed, because the government was not as ruthless as it said it would be in closing unproductive plants. Even worse, if a plant was productive in areas A, B, and C and was terrible in D and E, then as long as they made a profit, they continued their operations without shutting down areas D and E. So the system faced a built-in resistance to increased unemployment.

Finally, he looked at foreign exchange, which he saw as a balancing force. As the exchange rate got worse, increasing from 700 zlotys per dollar to 1,500 zlotys per dollar, people would find foreign goods too expensive so they would buy more Polish items. Similarly, outsiders would find that Polish-made items were a bargain, so exports would boom, increasing employment and improving economic health. He thought this might take a few years to accomplish, if at all. He expected that during 1990, the exchange rate would continue to increase, eventually to 1,400 zlotys per dollar. He expected that the government would intervene at that point. During the year I noted that the zlotys went up to around 900 per dollar and stayed there. Andrzej had been too pessimistic. In 1991, I discussed this with him, and he felt that the problem again was that the government was softening the blows. Had the full market economy shift been made as advertised, the rate would have increased much faster, and the shift would have been finished much quicker.

This mental simulation depended on three factors and on a few transitions (rapid inflation, reduced level of inflation, gradual rise in unemployment and loss in exchange rate, improved employment, and finally, stabilized exchange rate).

Andrzej was not finished. He estimated the likelihood of success for this market economy experiment at 60 percent. A virtuoso at simulating Polish futures, he generated pessimistic mental simulations and showed how the experiment could fail. He switched to political simulations.

Buoyed by this example, I lined up two more people to interview, neither as expert as Andrzej. The first was one of Andrzej's best students, who had visited Eastern Europe recently. The other was a professor of political science at another university; this man had spent a sabbatical in Poland many years earlier. Neither could generate any mental simulations at all. They considered only two variables, inflation and unemployment, so there was no balancing factor such as foreign exchange. Worse, they did not know the current rate of inflation or unemployment, and they had no sense for what would count as a high rate for either variable. The student thought that there would be tough times but that the experiment would succeed, which made him happy. The professor was a Marxist who thought the Poles were making a big mistake by retreating from the wave of the future. He thought there would be tough times and that the government would have to dismantle the market economy, which made him happy.

The implications of this minor sideline in an exploratory study are clear: without a sufficient amount of expertise and background knowledge, it may be difficult or impossible to build a mental simulation. The expert, despite his desire to see the market economy experiment work, could imagine different ways for it to fail and to anticipate early warning signs. He told me about several (e.g., if the rate of inflation does not come down below an annual rate of 50 percent by April, start worrying).

Incidentally, the Polish economy did fairly well during its first year as a market economy. Inflation stayed at a reasonable level, unemployment did not increase too much, and foreign exchange remained stronger than expected. The experiment seems to be working, and as of this writing Poland has become the first former communist country to enjoy economic growth.

The example of the Polish economy shows how difficult it is to construct a useful mental simulation. But once it is constructed, it is impressive. We do this all the time in areas about which we are knowledgeable. We do it to imagine how a supervisor will react, or how to repair a car, or to explain the way a neighbor has been behaving. We do it without giving much thought to what an important source of power we have in our ability to construct mental simulations on demand. In technical fields, people may spend hundreds of thousands of dollars, and sometimes over a million dollars, to build computer simulations of complex phenomena. The computer is needed to keep track of all the variables and the interactions and all the different pathways that are possible. The programs are not as limited by memory capacity as we are. However, these programs are extremely specialized. They run simulations only in the single area for which they have been programmed. In contrast, you and I carry around a multipurpose mental simulator that adapts to all kinds of different problems and requires virtually no reprogramming time. True, it has a limited memory capacity, but its versatility is astounding.

Models of Mental Simulation

Figure 5.3 shows a generic model of mental simulation. It shows the two types of needs: to explain the past and project the future. It shows that we specify the parameters by pinning down the initial state (if we are projecting the future), the terminal state (if we are explaining the past), both initial and terminal states (if we are trying to figure out how the transformation occurred), and the causal factors that drove the transformation.

In assembling the action sequence, figure 5.3 reminds us that mental simulations generally move through six transitions, driven by around three causal factors. Once the person tries to assemble the action sequence, he or she evaluates it for coherence (Does it make sense?), applicability (Will

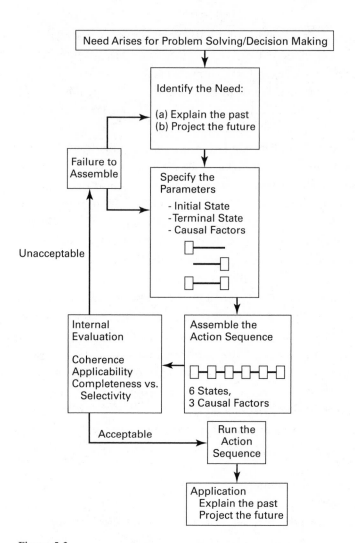

Figure 5.3

Generic model of mental simulation

it get what I need?), and completeness (Does it include too much or too little?). If everything checks out, the action sequence is run and applied to form an explanation, model, or projection. If the internal evaluation turns up difficulties, the person may reexamine the need and/or the parameters and try again.

The cases Beth and I reviewed fit into two major categories: the person was trying to explain what had happened in the past, or trying to imagine what was going to happen in the future. We developed models of each that were variants of the generic model. Incidentally, we coded the seventy-nine incidents of mental simulation independently and found that we could reliably code the incidents into the same categories.

Explaining a Situation

For cases where a person was trying to explain what had happened in the past, the reason was either to make sense of a specific event (such as a juror's trying to figure out if the evidence showed that the defendant had committed the crime) or to make sense of a general class of events by deriving a model (such as Einstein's imagining how a beam of light shining through a hole in an elevator might seem to curve if the elevator was moving). Figure 5.4 shows a specific version of the model that describes how we explain a chain of prior events, or a state of the world.

Consider this example. Some need arises for building a mental simulation; let us say a coworker has suddenly started acting rudely toward you. The simulation has to let you infer what the original situation that led to the events you are observing. You assemble the action sequence: the set of transitions that make up the simulation. Perhaps you recall an incident that same morning when you were chatting with some other people in your office and said something that made them laugh. Perhaps you also recall that earlier that morning, your coworker had confided some embarrassing secret to you. So you construct a sequence in which your coworker trusts you with a confidence, then regrets it immediately afterward and feels a little awkward around you, then sees you possibly entertaining some other people with the secret, and then feels that it is going to be unbearable to live with you in the same setting. Now you can even remember that after you made the other people laugh, you looked up and saw the coworker giving you a look that made you feel uneasy.

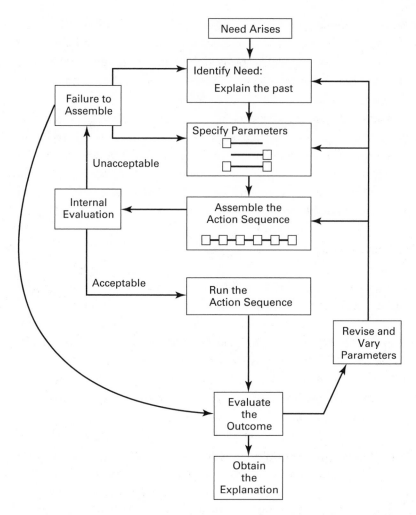

Figure 5.4

Using mental simulation to generate an explanation

This set of states and transitions is the *action sequence,* the mental simulation that explains the rude behavior.

The next step is to evaluate the action sequence at a surface level. Is it coherent (Do the steps follow from each other)? Yes, it is. Does it apply (Does the sequence account for the rudeness)? Yes, it does. How complete is it (Does it leave out any important factors, such as the excellent performance evaluation you have just received)? Yes, there are some more pieces that might belong to the puzzle. But in general, the mental simulation passes the internal evaluation. It is an acceptable explanation. That does not mean it is correct.

Sometimes the mental simulation will not pass the internal evaluation, and that also helps you make sense of things. Example 5.3 illustrates this with a story reported in a newspaper.

Example 5.3
The IRA Terrorist

A well-respected lawyer has agreed to defend a man accused of committing an act of terrorism: planting a bomb for the IRA. The lawyer, asked why he would take the case, answers that he interviewed the accused man, who was shaking and literally overcome with panic. He was surprised to see the man fall apart like that. He tried to imagine the IRA's recruiting such a person for a dangerous mission and found that he could not. He cannot conjure up a scenario in which the IRA would give a terrorism assignment to a man like this, so his conclusion is that the man is innocent.

This lawyer could not generate an action sequence that passed his internal evaluation—specifically, the requirement that the transition between steps be plausible. His failure to assemble a plausible sequence of steps led him to a different explanation than the prosecutors had formed. That's why you see a long, curving arc in figure 5.4: the failure to assemble the mental simulation was the basis of the conclusion.

There are also times when you use mental simulation to try to increase your understanding of situations like these. You are trying to build up better models. When you run the action sequence in your mind, you may notice parts that still seem vague. Maybe you can figure out how to set up a better action sequence, or maybe there are some more details about the present state that you should gather. Going back to the example of your coworker, your explanation has not included the fact that you received such a good performance evaluation. What was your coworker's performance evaluation? Possibly the coworker felt you had gotten recognition for work that someone else had done. Perhaps you can get a general sense of the situation by talking to your boss. That might give you some more data points for building your explanations.

Projecting into the Future

In many cases, decision makers try to project into the future, either to predict what is going to happen and perhaps to prepare for it (manufacturers bidding on a new part who try to imagine how they will make the part and how long that will take) or to watch a potential course of action to find out if it has any flaws (e.g., the car rescue).

Figure 5.5 shows how you can try to build a bridge from your present condition to a future one. You know the initial state and you are trying to imagine the target state. Sometimes you also have a good picture of the target state, as in the truck example, and your job is to figure out how to convert one into the other. What is new here is the way you run and review the action sequence. Recall the car rescue. The team leader put his plan under a microscope, scrutinizing each step to see if there could be a problem. He was trying to find pitfalls in advance. In the end, he evaluated his plan based on the nature and severity of the problems that he found.

Sometimes we form a general impression that a plan is going to work out, without putting the plan under a microscope. We recognize aspects of it that match typical cases that worked for us in the past or led to difficulties. So we use intuition to form an emotional reaction of optimism or worry. In his research with chess masters, Adriaan de Groot found that they frequently formed these global impressions of whether a line of play was going to work, even before they studied the sequence.

Once you have evaluated the action sequence, which is usually a planned course of action, you may try to modify the plan to overcome the pitfalls; or you may decide it cannot be salvaged, so you reject it; or you may carry it out. In some cases, the purpose of the mental simulation is to make a prediction (e.g., how long a process will take), so you run the action sequence through in your mind and form a judgment. Finally, you can use mental simulation to prepare for carrying out a course of action, by rehearsing what you are going to do.

We have left the truck in figure 5.2 dangling in the air long enough. The parameters are that you know the initial state and the target state; your job is to transform one into the other. You assemble the action sequence of what is going to change from one state to the next. Then you evaluate this sequence. Does it make sense? If you are simply trying to make up

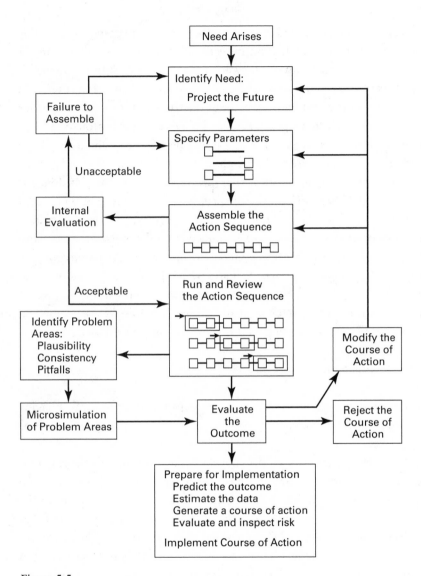

Figure 5.5

Using mental simulation to project into the future

a plausible plan, then you have succeeded. If you are going to carry this plan out, then your evaluation must be a little more careful. You might notice that the truck can roll forward or backward each time you jack it up. Maybe you can use some of the blocks to wedge around the tires. You might also notice that all the weight of the truck in the target state seems to be resting on a single point. Is there any place on the bottom of a truck that can bear such weight? Perhaps it will be safest to build a very large central platform to spread the weight out more.

The mental simulation study that I have been describing was done for purposes of exploration, and so the proposed model has to be considered tentative until we conduct more research. Nevertheless, since completing this exploratory study, we have examined mental simulation more carefully in other research projects and have not come across anything to contradict the models shown in figures 5.3, 5.4, and 5.5.

Mental simulations, run from the past into the present or the present into the future, can stretch to help us infer a missing cause, a missing effect, or a bridge between the two. They can also mislead us.

How Mental Simulations Can Fail

The biggest danger of using mental simulation is that you can imagine any contradictory evidence away. The power of mental simulation can be used against itself.

Consider the example of the rude coworker. You believe the rudeness comes from paranoia that you have divulged the coworker's secret. To test this explanation, you ask a mutual friend to ask the coworker the reason for the rude behavior. The friend reports back that your coworker was not aware of any rudeness, harbors no anger toward you, and never thought that you might reveal confidential information. Does that stop you? Not for a second. The coworker was not aware of rudeness, but who ever is? Similarly, not feeling any anger at all sounds suspiciously like denial. That makes you even more convinced of your explanation. You do not really believe the claim that the coworker never thought you might divulge a confidence, since everyone who tells a secret must have these worries; more likely, the coworker did not want to appear paranoid in front of the mutual friend and was faking good. Or maybe the mutual friend is not so trustworthy after all. Maybe this so-called mutual friend is not telling you the truth on purpose, to lull you into a trap, perhaps to get you to tell the precious secret. Maybe they are all in on it!

We can ask what evidence you would need to give up your explanation. Sadly, the answer is that if you are determined enough, you might never give it up. You can continually save the explanation by making it more comprehensive and complicated. In the nineteenth century the British scientist Sir Francis Galton tried an experiment to see if he could experience what it was like to be paranoid. He tried to maintain the belief that everyone he encountered was plotting against him. Two people talking suddenly look up at him? They are part of the plot. A horse in the park shies away when he comes into view? Even the animals are against him. Galton continued this for part of the day but had to give up the exercise before the day was over. His paranoid explanations were becoming so convincing that they were beginning to get out of control, and he became frightened for his own sanity.

Perrow (1984) has described similar cases that have resulted in major accidents. He refers to them as *de minimus* explanations—explanations that try to minimize the inconsistency.[3] The operator forms an explanation and then proceeds to explain away disconfirming evidence. The following example was an incident that took place on the Mississippi River.[4] Figure 5.6 depicts the incident.

Example 5.4
The *Trademaster* and the *Pisces*

The plot is simple: a ship in a safe passing situation suddenly turned and was impaled by a cargo ship.

To understand how such a thing could occur, remember all the times you have been walking down a hall, approaching someone coming from the other direction. You try to move aside, only to find the other person has moved in the same direction, zigging back at the same time, zagging in unison again. Finally you both come to a full stop, smiling, and resorting to hand signals to sort out the passage. In the case of the *Trademaster* and *Pisces,* the momentum did not allow them to stop.

The Mississippi is sufficiently well mapped for ships as large as these (600 feet long, 24,000 and 33,000 tons) to be able to figure out their passing patterns. Even before they see each other, even as they are rounding the final bend, the two captains radio their arrangement to pass starboard to starboard (with their right sides closest).

Example 5.4 (continued)

Then the complications start. The captain of the *Pisces* sees that he is going to be overtaken by a tug and will have to steer too closely to rafts of barges on his left. Therefore, he uses his radio to request a port-to-port passage with the *Trademaster,* at the same time turning to his right to get in position. Unhappily, the captain of the *Trademaster* never gets the message. He sees the *Pisces* swing out and figures that the captain will correct his error soon enough. He does not want to turn right, since he expects the *Pisces* to go in that direction any moment. Instead, he turns farther left himself, to give the *Pisces* more room to shift back. The *Pisces,* wondering why the *Trademaster* was swerving out so far, turned even more sharply to give the *Trademaster* more room. That is how they collided.

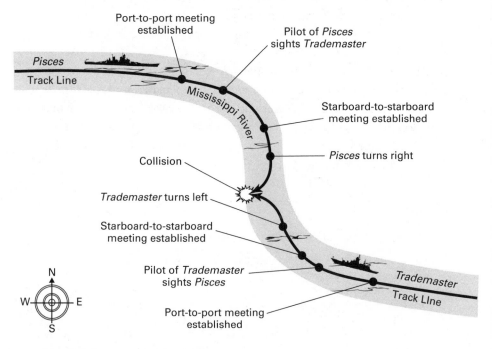

Figure 5.6

Track lines of *Trademaster* and *Pisces*

This simple case shows how disconfirming evidence is explained away. A ship that should be staying to your right swings over to your left? No problem; you have seen it before. There is no reason to think anything might be wrong, until it is too late.

Scientists also fall prey to de minimus explanations. The following example shows how easy it is to invent an explanation that discounts some inconvenient observations.[5]

Example 5.5
The Disoriented Physicists

Two physicists associated with the Aspen Center for Physics are climbing in the Maroon Bells Wilderness near Aspen, Colorado. While descending, they lose their bearings and come down on the south side of the mountain instead of the north side, near Aspen. They look below them and see what they identify as Crater Lake, which they would have spotted from the trail leading home. One of them remarks that there is a dock on the lake. Crater Lake does not have a dock. The other physicist replies, "They must have built it since we left this morning."

A couple of days later they reach home.

I do not count it as a weakness of mental simulations that they are sometimes wrong. My estimate is that most of the time they are fairly accurate. Besides, they are a means of generating explanations, not for generating proofs.

I do count it as a weakness of mental simulations that we become too confident in the ones we construct. One reason for problems such as de minimus explanations that discard disconfirming evidence is that once we have built a mental simulation, we tend to fall in love with it. Whether we use it as an explanation or for prediction, once it is completed, we may give it more credibility than it deserves, especially if we are not highly experienced in the area and do not have a good sense of typicality. This "overconfidence" effect has been shown in the laboratory by Hirt and Sherman (1985). They asked subjects to generate cartoon sequences for the big Penn State versus University of Pittsburgh football game. The subjects were then asked to rate their confidence in one of these teams' actually winning the game. The result was that the confidence rating was affected by the cartoon sequence. Subjects who imagined a sequence in which Penn State won the game rated Penn State's actual chance as higher than the subjects who imagined a sequence where the University of Pittsburgh won the game.

Mental simulation takes effort. Using it is different from looking at a situation and knowing what is happening. Mental simulation is needed when you are not sure what is happening so you have to puzzle it out. When you are pressed for time, you may not do as careful a job in building or inspecting the mental simulations you have constructed. That shortcoming, however, does not argue for any other approach. If you want to deduce every inference logically, you will still run into time barriers.

A final shortcoming is that we have trouble constructing mental simulations when the pieces of the puzzle get too complicated—there are too many parts, and these parts interact with each other. If we are trying to repair a piece of equipment and keep testing it to find out what is wrong, we have a lot of trouble if more than one thing is broken. Once we find one fault, we may be tempted to attribute all the symptoms to it and miss the other fault, so we fix just the problem we know about, and the result is that the equipment still does not work.

Despite these limitations, mental simulation allows us to make decisions skillfully and solve problems under conditions where traditional decision analytic strategies do not apply.

People can also draw on some self-correcting characteristics of mental simulation, to overcome some of the limitations that were described above. We often have a general sense of whether the simulation is becoming unrealistic.

Marvin Cohen (1997) believes that mental simulation is usually self-correcting through a process he has called *snap-back*. Mental simulation can explain away disconfirming evidence, but Cohen has concluded that it is often wise to explain away mild discrepancies since the evidence itself might not be trustworthy. However, there is a point when we have explained away so much that the mental simulation becomes very complicated.[6] At this point, we begin to lose faith in the mental simulation and reexamine it. We look at all of the new evidence that had been explained away to see if maybe there is not another simulation that makes more sense. Cohen believes that until we have an alternate mental simulation, we will keep patching the original one. We will not be motivated to assemble an alternate simulation until there is too much to be explained away. The strategy makes sense. The problem is that we lose track of how much contrary evidence we have explained away so the usual alarms do not go off. This has also been called the garden path fallacy: taking one step that seems very straightforward, and then another, and each step makes so much sense that you do not notice how far you are getting from the main road. Cohen is developing training methods that will help people keep track of their thinking and become more aware of how much contrary evidence they have explained away so they can see when to start looking for alternate explanations or predictions.

Here is an example of snap-back. Occasionally I engage in orienteering, which takes place in nature preserves. I am given a map with markers at designated points. I need to find those points, punch the card with the special punches located at each to show that I was there, and orient my way around the course. For beginners, the course follows paths in the woods. When you move to a higher level, you are on your own, crossing streams and scrambling up hills. Once when I was leaving a designated way point, I absentmindedly turned west when I meant to turn east. Soon none of the terrain features matched my topological map. Nevertheless, I was able to continue for a surprisingly long time. A small creek appeared where none was marked. Must have been new since the map was made. A curving path was supposed to be straight. It was sort of straight, for a small section. On I plunged, forcing the terrain to fit my map, reinterpreting the cues I was supposed to be seeing. Eventually I came to a section that I could not explain away except by turning the map 180 degrees, and that violated north and south unless my compass had also broken. That was the moment of snap-back; the accumulated strain of pushing away inconvenient evidence caught up with me.

Applications

Cohen, Freeman, and Thompson (1998) have been working on a "crystal ball" method to help people become sensitive to alternate interpretations of a situation. They ask officers to describe an explanation in which they felt high confidence. Then they pretend to peer into a crystal ball and inform them that their explanation was wrong. The crystal ball does not show why it was wrong. The officers have to sift through the evidence and come up with another explanation, and perhaps another. In doing so, they see that the same evidence can be interpreted in different ways.

My coworkers and I use a similar method to help people anticipate what will happen when a plan is put into action. We call it the premortem strategy. The idea comes from some work we did on the amount of confidence people place in a plan they had imagined. We hypothesized that people may feel too confident once they have arrived at a plan, especially if they are not highly experienced. You can ask them to review the plan for flaws, but such an inspection may be halfhearted since the planners really want to believe that the plan lacks flaws. We devised an exercise to take them out of the perspective of defending their plan and shielding themselves from flaws. We tried to give them a perspective where they would be actively searching for flaws in their own plan. This is the premortem exercise: the use of mental simulation to find the flaws in a plan.[7]

Our exercise is to ask planners to imagine that it is months into the future and that their plan has been carried out. And it has failed. That is all they know; they have to explain why they think it failed. They have to look for the causes that would make them say, "Of course, it wasn't going to work, because ... ." The idea is that they are breaking the emotional attachment to the plan's success by taking on the challenge of showing their creativity and competence by identifying likely sources of breakdown.

It takes less than ten minutes to get people to imagine the failure and its most likely causes. The discussion that follows can go on for an hour. We have tested this premortem method, and it seems to reduce confidence in the original plan, as we expected. We have also come to include it as a part of the kickoff meeting for new projects, to help us identify the trouble spots.

We have also suggested that the premortem approach be used during military planning exercises. In a study of team decision making in army helicopter missions, we observed the mission rehearsal. The simulated mission was to cross the battle lines into enemy territory, drop off some troops, and return to home base. The drop zone was being pounded by artillery; a one-minute period was defined during which the artillery would stop and the troops would be delivered. This sounds simple enough, but imagine flying around hills, avoiding enemy anti-air batteries, getting lost, getting found, and still arriving at the drop zone during the one-minute window. Out of twenty crews, only one made it through the window. Yet during the mission rehearsal, none of the crews we observed asked what they should do if they arrived too early or too late. It never occurred to them that the plan might not work and that they should prepare some contingency plans. Our recommendation was that mission rehearsal should include a premortem rehearsal to imagine ways the mission could run into trouble.

Royal Dutch/Shell, a large European petroleum company, has described how it used mental simulation to construct future scenarios of the world economy. During the early 1970s, executives of oil companies expected that the future would be like the past: consistent growth in supply and demand, with a small amount of variability. The Royal Dutch/Shell Group planning department discovered that there was going to be a discontinuity. Supplies would fall as demand increased, so that by 1975 there would be a major increase in the cost of oil. (The forecast was made before the 1973 oil crisis in which political events speeded up the adjustment.) Anticipating the jump in prices was the easy part. The hard part was to convey this change to the executives at Royal Dutch/Shell.

Pierre Wack (1985a, 1985b), the head of the planning department, described their strategy of building decision scenarios. These scenarios are like mental models except that they are written down, charted out, and developed to change the way executives think. The problem with forecasts and conventional scenarios is that they try to provide answers. Decision scenarios, in contrast, were built to describe the forces that were operating so the executives could use their own judgment. "Scenarios," wrote Wack (1985a), "must help decision makers develop their own feel for the nature of the system, the forces at work within it, the uncertainties that underlie the alternate scenarios, and the concepts useful for interpreting key data" (p. 1 40). Typically the decision scenarios featured only a few variables, usually around three, and a few transitions, rarely more than five or six.

The planning group presented a set of scenarios so the senior executives would not fixate on one. The ideal number of scenarios in this setting was three. The first one corresponded to the mental model actually held by the higher executives. This scenario was dubbed the "three-miracle scenario," since it revealed that the model depended on three unlikely assumptions that all had to hold for that scenario to work. The other two scenarios showed different ways of seeing the world. The point of these scenarios was not to get it right but to illustrate the forces at work. Moreover, the two alternate views rested on different plausible assumptions. The planning group found that if the two alternatives differed on a single dimension, managers would just split the difference. This example shows how mental simulations can gain force when made explicit; the executives responded more favorably to decision scenarios than to forecasts based on statistics and error probabilities. They abandoned their incremental strategy, and their response successfully anticipated the sharp price increases.[8]

The study of mental simulation is also relevant to consumer psychology. In a marketing research project for a large company, we studied how consumers imagined a product in action. We were trying to learn why they adopted different practices for using the product and to anticipate how they might react to a new type of product. Many consumers could not formulate a mental simulation to describe how some common products really worked. If they came up with any answer, it was likely to be a snippet of animation from a commercial. The consumers were like the novices who could not construct simulations of the Polish economy. We should be careful in assuming that consumers know how products work. Some were using the product inappropriately, getting unsatisfactory results, and blaming the product.

Key Points

- Mental simulation lets us explain how events have moved from the past into the present.
- Mental simulation lets us project how the present will move into the future.
- Constructing a mental simulation involves forming an action sequence in which one state of affairs is transformed into another.
- Because of memory limitations, people usually construct mental simulations using around three variables and around six transitions.

- It takes a fair amount of experience to construct a useful mental simulation.

- Mental simulations can run into trouble when the situation becomes too complicated or when time pressure, noise, or other factors interfere.

- Mental simulation can be misleading when a person argues away evidence that challenges the interpretation.

- There are methods for improving mental simulations, such as using crystal ball and premortem strategies and decision scenarios.

6

The *Vincennes* Shootdown

The same person can use mental simulation in different instances to achieve success one time yet meet failure the next. Will Rogers III is the former commanding officer of an AEGIS cruiser, the USS *Vincennes*. As part of a project we did for the U.S. Office of Naval Research, I interviewed him about several incidents involving time-pressured decision making.

Example 6.1
The Circling F-4s

The *Vincennes* has had to cut short its training exercise in April 1988 to go to the Persian Gulf during the Iran-Iraq War. The war has escalated, and each side has been attacking merchant shipping. The U.S. Navy has intervened to protect the merchant ships, the oil tankers from Kuwait, and all the other maritime traffic. The Iranians have purchased Silkworm missiles from China, which are capable of attacking the U.S. Navy forces. At that time, the navy has only one type of vessel capable of neutralizing the Silkworms: the AEGIS cruiser, designed to handle numerous attacking airplanes in a blue ocean setting. That means that they were designed to operate in the open seas, not for narrow bodies of water such as the Persian Gulf. Nevertheless, because no other ship can do the job, the *Vincennes* is in the thick of the Iran-Iraq War.

The *Vincennes* is given a mission to escort the flagship *Coronado* through the Strait of Hormuz during daylight. During this mission, Captain Rogers notes that two Iranian F-4s are taking off from Bandar Abbas airport, to the east. He expects that they are on a routine patrol and waits for them to head north or south. They violate his expectancies by circling the end of the runway. He notices that the circles are getting wider and wider, and with each widening, the F-4s are getting closer to the *Vincennes* and the *Coronado*. Suddenly the lead F-4 turns and shifts from its search to its target acquisition mode on its radar (used to lock on to a target when

Example 6.1 (continued)

preparing to fire a missile at it). These are not friendly actions. Under the then-existing rules of engagement for the Persian Gulf, aircraft using radars to lock onto ships were considered to have committed hostile acts.

Rogers has the prerogative to respond in kind, to protect his ship; however, he does not believe they will attack. They are so visible, so vulnerable, that he believes they are merely harassing him. Besides, the U.S. Navy is in the Persian Gulf to reduce hostilities, not to increase them. He puts himself in the boots of the pilots. Would he come out, with no maneuvering and no distractions and no covering force, in daylight, and attack a ship with better missiles and better radar? Or would he play some simple games with a U.S. Navy ship? That is something Rogers could imagine. So instead of shooting the two airplanes down, the *Vincennes* uses its advanced electronics to jam their radar.

Captain Rogers is careful to monitor the range of the F-4s in case they do get too close. He will not put his ship or the Coronado in danger. Soon the Iranian airplanes have had enough, and they fly off.

Captain Rogers achieved what he wanted: to protect his flagship and defend his own ship, without shooting at the F-4s. He was able to draw on his experience to imagine what was going on inside the minds of the pilots. Because he could not imagine how the Iranian pilots could realistically be preparing to attack him, he believed he had the situation well in hand and did not allow himself to become provoked. Sometimes we diagram incidents like this. Figure 6.1 gives an example. The incident starts at the top left and moves to the right. New information is shown along the top. The columns represent how Captain Rogers was thinking about the situation.

Captain Rogers was involved in another incident; the shooting down of an Iranian airliner. He used the same strategy, trying to imagine what the pilot was thinking, what the pilot's intent was. He was again able to rule out one explanation as implausible. Based on his mental simulation, he made a diagnosis that the track on his screen was not a commercial airliner. This time he was mistaken.

Chronology of the *Vincennes* Shootdown

On the morning of July 3, 1988, the USS *Vincennes* fired two missiles at an Airbus 300, Iran Air flight 655, which had taken off from the Bandar

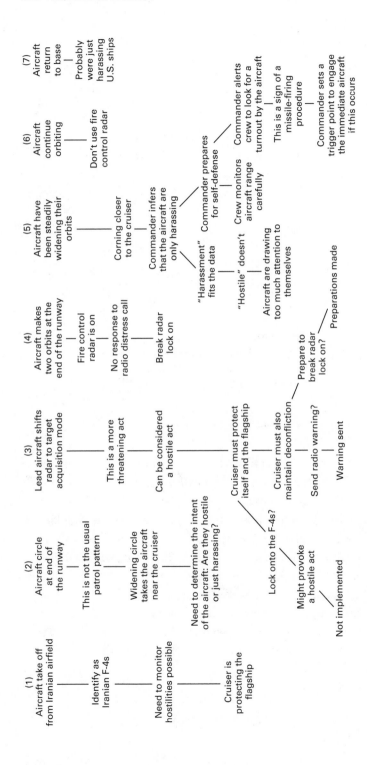

Figure 6.1

The harassing F-4s: How the situation was perceived as it evolved

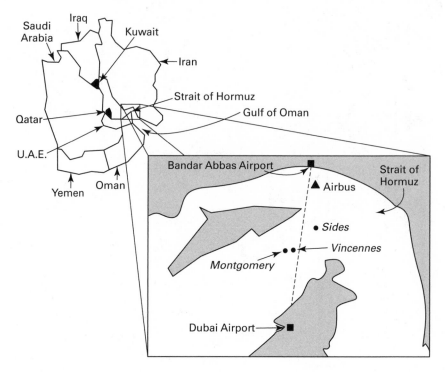

Figure 6.2

Map detail of the *Vincennes* incident

Abbas airport. (The map detail is shown in figure 6.2.) The departure time was 10: 17 A.M. local time. The missiles were fired at 10:24. The entire flight lasted seven minutes, eight seconds. Approximately three minutes, nine seconds elapsed from the time the air track was judged to be tactically significant until the missiles were launched. Shortly after, the *Vincennes* and the rest of the world learned that the track had been a commercial airliner on a regularly scheduled flight from Bandar Abbas to Dubai, in the United Arab Emirates.

This incident is widely used as a demonstration of faulty decision making under stress. There was time pressure, fear, and uncertainty. Many have claimed that there were dear flaws or biases in the decision making of the crew of the *Vincennes*.

Prior Events

Hostilities between the Iranian military and the U.S. Navy had been steadily worsening. Besides the case of the circling FAs, on April 18, 1988, there had been a battle in the same area in the Persian Gulf, involving another Navy ship, the USS *Wainwright*. At that time missiles had been fired at an Iranian F-4, damaging it. In mid-June 1988, the Iranians had transferred F-14s to the Bandar Abbas airport, which was used for both military and commercial activities. In one case an Iranian F-14 flying toward a U.S. cruiser had been warned and had broken off after the cruiser locked onto it with fire control radar. In another incident, a commercial airliner had taken off from Bandar Abbas with an Iranian F-4 flying just below, tucked underneath it to avoid radar detection. The U.S. Navy had modified its rules of engagement after the USS *Stark* had been hit by an Iraqi fighter. The new rules gave commanders more freedom to take steps to defend themselves, even if the attacker did not fire first.

Another issue was the use of an Identification Friend or Foe (IFF) system to distinguish aircraft. Commercial and military airplanes are outfitted with electronic devices to signal their characteristics. If another piece of electronic gear sends a signal, the electronic device will respond. In the United States, if the response is a Mode IV type, that shows that the aircraft is military and friendly, having been configured with the code word of the day. Commercial airplanes are rigged to send Mode III signals back when queried. Military aircraft from other countries will send back a Mode II signal. However, in the past, Iranian military aircraft had been observed to send Mode III signals, pretending that they were commercial.

Also, there had been recent U.S. operations against the Iranians, the Iraqis had just scored some military successes, and intelligence information suggested that the Iranians intended to take some provocative action during the July 4 weekend, perhaps kamikaze-type attacks on shipping. The Iranian Revolutionary Guard Corps began a series of attacks on commercial shipping the evening of July 2, 1988, prestaging some larger actions. The stage was set.

On July 3, 1988, the USS *Elmer Montgomery* was surrounded and attacked by thirteen gunboats belonging to the Iranian Navy. At 10:00 A.M. the *Vincennes* was thirty-five to forty miles away from the *Montgomery*.

It headed over to help, and sent a helicopter ahead to inspect the situation. The helicopter was fired on, and as the *Vincennes* reached the area, it too was attacked by the gunboats. The gunboats split into two groups, and a surface battle commenced.

It may seem strange that the *Vincennes*, a large U.S. Navy cruiser, would feel threatened by small gunboats, but its job was anti-air warfare. It was not built to deal with small and fast surface targets; fire from the gunboats was capable of damaging the *Vincennes*'s superstructure and injuring sailors. The *Vincennes* had only two guns that were useful in firing at the gunboats. One of these fouled, forcing the ship to maneuver sharply to bring the other gun into play. This was the surface situation into which the Airbus flew.

Example 6.2
The Flight of the Airbus

The Iranian Airbus took off at 10:17 A.M. local time, twenty-seven minutes after its scheduled departure time. Its flight path carried it directly over the *Vincennes*. Flight 655 climbed throughout its flight and had reached 12,000 feet, on its way to 14,000 feet, when it was hit. Here is the chronology of how it all happened that morning.

10:17 The computer system onboard the *Vincennes* classified the track as "unknown, presumed enemy," because the plane was taking off from an Iranian mixed-use airport. The *Vincennes* assigned it track number 4474. (Each object in the computer—whether an airplane, surface ship, or submarine—is given a track number, which is its name. This track number enables different crew members to know they are talking about the same object when they discuss it.)

10:18 A second ship in the area, the USS *Sides*, picked up the track of Flight 655 and gave it a different track number, 4131. The computer system network judged that tracks 4474 and 4131 were the same aircraft. The computer assigned it track 4131, the one selected by the *Sides*, rather than the track number the *Vincennes* had been using. It is unclear whether this shift in track number was announced over the *Vincennes*'s internal communications net. At the same time, one of the *Vincennes* crew members checked the commercial air schedules and noted that Flight 655 was supposed to depart at 9:50 A.M. No airliners were scheduled to depart Bandar Abbas at 10:17. Also during this minute, the *Vincennes* noted that an Iranian P-3 airplane was in the area. P-3s serve surveillance functions and can be used to direct other aircraft during missions. The Airbus was forty-four nautical miles away from the *Vincennes* at this point.

Example 6.2 (continued)

10:19 The *Vincennes* issued its first challenge to the unknown aircraft, warning it to avoid the area. During the following minutes, it issued several more challenges using both military and commercial radio frequencies. The track never responded to any of these challenges. Captain Rogers found this unusual. In the past he had twice issued warnings to commercial airplanes, and each time he had received an answer. He assumed that commercial pilots routinely monitored the international distress frequency as they were supposed to. The *Vincennes* might have tried calling air traffic control, but it did not have an extra radio on board to let it contact both air traffic control and the track of interest.

10:20 At this point several crew members in the *Vincennes* Combat Information Center reported they saw a Mode II return from the IFF, suggesting that they were dealing with an Iranian military aircraft, probably an F-14. We now know that this identification was mistaken. Throughout the incident, the crew in the Combat Information Center of the *Vincennes* believed that it was dealing with an Iranian F-14. The AEGIS computer system does not incorporate data about IFF returns, so it did not have this erroneous piece of information. The designation was entered into the large screen displays. The identification was also communicated over the internal voice net. The air engagement decision properly begins at this point, with the idea that the *Vincennes* was facing an F-14 flying directly at it and ignoring radio warnings. Not everyone accepted this judgment. One crew member told Captain Rogers that he thought the track was a commercial airliner.

The tactical action officer in charge of managing the air war requested that the *Vincennes* defend itself by firing missiles at the track when it reached twenty nautical miles. Captain Rogers denied the request. The aircraft was not using any systems that would normally be associated with aggressive actions, such as search radar or fire control radar. Rogers's mission was to reduce conflicts, not increase them. He wanted more information before firing, even if it meant adding to the risks. He had confidence in the AEGIS system. Besides, he did not believe a fighter pilot would attack a ship as sophisticated as the *Vincennes* in such a reckless way. The *Vincennes* turned on its fire control radar, to prepare to fire at the aircraft if necessary, but also to send a message to the pilot that he was in the *Vincennes's* sights. The aircraft still was not responding to radio warnings. Moreover, it was departing from the centerline of the commercial air corridor. The corridor was 10 miles wide and the track was within this space, but as a rule commercial aircraft flew down the center "like a bug on a wire," as Captain Rogers described it. By the time it was hit by the missiles, the aircraft was 3.35 nautical miles off of center, in the direction of the *Vincennes*.

10:22 Captain Rogers asked, "What is 4474 doing?" Several crew members onboard the *Vincennes* reported that the aircraft was now descending, an

> **Example 6.2** (continued)
>
> unhappy sign, since a commercial airliner would have still been ascending. According to these crew members, the track was assuming a classical attack profile of increasing speed, decreasing altitude, and closing range. However, some crew members saw the track as still increasing in altitude. At any rate, the *Vincennes* was now within range of air-to-surface missiles that the aircraft might be carrying.
>
> *10:24* Captain Rogers could wait no longer. His own weapons systems would become ineffective if he let the aircraft get any closer. He had waited until the last possible moment. Now he ordered that the missiles be fired. The Airbus was hit at 13,500 feet, eight nautical miles away.

As far as I can see, the decision to fire was fairly straightforward, based on mental simulation. The cues were all consistent with a hostile aircraft:

- The IFF report showing that it was an F-14.
- The failure to respond to radio warnings.
- The timing of the takeoff to correspond to the attack by the gunboats.
- The final descent toward the *Vincennes*.

This story all fits. There were some discrepancies, as shown in table 6.1, but these were small and easily explained away. The aircraft was not using radar or other electronic means of targeting, but this could be explained because the Iranian P-3 in the area could be providing targeting data. Or the pilot might have been trying for visual identification, intending to use fire control radar when he got closer. A second discrepancy was that the aircraft showed Mode III IFF, as if it was a commercial airliner, but Iranian fighters had played that trick before. Third, the aircraft ignored the radio warnings, as expected if it was up to no good.

In contrast, the story that the plane was a commercial airliner had too many holes in it. Why would air traffic control vector an airplane directly into the center of a surface battle? Why didn't the pilot fly straight down the center of the air corridor? Why didn't the takeoff correspond to the commercial schedule? Why did the cockpit ignore the radio warnings issued over the international distress frequency? More troubling, why was it sending Mode II IFF signals? Most troubling of all, why was the airplane descending (as was reported by the majority of crew members)?

Table 6.1

The *Vincennes* Shootdown: Story Discrepancies

Attacking F-14 Story Discrepancies	Commercial Airline Story Discrepancies
Not generating any radar emissions	Flying into the middle of a surface battle
Generating a Mode III IFF signal	Not on the centerline of the air corridor
Ignoring the *Vincennes's* military air distress radio calls	Takeoff was not on the schedule
	Ignoring the *Vincennes's* international air distress radio calls
	Generating a Mode II IFF signal[a]
	Descending toward the *Vincennes*[a]

a. Later determined to be incorrect.

It is hard to build a story that can fit all of these discrepancies. The diagnosis that the track was a commercial airliner was rejected without difficulty.

It is easy to blame Captain Rogers for making the wrong decision, since hindsight shows that he was mistaken. But we do not need hindsight. The commander of the USS *Sides*, viewing the same picture, concluded that the aircraft was a commercial airliner. Certainly the *Sides* did not have a potential F-14 bearing down on it and was not being attacked by a fleet of gunboats. Still, the *Sides* read the situation correctly, even under time pressure. Why?

The *Vincennes* was working with two pieces of inaccurate data: Flight 655 never squawked Mode II IFF, and it never descended. The *Sides* had accurate readings on both issues. Once the *Vincennes's* crew became convinced that the track belonged to an F-14, that assumption colored the way they treated it and thought about it. Once they believed it was descending toward them, there was nothing more to wonder about. Of these two mistakes, the first was the more important. If the *Vincennes* had never received any Mode II IFF signals, the crew would have been more likely to believe that it might be a commercial airliner.

The first mistake is easy to explain. One of the crew members in the *Vincennes's* Combat Information Center was in charge of identifying tracks. He used his remote control indicator to query the aircraft's transponder, working with the IFF system. He successfully hooked Flight 655 as it departed from the airport, but left it hooked for almost ninety seconds. The way the system worked, the range gate stayed positioned at the end of the runway of Bandar Abbas airport, even as Flight 655 moved toward the *Vincennes*. During that time, airplanes on the ground would be interrogated by the IFF system. If a military aircraft happened to be positioned within the area covered by the range gate, it would reply with a Mode II response. By coincidence, an Iranian military aircraft did take off from Bandar Abbas just when the *Vincennes* received the Mode II response. The military airplane was squawking Mode II. So there was no decision error here, just a human error that let the Airbus become correlated with a Mode II signal reserved for military airplanes.

The second mistake is the more controversial one: judging that the Airbus was descending. In fact it ascended throughout its entire flight until hit by the missiles. The computer system reported continual ascent, and the USS *Sides* saw continual ascent. The Fogarty report, the official U.S. Navy analysis of the incident, concluded that "stress, task fixation, an unconscious distortion of data may have played a major role in this incident. [Crew members] became convinced that track 4131 was an Iranian F-14 after receiving the ... report of a momentary Mode II. After this report of the Mode II, [a crew member] appear[ed] to have distorted data flow in an unconscious attempt to make available evidence fit a preconceived scenario ('Scenario fulfillment')."

This explanation seems to fit in with the idea that mental simulation can lead you down a garden path to where you try to explain away inconvenient data. Nevertheless, trained crew members are not supposed to distort unambiguous data. According to the Fogarty report, the crew members were not trying to explain away the data, as in a *de minimus* explanation. They were flat out distorting the numbers. This conclusion does not feel right.

The conclusion of the Fogarty report was echoed by some members of a five-person panel of leading decision researchers, who were invited to review the evidence and report to a congressional subcommittee. Two members of the panel specifically attributed the mistake to faulty decision making. One described how the mistake seemed to be a clear case of expectancy bias, in which a person sees what he is expecting to see, even when it departs from the actual stimulus. He cited a study by Bruner and Postman (1949) in which subjects were shown brief flashes of playing cards and asked to identify each. When cards such as the Jack of Diamonds were printed in black, subjects would still identify it as the Jack of Diamonds without noticing the distortion. The researcher concluded that the mistake about altitude seemed to match these data; subjects cannot be trusted to make accurate identifications because their expectancies get in the way.

I have talked with this decision researcher, who explained how the whole Vincennes incident showed a Combat Information Center riddled with decision biases. That is not how I understand the incident. My reading of the Fogarty report shows a team of men struggling with an unexpected battle, trying to guess whether an F-14 is coming over to blow them out of the water, waiting until the very last moment for fear of making a mistake, hoping the pilot will heed the radio warnings, accepting the risk to their lives in order to buy some more time.

To consider this alleged expectancy bias more carefully, imagine what would have happened if the *Vincennes* had not fired and in fact had been attacked by an F-14. The Fogarty report stated that in the Persian Gulf, from June 2, 1988, to July 2, 1988, the U.S. Middle East Forces had issued 150 challenges to aircraft. Of these, it was determined that 83 percent were issued to Iranian military aircraft and only 1.3 percent to aircraft that turned out to be commercial. So we can infer that if a challenge is issued in the gulf, the odds are that the airplane is Iranian military. If we continue with our scenario, that the *Vincennes* had not fired and had been attacked by an F-14, the decision researchers would have still claimed that it was a dear case of bias, except this time the bias would have been to ignore the base rates, to ignore the expectancies. No one can win. If you act on expectancies and you are wrong, you are guilty of expectancy bias. If you ignore expectancies and are wrong, you are guilty of ignoring base rates and expectancies. This means that the decision bias approach explains too much (Klein, 1989). If an appeal to decision bias can explain everything after the fact, no matter what has happened, then there is no credible explanation.

In order to reject this scenario fulfillment or expectancy bias explanation, we need to come up with a better one. The Fogarty report pointed out an obvious culprit: the computer screens that the crew members worked with were not easy to read. A very large screen display showed the big picture, but this display did not show altitude. Instead, altitude was listed on a small alphanumeric display off to the side of the primary display. The altitude of a track was given as a four-digit number, so 13,000 feet would appear as 1300. This number was embedded in a list of other numbers showing range, speed, bearing, and so on. This small screen was hard to read, especially if a crew member had to abandon what he was watching on the large screen to search through the small one. The more critical problem noted by the Fogarty report was that the trend was not given. Crew members could not easily check whether an airplane was ascending or descending. To figure that out, the crew members had to study the changes in the four-digit altitude readout. I asked Captain Rogers how long it might take to infer altitude. He said perhaps five to ten seconds. That may not sound like a long time, but consider these sailors in a noisy room, wearing headphones with one message coming in over one ear and another over the second ear, and a third set of messages coming in over the loudspeakers in the room, and perhaps a fourth from someone else; it may be hard to remember what the original numbers were in trying to keep track of the trend. The key part of the decision here took only 189 seconds, so 10 of those seconds can seem long. The Fogarty report recommended that trend data for altitude be shown on the large screen displays, a sensible idea. The *Vincennes's* crew may just have gotten confused by the welter of numbers. Yet this still leaves the problem of why so many crew members insisted that they saw the aircraft descending.

The answer may be that there was a second airplane that no one knew about, causing the confusion. I heard about the second airplane from Captain Rogers, who told me that something odd had occurred at the beginning of the incident. Recall that the *Vincennes* had given Flight 655 the track number 4474, while the *Sides* had identified the same airplane at the same time and used track number 4131. The computerized system figured out that 4474 and 4131 were the same airplane and needed to have a single track number. The computer selected the *Sides's* number for Flight 655, track number 4131. Rather than risk running out of track numbers, the computer system put track number 4474 in storage, to be recycled. A few minutes later it recycled the number, assigning it to a U.S. Navy A-6 several hundred miles away. As luck would have it, during the time period 10:20 to 10:24, that A-6 was flying a course that was descending and increasing in speed. At least that was what Rogers thought, but he did not want to attach too much credibility to it.

In the Fogarty report, the account of the *Vincennes* during the incident sounds like bedlam, with everyone having a different idea of what the track was doing.

Roberts and Dotterway (1995) reanalyzed the evidence and concluded that there were just two sets of impressions in the *Vincennes*. One set of crew members reported an aircraft steadily increasing in altitude. Their reports matched well with the Airbus's pattern. The other group reported an aircraft steadily descending, which matched well with the A-6 pattern. In other words, due to a system weakness, the *Vincennes's* crew may have been seeing two different airplanes. The fact that the track number had been changed had not been clearly announced at the time it occurred. To find out the altitude of a track, you can use a trackball to hook it on the screen. If the ship is pitching violently, as the *Vincennes* was, it might be safer to punch in the track number into a key pad. Apparently many of the crew chose to do that, and they punched in the wrong number. When Captain Rogers asked, "What is 4474 doing?" they proceeded to find out. It was descending. So we do not need to resort to scenario fulfillment explanations or expectancy biases. The crew members used a four-digit track number that turned out to be wrong.

Why did the Airbus fail to respond to the radio warnings? One guess is that on such a short flight, the pilots kept one ear of the headphone on the air traffic controller of the Bandar Abbas airport just departed and the other on the destination airport, Dubai. This strategy would leave the pilots without any ears free to be tuned to the international air distress frequency.

The *Vincennes* shootdown has some similarity to example 5.2, the Libyan airliner, another commercial airplane shot down because the pilot behaved in ways that were inexplicable to the people monitoring its flight. Both instances seem to follow the same pattern: the use of mental simulation to evaluate and rule out possible explanations.

7

Mental Simulation and Decision Making

Mental simulation serves several functions in nonroutine decision making. It helps us to explain the cues and information we have received so that we can figure out how to interpret a situation and diagnose a problem. It helps us to generate expectancies by providing a preview of events as they might unfold and by letting us run through a course of action in our minds so we can prepare for it. And it lets us evaluate a course of action by searching for pitfalls so we can decide whether to adopt it, change it, or look further.

Mental Simulation and the RPD Model

Mental simulation shows up in at least three places in the RPD model: diagnosing to form situation awareness, generating expectancies to help verify situation awareness, and evaluating a course of action.

Situation Awareness

The basic aspect of recognitional decision making is that people with experience can size up the situation and judge it as familiar or typical. Usually this assessment happens so quickly and automatically that we are not aware of it. Sometimes, though, we have to try to make sense of the different clues. Mental simulation is one way to make sense of events and form an explanation. When we use mental simulation to derive a plausible explanation, we feel that we have diagnosed the situation, the way a physician might diagnose a disease or an auto mechanic might diagnose an engine problem. The diagnosis is a mental simulation that weaves together different events into a story that shows how the causes led to the effects.

In example 6.1 Captain Rogers decided that the F-4s getting closer to his ship were probably not going to attack him. He was making a decision—a diagnosis of their intent. He was explaining their actions by using his understanding of their intent, and his explanation shaped his own actions. In example 6.2 when Captain Rogers decided that the pilot of the approaching aircraft, track number 4131/4474, probably intended to attack him, he was also making a decision. Rogers was diagnosing the intent of the pilot, but this time he was working with faulty data.

Situation awareness can be formed rapidly, through intuitive matching of features, or deliberately, through mental simulation. Sometimes a situation reminds us of a previous event, and we try to use this analogy to make sense of what is happening. At times there are several competing explanations, and we may have to compare them. Usually we will scan each explanation to see if there are elements that do not seem plausible, so we can reject the less likely ones and keep the best.

Nancy Pennington and Reid Hastie (1993) have studied the way people make sense of the facts when asked to make a jury decision about whether a defendant is guilty or innocent. During a trial, the attorneys for the prosecution and the defense may present a great deal of evidence. According to Pennington and Hastie, people making jury decisions would have trouble cataloging each piece of information and its implications. Instead, they build stories, or mental simulations, trying to fit the evidence into a plausible account of what happened leading up to the crime. The criteria for evaluating mental simulations described in chapter 5 come into play: consistency, plausibility, and so on. Instead of passively listening to the attorneys, the jurors are actively trying to build their own stories, their own explanations. Then they compare their stories to those presented by the two attorneys, and select the one that more closely matches their own story. Pennington and Hastie call this a story model, because the reasoning strategy is to build and evaluate different stories about why people acted in the ways they did.

This story model describes how we make diagnostic decisions. Once we have diagnosed the situation, we provide for the aspects of situation awareness shown in figure 7.1:

- We have a basis for expecting certain things to occur but not others.
- We pay attention to cues relevant to this diagnosis.

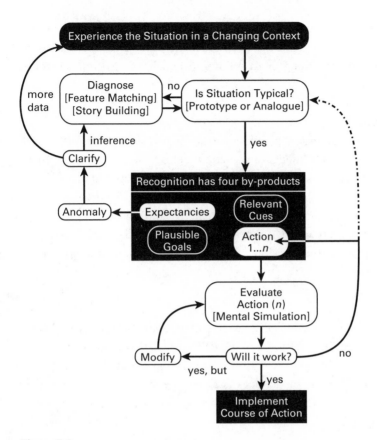

Figure 7.1

Integrated version of recognition-primed decision model

- We have some understanding of what goals are reasonable to achieve.
- We know which types of actions are likely to succeed.

Elstein, Shulman, and Sprafka (1978) studied the way physicians make diagnoses. Physicians are trained to suppress any explanations until they have studied all the symptoms, to make sure they do not overlook something. However, Elstein and his colleagues found that physicians are forming hypotheses and explanations from the very beginning and using these to direct their examinations. The ideal we sometimes have of a machine-like diagnostician carefully tagging new data and withholding judgment does not fit the reality of what people do. Asking decision makers to stifle their imaginations while recording data might well reduce efficiency, since stories give meaning to data, and without putting the data into stories, decision makers might find it harder to keep track of everything or to follow up hunches based on the stories that are forming.

Expectancies

In diagnosing a situation, people construct mental simulations of how the events have been evolving and will continue to evolve. The more experienced the decision makers are, the more clear-cut the expectancies are.

By checking whether the expectancies are satisfied, the decision maker can judge the adequacy of the mental simulation. The greater the violations and the more effort it takes to explain away conflicting evidence, the less confident the decision maker feels about the mental simulation and diagnosis.

Courses of Action

Someone who has sized up a situation will be aware of some typical ways of reacting to it. In variation 1 of the RPD model, the person just chooses the first action thought of, without deliberating about the little details. However, that simple model does not describe the major decisions. Few of us are so impulsive that we always act out the first thing that pops into our heads.

The car rescue example in example 5.1 showed how to use mental simulation to evaluate a new course of action, which is variation 3 of the RPD model. The overpass rescue (example 3.2) showed how a commander can evaluate several courses of action, one at a time, without ever comparing one to another. These are all cases of a singular evaluation: looking at one action at a time to see if it will work or can be made to work. Our research with the fireground commanders showed that when they did need to evaluate a course of action, they used the strategy of mental simulation.

Adriaan de Groot (1946) found the same result in his study of chess grand masters. We think of grand masters as rational and analytical. When de Groot asked them to think aloud while finding the best move in a chess problem, they relied on mental simulation to evaluate promising courses of action. In de Groot's published records, only five cases out of forty games, each containing several moves to consider, show the grand masters comparing the strengths and weaknesses of one option to another. The rest of the time they were rejecting moves or figuring out their consequences.

Certainly there are times to use a comparative rather than a singular evaluation of options. Orasanu and Fischer (1997) presented one clear example: commercial airline pilots forced to divert their course because of weather or malfunction, trying to determine which airport to select. This is not a decision made using an RPD strategy, although mental simulation can play a role. The RPD model describes how people can make decisions without comparing options, but the RPD model does not describe the only strategy people use in naturalistic settings. Even with time pressure, there will be times when you may need to compare different options. If you have moved to a new city and a realtor has shown you several different houses for sale, you will try to pick the best one by comparing options. Some decision researchers have investigated the ways people actually do contrast options when the task requires a comparison.

The following example shows a successful use of the rational choice method.[1]

Example 7.1
The Denver Bullets

The chief of the Denver Police Department recommends changing the handgun bullet police officers use, in particular, switching to a hollow-point bullet that will be more effective in stopping criminals. Some citizen groups become upset by the choice because they think that a hollow-point bullet will also increase the severity of injury to an unacceptable level. They protest the choice. A political standoff follows, and the city turns for help to Ken Hammond, a leading judgment and decision researcher at the University of Colorado.

Hammond and his research staff accept the challenge and use formal analysis methods to resolve the dispute. They begin by identifying the mayor's and the city council members' social value trade-offs regarding the relative importance of stopping effectiveness, severity of injury, and threat to innocent bystanders for selecting police handgun ammunition. Next, they convene a panel composed of one firearms expert, one ballistics expert, and three wound ballistics experts to make scientific judgments regarding the stopping effectiveness, severity of injury, and threat to innocent bystanders of eighty different ballistics tested at the National Bureau of Standards in Washington, D.C. The experts' judgments are based solely on the technical

Example 7.1 (continued)

characteristics of the bullets, particularly the bullets' performance in ballistic gelatin, a substance that simulates human tissue. The experts do not know the value judgments of the political representatives. Finally, Hammond and his staff analytically combine the social value judgments and the scientific judgments by using a model that equally weights the importance of stopping effectiveness, severity of injury, and threat to innocent bystanders.

The model identifies a third bullet to consider. Compared to the bullet that the Denver Police Department is using at the time, this one increases stopping effectiveness without increasing the severity of injury. Compared to the hollow-point bullet recommended by the Denver Police Department, the bullet has the same level of increased stopping effectiveness without increasing the severity of injury. Compared to both the current and the recommended bullets, the bullet identified by the analysis poses less threat to innocent bystanders.

The mayor, Denver City Council, Denver Police Department, and city groups accept the bullet identified by the analysis. Although it too is a hollow-point bullet, its other technical characteristics, including its lighter weight as compared to the bullet recommended by the Denver Police Department, result in levels of stopping effectiveness, severity of injury, and threat to innocent bystanders that are more acceptable to the community. The dispute is resolved.

The rational choice model is termed a compensatory strategy, since a weakness on one evaluation dimension can be offset by strengths on other dimensions. Researchers (see Svenson, 1979) have also identified a number of noncompensatory strategies that are simpler to use. Studies have shown that decision makers in natural settings use these simpler noncompensatory strategies. Instead of trying to see if the strengths on one dimension compensate for the weaknesses on others, we may use methods such as selecting the option that is the best on the dimension that is most important and ignoring the other dimensions. Another simple strategy is called elimination by aspects (Tversky, 1972), in which all the options are evaluated on the most important dimension; the ones that fail to meet a standard are dropped, and the surviving options are evaluated on the next-most-important evaluation dimension, and the ones that do not meet that standard are dropped, filtering and filtering until only one is left. Yet another strategy is a face-off procedure in which one option is compared to a second, and the winner gets compared to a third, and then the winner of that face-off is compared to a fourth, and so on. Here, the comparison considers only two options at a time.[2]

Example 7.1 described a successful use of formal analysis methods. There are times to use comparative strategies and times to use singular evaluation strategies such as the one described by the RPD model. Table 7.1 shows some predictions about when people will use the different types of strategies, drawing on the observations we have made in different studies. It lists the boundary conditions for the two approaches to evaluating courses of action.

People seem more likely to use singular strategies in the following situations:

- When *time pressure* is greater, evaluating one option at a time until an acceptable one is found. The reason is that it takes too much time to lay out the alternatives and analyze the evaluation criteria.

- When people are more *experienced* in the domain. With experience, they can be more confident in their ability to size up the situation and recognize plausible courses of action as the first ones they consider.

- When the conditions are more *dynamic*. The time and effort needed to set up an analysis can be rendered useless when the context shifts.

Table 7.1
Boundary Conditions for Different Decision Strategies

Task Conditions	Recognition-Primed Decisions	Rational Choice Strategy
Greater time pressure	More likely	
Higher experience level	More likely	
Dynamic conditions	More likely	
Ill-defined goals	More likely	
Need for justification		More likely
Conflict resolution		More likely
Optimization		More likely
Greater computational complexity		More likely

- When the goals are *ill defined*. Ambiguity makes it hard to come up with evaluation criteria that apply across all options.

In contrast, people seem more likely to use comparative evaluation in these situations:

- When they have to *justify* their choice. Higher authorities usually look for evidence that alternatives were considered.

- When *conflict resolution* is a factor. In the case of the Denver bullets, different stakeholders held different priorities, and a common analytical metric was needed to place all the considerations into a common format.

- When the decision maker is trying to *optimize*, finding the best course of action. This is what the comparison is all about. The singular evaluation that uses mental simulation tries to find the first workable option, not necessarily the best.

- When the situation is *computationally complex*. This is not something anyone can easily recognize, such as analyzing an investment portfolio to select the best strategy.

But even when decision makers are comparing options and trying to find the best one, they may not be using rational choice strategies such as assessing each option on a common set of criteria. The process may be more like running a mental simulation of each course of action and comparing the emotional reactions—the discomfort or worry or enthusiasm—that each option produces when it is imagined. De Groot's (1946) study of chess players shows this. The chess grand masters were trying to find the best move in a position, yet they were not comparing the options on a common set of criteria (e.g., center control, defensive security). They were using progressive deepening to imagine how the option would be developed, and forming a judgment and emotional reaction to these potential outcomes.

Table 7.1 suggests that we will be more likely to compare options when faced with unfamiliar situations. The reason is that a lack of experience will prevent us from generating reasonable options, or will at least reduce our confidence in the options we do generate. If time pressure is low, the conditions are fairly stable, and the goals arc clear, then we should expect to find the highest level of option comparisons.

Testing the RPD Model in Different Domains

I based the boundary conditions shown in table 7.1 on a set of studies that looked at decision making in different domains. The goal of this research program was to find out if the **RPD** model held for other decision makers besides firefighters. We also kept searching for situations where the RPD model breaks down, to test its limits.

After we conducted the first study with the fireground commanders, my colleagues and I compiled all the decision points and totaled up the number of times the commander had used a recognitional decision strategy with singular evaluation rather than comparative evaluation. The percentage was 80 percent, for 156 decision points. This is entered into the top line of table 7.2, to compare it to other naturalistic decision-making studies we performed. (Most of the studies in table 7.2 were funded by the Army Research Institute.) Next, Roberta Calderwood, Marvin Thordsen, Beth Crandall, and I contrasted experienced versus very new commanders, expecting that the percentage of recognitional decisions would be low for the new commanders. We tabulated only the toughest decision points in the nonroutine incidents, to make things a little more difficult

Table 7.2

Frequency of RPD Strategies across Domains

Study	Number of Decision Points	Decision Points Handled Using RPD Strategy (%)
1. Urban fireground commanders	156	80
2. Expert fireground commanders	48	58
Novice fireground commanders	33	46
3. Tank platoon leaders	110	42
4. Wildfire incident commanders	110	51
Functional decisions		56
Organizational decisions	31	
5. Design engineers	51	60
6. Battle command teams	27	96
7. AEGIS commanders	78	95

on the RPD model. By using the tighter selection on decision points, the percentage of RPD observations dropped below 60 percent, and it was lower for the novices than for the expert commanders.

In the next study, we sought more novice decision makers. We assessed tank platoon leaders who were going through their first instruction course at Fort Knox. Some had never ridden in a tank before. Here the percentage of recognitional decisions fell below 50 percent. (This was the project where Chris Brezovic had tear-gassed himself.) It had been a tough study. Part of the time we were riding with the tank platoon leaders, in the loader's position of the M-1 tanks, so we could conduct the interview immediately after each exercise and before the tank platoon leader could hear the after-action review of the instructors.

We wondered if recognitional decision making was more common in individuals or in leaders working with small teams. Therefore, we next studied incident commanders who worked for the Forest Service and were in charge of managing large forest fires. By good fortune, we were able to obtain firsthand observations of incident commanders and their teams in action against a very large fire. The entire organization was composed of four thousand people. Units from all over the country were flown in on short notice and had to be organized and managed. In a setting such as this, we speculated that people would see things differently, would argue with each other more, and would force a strategy by which different options were identified and compared. We were only partially right. As you can see in table 7.2, when the incident commanders were making operational decisions about the firefighting itself, the percentage of RPD strategies was about the same as with the fireground commanders. But when they were working on organizational decisions, such as how to discipline someone for doing a poor job, the percentage of recognitional decisions went down. One possible reason is that the incident commanders were less expert with these kinds of decisions.

The next possibility we considered was that the RPD model held only during time-pressured decisions. To test this hypothesis, Chris Brezovic and I studied the way design engineers made decisions about interfaces. (This project was conducted for the U.S. Air Force's Armstrong Laboratory.) These decisions could stretch out over days, or even months, rather than seconds and minutes. Even here, the majority of tough decisions were coded as RPD strategies. Furthermore, in many cases that we coded as comparative evaluations, the design engineers had started to compare options, filtered out some alternatives, and then switched to a different strategy such as physically simulating the option and trying it out.

Perhaps we were getting distorted data because of our interview method. So Marvin Thordsen and Chris Brezovic traveled to Fort Hood, Texas, to watch command and control teams at the army brigade level go through a training exercise. The decisions were going to be made by teams, not individuals, and we thought this might further reduce the rate of RPD strategies. Marvin and Chris stationed themselves in the small trailers where the battle command teams were located. We got a complete record of one five-hour planning session. Going through the tapes, Marvin identified and coded twenty-seven distinct decision points. Only one of those points showed evidence of comparing options—particularly surprising since army planners are indoctrinated to generate a set of several different options, usually three.

George Kaempf, Marvin Thordsen, Steve Wolf, and I interviewed U.S. Navy commanders and captains, seeking to find out how they had made difficult decisions involving low-intensity conflicts (1996). The navy officers had served on AEGIS cruisers. This research project had a specific purpose: the Office of Naval Research wanted to learn how to build better human—computer interfaces, to reduce accidents such as the *Vincennes* shootdown.

If there was ever a setting that called for recognitional decision making, it was this one. The time pressure was severe. The skill level was moderately high; people generally had a year or more in their positions and many years of related experience working up to their positions. The situations changed rapidly. Moreover, there were very few courses of action available to the officers, and there were clear guidelines, including official rules of engagement, telling them how they must react. Table 7.2 shows that 95 percent of the decision points were coded as recognitional. In these cases, the decision maker reported he had not compared any options and that his course of action was not a novel one.[3]

To date we have formally coded more than six hundred decision points, for the nonroutine and challenging decisions that people have faced in natural settings. In a large percentage of cases, ranging from 46 percent to 96 percent, people have used recognitional strategies. Only in a small number of instances have we found evidence for comparative evaluation of options. Even this number might be overstated since the comparison was often abandoned before the final choice. For all of these reasons, we believe that the RPD model is a general strategy found in most domains.

The data I have described in this chapter make a strong claim that recognitional decision making is a common strategy and that comparing options is fairly infrequent. Because of the important implications of this claim, other researchers have independently investigated the issue, to determine if they could replicate our findings.

Mosier (1991) studied videotapes of twenty-three three-person crews, consisting of qualified commercial airline crews, flying a full-mission simulation in a Boeing 727 simulator. She found that "most crews did not wait until they had a complete understanding of the situation to make and implement decisions. Rather, they seemed to make a recognitional, almost reflexive judgment, based upon a few, critical items of information; and then spent additional time and effort verifying its correctness through continued situational investigation. If later information changed situation assessment enough to prompt a change of decision, a second option was generated and implemented. *Virtually no time* was spent in any comparisons of options. In fact, the bulk of time was spent in situation assessment rather than alternative generation for *all crews*" (p. 269).

Flin, Slaven, and Stewart (1996) studied emergency decision making in the offshore oil industry. Their study used experienced offshore installation managers (managers of oil platforms). The six participants described how they would deal with a hypothetical crisis scenario, adapted from a standard industry training exercise. The data were coded for number of decision points and for type of decision strategy used with each of the 107 decision points. The results show little evidence of generating multiple options when faced with crisis decisions. The mean for the six participants was 10 percent, whereas 90 percent of the strategies were classified as being consistent with the RPD model. "The majority of their decisions," wrote Flin et al., "seem to be based on recognition of a particular problem and the generation of a single course of action drawn from their company's standard operating procedures" (p. 275).

Pascual and Henderson (1997) collected data from fifteen experienced commissioned and noncommissioned officers from the British Army, using a set of controlled but functionally realistic simulated exercises. All experimental sessions were video and audio recorded, and subjects were requested to verbalize the actions they were taking as the scenario unfolded (e.g., when they were sending or receiving information, planning, setting goals, or processing information). Subjects were not asked to explain the reasoning behind any of their actions or judgments. "A primary finding from the analysis of the coded responses across all scenarios was the dominance of naturalistic strategy utilization (87%) over classical (2%), hybrid (3%), and other (8%) strategies. " In assessing the form of the naturalistic strategies found, Pascual and Henderson concluded that "Recognition Primed Decision-making (RPD)...dearly dominated. ...It is felt that the RPD model provides the most appropriate, accurate, and utilitarian concepts for describing a broad range of C2 [command and control] decision making behavior, particularly for those subjects with considerable military experience" (p. 220).

Randel, Pugh, and Reed (1996) studied twenty-eight electronic warfare technicians who varied in experience level from six months to seven years. Data were collected using scenarios conducted with a simulator that has high physical and audio fidelity to the equipment found on board ships. They used the critical decision method to identify decision points and study the strategies used.

> The experts placed a greater emphasis on situation assessment, while the majority of the novices emphasized deciding on the course of action. ... This finding is consistent with the RPD model which proposed that experts based their decisions on situation assessment.
> The majority of the decisions discussed (93%) involved serial rather than concurrent deliberations, whether assessing the situation or deciding on a course of action. We found no differences between experts and novices in their use of serial deliberations over concurrent deliberations. All three groups—experts, intermediates, and novices—used predominately serial deliberations as specified by the RPD model. (p. 592)

To summarize, the RPD model was developed on the basis of field studies of the way that experienced personnel actually make decisions. The model explains how people can use experience to react rapidly and make good decisions without having to contrast options. The model has been tested and has been supported by different research teams working in a variety of settings.

The RPD model is not synonymous with NDM research. There are other NDM models (see Klein, Orasanu, Calderwood, & Zsambok, 1993 for descriptions). Moreover, the RPD model is incomplete; it does not cover teams, organizations, issues of managing workload and attention. The RPD model does not describe the strategies people use when they do have to compare options in natural settings. The significance of the RPD model is that:

- It appears to describe the decision strategy used most frequently by people with experience.
- It explains how people can use experience to make difficult decisions.
- It demonstrates that people can make effective decisions without using a rational choice strategy.

Prior to the RPD model and others like it, traditional decision researchers speculated that under certain task conditions, people would not use a rational choice strategy, but no one presented a coherent idea of what the alternative might be. Most researchers assumed that it would be a defective version of the rational choice strategy or some sort of random process. The description of the RPD model provides a counterexample to rational choice and makes it easier to take natural decision strategies more seriously.

Applications

This section describes two kinds of implications growing out of the RPD model: recommendations about training and about designing systems. For a detailed discussion of the applications of the NDM framework, Flin (1996) provides an excellent survey of the implications of NDM research for decision support system design, training, and personnel selection for critical incident managers such as police officers, firefighters, and offshore oil installation managers.

The standard advice for making better decisions is to identify all the relevant options, define all the important evaluation criteria, weight the importance of each evaluation criterion, evaluate each option on each criterion, tabulate the results, and select the winner. In one form or another, this paradigm finds its way into training programs the world over. Again and again, the message is repeated: careful analysis is good, incomplete analysis is bad. And again and again, the message is ignored; trainees listen dutifully, then go out of the classes and act on the first option they think of. The reasons are dear. First, the rigorous, analytical approach cannot be used in most natural settings. Second, the recognitional strategies that take advantage of experience are generally successful, not as a substitute for the analytical methods, but as an improvement on them. The analytical methods are not the ideal; they are the fallback for those without enough experience to know what to do.

One application of the RPD model is to be skeptical of courses or books about powerful methods for making effective decisions, thirty days guaranteed or your money back. I doubt whether such methods exist. Means, Salas, Crandall, and Jacobs (1993) reviewed the literature on the effectiveness of such analytical decision training and found that the results have been disappointing. Johnson, Driskell, and Salas (1997) have collected data showing that subjects did better using unsystematic strategies than analytical strategies for identifying and comparing options.

A second application of this chapter is to suggest that analytical methods may be helpful for people who lack experience. Decision training courses may be valuable as aids for novices or for complex cases with many different stakeholders. When I have used analytic methods in such settings, they have been helpful for setting out different factors and helping everyone achieve a shared perspective. Pious (1993) and Russo and Shoemaker (1989) present well-written guides to using analytical methods.[4]

A third application is to consider which decisions are worth making. When options are very close together in value, we can call this a zone of indifference: the closer together the advantages and disadvantages of competing options, the harder it will be to make a decision but the less it will matter.[5] For these situations, it is probably a waste of time to try to make the best decision. If we can sense that we are within this zone of indifference, we should make the choice any way we can and move on to other matters.

A situation that is like the zone of indifference can occur under conditions such as combat. A squad leader may have to decide whether to take an uphill or a downhill route, knowing that one will probably lead to safety and the other to an ambush. But he or she may have no information about which route to take and may be under attack and unable to remain in the current position. Here, the difficulty is created by the lack of information rather than the closeness of the two outcomes. We can think of this as a zone of ignorance: the squad leader will have to choose one route, primarily by chance.[6] In many cases, this situation will transform into a problem-solving activity with the apprehensive squad leader taking precautions such as assigning people with more experience as scouts, making sure that the troops are dispersed, and so forth.

A fourth application is *not* to teach someone to use the RPD model. There is no reason to teach someone to follow the RPD model, since the model is descriptive. It shows what experienced decision makers already do.

A fifth application is to improve decision skills. Because the key to effective decision making is to build up expertise, one temptation is to develop training to teach people to think like experts. But in most settings, this can be too time-consuming and expensive. However, if we cannot teach people to think like experts, perhaps we can teach them to learn like experts. After reviewing the literature, I identified a number of ways that experts in different fields learn Klein (1997):

- They engage in deliberate practice, so that each opportunity for practice has a goal and evaluation criteria.

- They compile an extensive experience bank.

- They obtain feedback that is accurate, diagnostic, and reasonably timely.

- They enrich their experiences by reviewing prior experiences to derive new insights and lessons from mistakes.

The first strategy is to engage in deliberate practice.[7] In order to do this, people must articulate goals and identify the types of judgment and decision skills they need to improve.

The strategy of compiling an extensive experience bank appears important. But the mere accumulation of experiences may not be sufficient. The experiences need to include feedback that is accurate, diagnostic, and timely.[8] In domains were it is possible to obtain such feedback (e.g., weather forecasting), decision-making expertise develops. In domains that are not marked by opportunities for effective feedback (e.g., clinical psychology), mere accumulation of experience does not appear to result in growth of decision expertise.

In addition to feedback, expertise may be affected by the opportunity to reflect on experiences. For example, chess masters do not spend all their time playing games against each other. The bulk of their time is spent studying positions and games. During a tournament, a grand master will be working against the clock and will not be reflecting on the implications of the game. But afterward, there is time to go over the game record to look for opportunities that were missed, early signals that were not noticed, or assessments and assumptions that were incorrect. In this way, an experience (even a single game) can be recycled and reused. In many field settings where there are limited opportunities for experience, developing the discipline of reviewing the decision-making processes for each incident can be valuable.

The strategies provide a concept that is consistent with principles of adult learning in which the learner is assumed to be motivated, and the emphasis is on granting autonomy and ownership to the learner rather than having the trainers maintain tight control.

So far, I have been describing our theoretical framework. How does this get translated into action? We recently had an opportunity to develop and implement a decision skills training program. The goal of the effort was to train approximately thirty U.S. Marine Corps squad leaders to handle a variety of decisions during a field exercise. The period of the training was three and a half months, but only a few hours each week could be allocated to the training. The squad leaders were enlisted men with high school, but not college, experience and between four and eight years in the Marine Corps.

John Schmitt, Mike McCloskey, and I put together a decision skills training approach consisting of several exercises. Three of those exercises were to identify decision requirements, practice with tactical decision games, and review experiences using a cognitive critique.

The *decision requirements* exercise is for the squad leaders to identify the key judgments and decisions facing them, why they are difficult, and where they can go wrong. These decision requirements are the high drivers, the specific decision skills that they need to polish. In addition, by identifying the decision requirements of their mission (e.g., identifying a good landing zone for helicopters, judging the amount of time it will take a squad to move from one position to another), the squad leaders could find ways to practice these judgments, such as getting feedback from helicopter pilots about the adequacy of a landing zone, or timing different squads as they moved across terrain, to become more sensitive to factors such as the nature of the terrain, the effect of weather, and the amount of equipment carried. Thus, the decision requirements let the squad leaders identify their own needs, for their own missions, and let them discover ways to engage in deliberate practice and obtain feedback for their judgments and decisions.

Tactical decision games are low-fidelity, paper-and-pencil simulations of incidents that might occur in the field (Schmitt, 1994). Each game consists of a map showing the setting for the incident and the location of the teams involved, and a brief verbal description of what is transpiring. The verbal description presents a dilemma with high levels of uncertainty. Upon completing the verbal description of the dilemma, the person leading the tactical decision game asks each of the participants to take three to five minutes to consider how he or she would react. The U.S. Marines do regular physical conditioning; working with the tactical decision games is like a mental conditioning program.

Cognitive critiques help the squad leaders reflect on what went well and not so well during an exercise, and to use this reflection to increase how much they learned from experience. The critique is a simple exercise, consisting of questions about how the squad leader had estimated the situation (Was it accurate?), uncertainty (Where was it a problem, and how was it handled?), intent and rationale (What was the focus of the effort?), and contingencies (reactions to what-if probes). The checklist could be used after tactical decision games as a way for the squad leaders to compare notes, get feedback, and see how others were perceiving the situation. The checklist, primarily designed to be used after field training exercises, was a way to enrich experiences by reviewing them, much as a chess master goes over a game record. Reviews generally occur after mistakes, and not as a routine. And when they do occur, they seem to be directed at what happened, whereas the cognitive critiques are aimed at the thought processes of the key decision makers. Moreover, reviews are conducted in a forum that is usually not conducive to reflection. Also, in most settings there are not always enough real incidents to build expertise quickly enough. That is why it is important to make effective use the incidents that occur.

The squad leaders were initially skeptical about the decision skills training program but soon became enthusiastic. They believed that the training helped to boost expertise in decision making and judgment, so that they felt more prepared to make difficult decisions under uncertainty and time pressure.

A sixth application is to use decision requirements for designing software systems. For a given task, the decision requirements are the key decisions and how they are made.[9] This includes the decisions that are required by the task, as well as the cues, information, and strategies required to make the decisions. When design engineers are given a new project, they are usually told what the system is supposed to accomplish, that is, what it will do if it works the way it is supposed to. Yet they are rarely told what the key decisions are that the system must help the operator make or the types of strategies or rules of thumb that the operator is likely to use. Left without any way to visualize the operator, designers do the best job they can to pack information onto screens so that it will all be there when needed. All the relevant information was available to the crew during the *Vincennes* shootdown, but the format of the information was difficult to interpret. The crucial altitude information was presented as a static four-digit number on a separate monitor.

In several projects we have been using decision requirements to design knowledge-based systems and human system interfaces. In one project we identified the decision requirements of U.S. Air Force weapons directors who fly in the AWACS (airborne warning and command system) airplane.[10] The weapons directors monitor the radar picture of the air for hundreds of miles, vectoring planes to different destinations. AWACS is a large airplane with a radar dish on its back. It is a flying command post, and the weapons directors are air traffic controllers working in the middle of a battle. By identifying their decision requirements in defensive operations, we could make some simple modifications of their interface with their workstations.

Example 7.2
The AWACS Weapons Directors

In 1991 we started a demonstration project to find out how useful it is to apply a cognitive approach to design. The charge of the project, funded by the Armstrong Laboratory of the air force's Human Systems Division, was to design a computer interface from the vantage point of the user, not the equipment.

On our team was Steve Andriole of Drexel University, to recommend technological solutions, and Len Adelman of George Mason University, who had written the book on evaluating decision support systems (Adelman, 1992). The project leader was David Klinger, who was supported by Laura Militello and Marvin Thordsen.

The reason for using AWACS to demonstrate the cognitive design approach was that there was a good AWACS simulator (a computer-driven mock-up of the AWACS workstations) at Brooks Air Force Base in San Antonio. It would be easy to modify the simulator and then to run several weapons directors through it to test how much the new system helped them.

A meeting with the AWACS specialists in San Antonio helped us solidify the plans to conduct interviews, redesign the interface, and conduct the tests. After the testing, we conducted the interviews, codified the interview data, and then worked to figure out what should go into the interface. We shipped these requirements to the Systems Research Laboratory programmers in San Antonio, who reprogrammed the AWACS simulator for testing of the new system.

When we began, most of the people on our team had no experience with AWACS at all. We had no idea about what we were going to improve, or even if any improvements were needed. The challenge was to find out if identifying decision requirements made a difference.

One of the key decision requirements was situation awareness. We learned that the weapons directors had to be especially vigilant for the high, fast flyers—the enemy aircraft that were the greatest threats.

The decision requirements also indicated a few key factors that could be used to identify these high-threats. That let us develop a simple algorithm to let the system outline each high-threat aircraft in a red circle. We were not trying to use very sophisticated methods but rather were searching for the simple fixes that could have an impact.

We had selected only a few changes for the interface. We highlighted critical tracks to make them more salient, used color to distinguish land and water, and moved a control panel onto the screen where it could more easily be used than in its previous position below the screen.

By May 1992, we were ready to test the interface to see if the new interface features made any difference at all. The evaluation tested the two interfaces: the current one, which had been used for many years, and our new one. The result was an improvement in performance of about 15 to

Example 7.2 (continued)

20 percent. In a simulated test, the weapons directors using our interface allowed:

- 20 percent fewer hostile strikes to be completed.
- A 15 percent reduction in the number of friendly aircraft shot down.
- A 36 percent decrease in the number of missiles fired that missed their target.
- A 9 percent increase in the overall kill ratio (hostile aircraft shot down versus friendly aircraft lost).
- A 76 percent increase in successful air refuelings.
- An 18 percent decrease in the number of aircraft having to return to base for refueling.

We got these effects using highly experienced weapons directors. Each director in the study used the standard interface for half of the simulated missions and our new interface for the other half. The directors had approximately fifteen hundred hours of practice with the standard interface. We could only give them four and a half hours to practice with the new interface, and still they did better. The redesigned interface satisfied their decision requirements.

In a relatively short amount of time (ten months), decision researchers with no domain experience were able to elicit information and redesign an interface to produce a large improvement in performance. It would have been very costly to achieve a 15 to 20 percent improvement in performance by developing faster and more powerful computers or providing more weapons director training.

8

The Power to Spot Leverage Points

Just as we are impressed when someone with expertise seems to know just what to do in a difficult situation, we are also impressed when someone invents a new procedure on the spot. This chapter explores the way people use leverage points—a small difference that makes a large difference, a small change that can turn a situation around—to create a new course of action, notice something that may cause a difficulty before there are any obvious signs of trouble, and figure out what is causing a difficulty.[1] If you have the task of moving a boulder, you can put your shoulder against the stone and strain to overcome its massive inertia, or you can survey the scene to find the opening that might let you exert a small amount of pressure to shift the center of gravity and topple the boulder. The search for leverage points is about finding those openings and making them work. We also want to find our vulnerabilities, the easy ways our plans can collapse, so that we can take steps to prevent the difficulty.

Example 8.1
Bubbling with Life

Norman Berlinger (1996), a physician, describes a case in which a fetus was diagnosed as having a large cystic hygroma, a tangled mass of lymph vessels, on the side of his neck. The sonogram suggested that the hygroma had grown inside the neck, wrapping around the trachea. If that were indeed the case, without emergency treatment the infant would die shortly after delivery because his air passage was blocked. As long as the fetus was in the uterus, receiving oxygen from the umbilical cord, he was safe. A cesarean section was scheduled for the following day.

During the delivery, Berlinger was going to determine if the baby was able to breathe on his own. If he could not, Berlinger's strategy was to intubate the infant, guiding a slender tube down his throat to clear a breathing

Example 8.1 (continued)

passage. But that might be impossible if the hygroma had grown so large as to obscure the opening of the windpipe. In that case, it might be necessary to do a tracheostomy—piercing the trachea and inserting the breathing tube into it. That would also be difficult. A tracheostomy is easy with an adult, but an infant's trachea is less than a quarter-inch wide, and soft and spongy. It is difficult to find. And other complications were likely. The incision would probably cut into the hygroma, possibly leading to infection of the lymphatic cysts and serious problems with abscesses in his chest. Moreover, the tracheostomy would have to be done under crisis conditions. It would be a last resort.

Upon delivery the infant gave a cry, suggesting a clear breathing passage. But then the passage sealed up. The infant could not even grunt. One of the nurses suctioned the infant's mouth and nose and placed him in front of Berlinger. Berlinger remembered an earlier situation, when he had been called in to operate on a young man who had run his snowmobile into a strand of barbed wire strung above the ground to discourage trespassers. The wire had jumbled the victim's neck tissue into sausage-like chunks. On that occasion, when Berlinger arrived, he found that the emergency technician had already inserted a breathing tube, and Berlinger had wondered how this was done. The technician later explained that he stuck the tube where he saw bubbles. Bubbles meant air coming out.

So in the delivery room, Berlinger looked into the mouth of the infant for bubbles. All he saw was a mass of yellow cysts, completely obscuring the air passage. No bubbles. Berlinger placed his palm on the infant's chest and pressed down, to force the last bit of air out of the infant's lungs. Berlinger saw a few tiny bubbles of saliva between some of the cysts and maneuvered the tube into that area. The laryngoscope has a miniature light on its tip, and Berlinger was able to guide it past the vocal cords, into the trachea. The infant quickly changed color from blue to a reassuring pink. The procedure had worked.

This example involves high-pressure problem solving. The physician did not have any procedures for inserting the breathing tube into the infant. He did recall an analogous case—a far-fetched one at that. It was about an adult, not an infant. It was about an accident, not a birth. It was about someone else's actions, not his own. The key point of similarity was discovering the air passage in an obscured throat. And even the analogy was not sufficient. There were no bubbles. The physician had to invent his own way to produce bubbles.

Skillful problem solving is impresive because after the fact, the solution seems obvious, yet we know that, without any guidance, most people would miss the answer. They would not even know that an answer was possible. We would look into the infant's mouth, see the mass of cysts, and abandon the idea of inserting a tube, immediately turning to the risky tracheostomy procedure, with no time to spare.

A leverage point is a focus for building a solution. It is the starting point for insightful problem solving. In example 8.1, the leverage point for the physician was the idea that bubbles could be used to find a breathing passage that otherwise could not be seen. In example 5.1, the leader of the emergency rescue team improvised a new way to rescue the motorist who was trapped in his car after it crashed into a concrete support. Some goals stayed the same (make the rescue quickly, do not endanger the victim, allow the victim to receive medical treatment), but some shifted. The goal of using the Jaws of Life to pry open the car doors was replaced by the goal of lifting the victim safely through the open top of the car. The strategy emerged on the spot, as both a goal (lift the victim through the top) and an action sequence (remove the top of the car, support the victim's neck and back, lift and turn the victim, and so on). The leverage point was the realization that the roof posts were fairly well severed, so that the rescue could be made from above the victim. In that study of decision making, we coded the incident described in example 5.1 as an example of constructive problem solving, not as a recognition-primed decision.

One way to think about leverage points is to use an example from the sport of rock climbing.

Example 8.2
Holding Firm

To move from one place to another, a climber makes use of holds. What are the features of a hold? It turns out that holds do not have context-free features, such as protruding at least two inches and extending at least four inches across. A hold, rather, is whatever I can use to propel myself forward. If I can kick off with some power and do not have to travel too far, the hold can be smaller. On a more horizontal surface, at the start of the climb, a simple ridge less than a quarter-inch wide may do. If my fingers are tired, the protrusion needs to be larger. If it has been raining, or the climb is more vertical, or I do not think the rock is strong enough, I need a larger surface. A hold doesn't have to protrude at all; a crack into which I can insert my hand will work. If the crack is too narrow to accommodate my hand but I

> **Example 8.2** (continued)
>
> can insert a finger and bend it so that the knuckle can be used as a brace, that may work too.
>
> For these reasons, no one can examine a photograph and identify the holds. What counts as a hold depends on the conditions of the climb and the climber. Similarly, in problem solving we build our plans and solutions from the holds that we recognize.[2]

My colleague Steve Wolf and I first noticed the use of leverage points in a study of chess players. Sometimes the chess players were trying to reach a goal ("If I can only get that rook off that open file"), and other times they would notice a happy accident. For example, one player was mentally simulating a sequence of moves and noticed that he could attack his opponent's queen. He did not find any way to capture the queen but started thinking of how to use this attack to gain some other advantage. The leverage point was in realizing that there might be an advantage gained in pressing the attack on the queen.

The decision maker, now acting as a problem solver, can try to use experience to identify leverage points and construct a new course of action. In evaluating whether the action will work, the decision maker now can try to improve it, or try to work with a different leverage point. Another approach is to try to modify the goals, which may result in the identification of different leverage points. The evaluation process can alter the understanding of the situation itself.[3]

Leverage points play an important role in a wide variety of domains. There are many examples from the field of business.[4] I present just a few illustrations, starting with the idea for pocket radios. In 1952, Masaru Ibuka, working for Tokyo Tsushin Kogyo (later to become Sony Corporation), saw an opportunity to use transistors for consumer products. He believed his company could somehow build and market a transistor radio that could fit in a shirt pocket. In the early 1950s, radios depended on vacuum tubes; transistors were largely restricted to military projects. Most people thought the idea of a transistor radio was impractical. We now know that the concept of using a transistor for a consumer product was a leverage point. Developing, applying, and building on that insight had tremendous implications.

The realization by Boeing engineers that commercial jetliners would have a big advantage over propeller-driven planes was another use of leverage points. The engineers had not designed such a plane and did not have a ready market for one. They had a concept and the interest and curiosity to see what would happen if they were to put jet engines into airliners. Rival companies such as Douglas Corporation (now incorporated into McDonnell Douglas) were not motivated to build on this leverage point to design their own jetliner, and they were not prepared to handle the market that opened up after Boeing introduced the 707.

Henry Ford's realization in 1907 that he could manufacture automobiles using mass production to cut costs so that most workers could afford one is a well-known example. At the time, Ford was just one of thirty competing automobile companies. His suspicion that mass production could cut costs dramatically was the leverage point.

In the early 1960s, Thomas J. Watson, Sr., at IBM, realized that a state-of-the-art system (to become the IBM 360) could change business in the way Henry Ford's standard model automobiles changed transportation. IBM invested more money to build the 360 model than the cost of the Manhattan project to build the first atomic weapon during World War II.

Peter Schwartz (1991) describes a project he performed for Royal Dutch/Shell. The question was about the Soviet Union's future policies on selling petroleum. Schwartz wondered whether there was any reason for the USSR to make dramatic policy changes. In reviewing some demographic data, he realized that the USSR could be headed for a sudden crisis. The population of elderly was increasing sharply, but the population of young adults entering the working class was decreasing. Schwartz wondered what this discontinuity might mean, and in exploring the implications, he was able to forecast, years ahead of the event, the possible destabilization of the USSR. He had discovered a leverage point for predicting a society under strain.

Scientists also rely heavily on leverage points. In a study of how successful human factors scientists and engineers first came up with their ideas (Klein & Hutton, 1995), we found that they were able to identify leverage points as opportunities where a need existed and the technology had become sufficiently mature. In other words, the scientists were not single-mindedly pursuing important topics. Unless they had a sense of how the problem could be solved, they did not get engaged. The leverage point provided them with a sense of the solvability of the problem. For example, for miniature visual displays, color would be better than black and white. However, color displays have lower resolution than black and white because it takes a mixture of three primary colors to produce a single pixel. Dave Post, a specialist in visual perception, wondered if he could use a subtractive method rather than an additive method, to get the same resolution as black and white. This hunch was enough to keep him working on the project and scavenging for funds for several years, until the technology was worked out.

In another example, Lee Task, a specialist in optics, noticed that pilots using night vision goggles could not read their instrument panels while landing their aircraft. He believed that the key data elements on the instrument panel could be incorporated into the night vision goggle display, so he identified this to his sponsors as a work project. Within a few months, he had developed a successful prototype.

Military commanders also need to detect leverage points. They need to find ways to exploit enemy weaknesses and detect signs that an adversary is preparing to do the same to them. The concept of maneuver warfare is to discover efficient opportunities for achieving powerful results. (It stands in contrast to attrition warfare, the approach of using force-on-force engagements to wear the enemy down.) A skilled commander is able to study a map and quickly detect the leverage points. Clausewitz refered to this capacity as the *coup d'oiel,* the rapid size-up that identifies the critical points in the terrain.

Leverage points are just possibilities—pressure points that might lead to something useful, or might go nowhere. Expertise may be valuable in noticing these leverage points. Certainly in games like chess, the experts are more likely to see them. In interpreting situations, experts seem attuned to the leverage points—both the opportunities and the threats facing them—rather than just being aware of the physical and spatial arrangement of objects.

In 1996, the world chess champion, Garry Kasparov, defeated the IBM chess computer Deep Blue in a six-game match. Observers noted that Deep Blue never adjusted its playing style. It always searched for the best move, even in positions where it knew it was behind. A human would have gambled on a strategy that was speculative rather than marching off to defeat. One of the IBM team members explained that the computer did not have a sense of "creative desperation"—the sense that drives chess players to search for leverage points, no matter how risky. In 1997, Deep Blue came back to defeat Kasparov. The machine still had not acquired a sense of creative desperation, but its developers had more than doubled the number of moves it searched and added some other refinements to make up for its limitations. The following example shows the use of creative desperation in spotting a leverage point.[5]

Example 8.3
The Impossible Crossing Points

Israel is being invaded by one of its neighbors. The Israeli Defense Force commanders decide that they need to infiltrate tanks across the battle lines to conduct a critical maneuver, but they cannot find an acceptable place for the tanks to cross. One of the commanders scrutinizes the map and points to the place where the tanks will cross. "Here," he says, "where it is marked 'Impossible.' That's where we cross." He knows that the terrain has been tested with platoons, which consist of four tanks, and they have failed to make the crossing. Accordingly, the map was annotated to show the failure. But he also knows the terrain sufficiently well to realize that they can send one or two tanks at a time and make it through. And they do.

This theme is repeated in many domains. Experts know how the official records are compiled, whether they are maps, computer manuals, diagnostic tests, or air crew checklists. They know when the steps have to be followed and when to make exceptions.

Leverage points provide fragmentary action sequences, kernel ideas, and procedures for formulating a solution. Experts seem to have a larger stock of procedures that they can think of to use as starting points in building a new plan or strategy. These can serve as holds to get the process moving, or in combination with other fragmentary actions. Novices, in contrast, are often at a loss about where to begin.

We also need to spot leverage points that can work against us, in order to learn the weaknesses in our plans. These are sometimes called *choke points*. For example, a manager of a production line might realize that the whole schedule could be disrupted if a key part is not delivered on time. At that moment, no problem exists, but rumors about an impending strike at the plant that is producing the part cannot be shrugged off. It may be prudent to find a backup supplier, just in case. By noticing leverage points that can work against us, we buy ourselves time to take preventive action before the emergency arises. Example 8.4 contrasts two pilots: one who spotted a vulnerability and one who did not.

Example 8.4
The Flight to Philadelphia

An airline crew takes off for a trip across the United States, from San Francisco to Philadelphia. A trained observer (himself a pilot) is riding in the cockpit, in the jumpseat. Before the airplane takes off, the crew conducts an inspection. The observer notes that the brakes and tires are fairly worn, almost to the limits for replacement. Once the crew members take their places in the cockpit, the preflight information package shows that they are carrying an extra 9,000 pounds of fuel. The observer asks the captain if he knows the reason, but it is a mystery. A few minutes later the captain radios the question to the dispatchers, but they do not know either.

After takeoff, about midway through the flight, the crew sees some flickering of the thrust reverser light. They do not believe that the thrust reversers are going to be accidently deployed, but the possibility exists that the thrust reversers may not be fully functioning to slow the aircraft down during the landing phase. Subsequently the crew learns that the weather in Philadelphia has deteriorated, with moderate winds and rain. The weather is not expected to get any worse, so the airplane should not need to divert. As they approach Philadelphia, the air traffic controller tells the crew which runway to expect for landing, so it can plan its approach.

The observer, realizing that the air traffic controller has selected the shortest runway at the airport, becomes disturbed: their stopping distance margin for error has been compromised, first by the worn tires and brakes, then by the extra weight, then by the possible thrust reverser malfunction, then by the wet runways, and now by the shortness of the assigned runway. Although still within the design limits for operating the airplane, the chances of stopping within the confines of the assigned runway have been reduced beyond his level of comfort. Knowing that the surface winds allow a longer runway to be used, the observer expects the captain to request it. Minutes go by, however, and the captain appears to be accepting the assigned runway. Wishing to call attention to the situation and to indicate his growing concern, the observer asks, "Which runway is that? It is that real short one?" The captain says that it is. Shortly, the captain initiates the radio call to air traffic control requesting a change in runway, which is granted.

The example shows two reactions to a potential problem. Both the captain and the observer had access to the same information. Both realized all the ways in which the landing was becoming risky. The observer identified the situation as problematic, requiring nonroutine action. In contrast, the captain appeared to be ignoring the warning signs and preparing to follow the air traffic controller's instructions.

Let us go back to the example of the rock climb. We have used the holds to make it up the initial part of the climb. Now the route is becoming more difficult. We look up to where the old path continues and wonder if we can find a series of holds to make it that far. There are some possibilities, but they look risky. Then we notice that a crack has opened up that would let us cross an area that used to be impassable and bring us to a section that always seemed like an interesting challenge, if we could only reach it. This seems to be the time to try it out. We cross over using the new crack that opened up and now have to find a way forward. We scan the rock to discover the possibilities it offers. Each time we notice a good hold, we use it to map out how the sequence might go.

Once we come up with leverage points, we need to fill in the remaining details. In the harness rescue example, the commander synthesized a course of action by starting with the fragment of attaching a ladder belt to the semiconscious woman. From that starting point, he worked out the details of how to attach the ladder belt to her and how to tie a rope to the ladder belt to lift her to safety. By adding these details, the commander had the new course of action.

In the rock climbing example, we need to tie the leverage points together into a path in which we can feel confidence. Once we see how to move from hold to hold, we have a plan. We also know we will be changing the plan during the climb as we notice new features. We may have gaps in the plan where we do not see the connection but trust that we will find it when we get that far.

9

Nonlinear Aspects of Problem Solving

People become problem solvers when they have to find a way to create a new course of action, improvise, notice difficulties way in advance, or figure out what is causing a difficulty. The concept of leverage points opens the way to think about problem solving as a constructive process. It is constructive in the sense that solutions can be built up from the leverage points and that the very nature of the goal can be clarified while the problem solver is trying to develop a solution. In rock climbing, there is no correct solution. The climber looks at the available holds and figures out what direction makes good sense.

This approach to problem solving can be traced back to the German research psychologist Karl Duncker, one of the central figures in the Gestalt psychology school in Europe. The Gestalt school emphasized perceptual approaches to thought. Rather than treating thought as calculating ways of manipulating symbols, the Gestaltists viewed thought as learning to see better, using skills such as pattern recognition.

Duncker (1935/1945) had asked people to think out loud (so he could gain insights into their thought processes) while solving well-defined and ill-defined problems. One of the tasks he used was the X-ray problem: you are a physician needing to treat a patient with a tumor. You can use X-rays to destroy the tumor, but the radiation will also damage healthy tissue. What can you do?

There are a few acceptable approaches (as befits an ill-defined problem). One of the more satisfactory solutions is to use several X-ray sources. Each could transmit low-level radiation that would not be harmful to healthy tissue yet could be aimed to converge on the tumor and destroy it. To find this solution, the subjects had to elaborate the goal of destroying the tumor. The goal included the property of not injuring healthy tissue.

Eventually the problem solver identified a new goal of exposing healthy tissue to only small amounts of radiation.

Duncker found that as his subjects worked on these problems, they simultaneously changed their understanding of the goal and assessed solutions. A subject might think of a solution, try it out, realize it would not work, realize what was missing, and then add to the definition of the goal. This new definition would suggest new approaches, and when these approaches failed, they helped to clarify the goal even further.

To solve ill-defined problems, we need to add to our understanding of the goal at the same time we generate and evaluate courses of action to accomplish it. When we use mental simulation to evaluate the course of action and find it inadequate, we learn more about the goal we are pursuing. Failures, when properly analyzed, are sources of new understanding about the goal.

The leverage point account of problem solving requires a nonlinear rather than a linear approach.[1] We can think of problem solving as consisting of four processes: problem detection, problem representation, option generation, and evaluation (see figure 9.1).

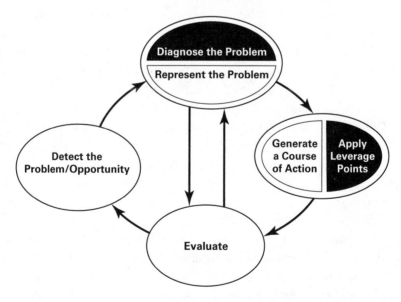

Figure 9.1

Nonlinear account of problem solving

The account shown in figure 9.1 does not have an output stage, because each of the components can lead to different types of outputs. Problem detection is itself an output, as in the warnings offices set up by governmental agencies whose job is to provide early detection of problems. Problem representation is another output, sometimes the necessary and sufficient output for determining how to proceed. There are medical diagnosticians whose responsibility is primarily to provide skillful problem representations. Generating forecasts is itself a professional specialty in many fields.

Constructing a course of action is the component most people think of as the output of problem solving: generating a plan for achieving a goal. Regardless of how the option is generated, it will need to be evaluated, often using mental simulation. The evaluation process can lead to adoption of the option, result in selecting between options, or identify new barriers and opportunities, thereby triggering additional problem solving.

The problem-solving process contains different types of outputs, depending on what is needed in the situation.

Figure 9.1 shows why this is an interactive account. The goals affect the way we evaluate courses of action, and the evaluation can help us learn to set better goals. The goals determine how we assess the situation, and the things we learn about the situation change the nature of the goals. Goals define the barriers and leverage points we search for, and the discovery of barriers and leverage points alters the goals themselves. The way we diagnose the causes leading to the situation also affects the types of goals adopted. Further, the leverage points (fragmentary action sequences) we notice grow out of our own experiences and abilities—another layer of interaction.

To review this nonlinear account, we will examine each of the components, starting with the *problem detection process*.[2] Something happens, something anomalous, and we may notice it. Perhaps a rock climber notices that the route has more debris on it than usual. Or an expectation is violated or something expected did not occur. In example 8.4, the pilot flying to Philadelphia did not seem to notice how much the margin of safety was being compromised.

The *problem representation function* covers the way a person identifies and represents the problem.[3] Is there a gap between what we have and what we want? Is there an opportunity to achieve more than we expected? Both gaps and opportunities can trigger problem-solving efforts, either to remove the gap (and obtain what you want) or to harvest the opportunity. Say that the rock climber gets a little higher and notices that there has been a small avalanche. The pitons she counted on using are covered up, so she may have to find another route, maybe retracing her steps. Or she can find better holds and keep going.

Leverage points are part of the problem representation. We try to detect the leverage points that can turn into solutions, as well as the choke points that can spell trouble ahead. In some cases, identifying the leverage points can count as the critical type of problem representation, emphasizing the lines of reasoning that may be most important.

Not all gaps or opportunities lead to problem solving. They must be important enough, and the problem solver must judge that the gap or opportunity will not be resolved without special effort. Then comes a difficult judgment: the solvability of the problem.[4] Somehow we use our experience to make this judgment even before we start working to come up with a solution. Part of our situation awareness is whether this is a problem we should be able to solve without too much work, versus a problem that can take days or weeks and get us nowhere.

Therefore, the function of problem representation includes goal setting because the problem solver must judge whether to try to come up with a solution or turn to other needs. For ill-defined goals, we can expect to see a lot of goal modification during the problem-solving effort.[5]

When a gap or opportunity is identified, often we will try to *diagnose* it.[6] This is the mental simulation function in which we try to weave together the causes that might have led to the current situation. Because diagnosis is not always required, it is portrayed as an elaboration of problem representation in figure 8.1 and is shaded. We may also want to project trends based on the diagnosis, to see how the situation may change. This is the forecasting process. In many situations, the primary need is to build a reliable forecast in order to determine whether the difficulty will disappear on its own, or will get worse and require action. The problem representation and diagnosis processes are linked to forecasting, which usually requires mental simulation.

The next function is directed at *generating a new course of action*, in many cases, a straightforward process: we recognize what to do, and do it. At other times, we do not recognize what to do and must rely on leverage points in order to construct a new course of action. If we blindly press forward trying to reach goals and remove barriers, we may miss these leverage points. Experience lets us detect them and provides a chance to improvise in order to take advantage of them. We also have to be careful not to pursue opportunities too enthusiastically since they might distract us from our more important goals. We have to balance between looking for ways to reach goals and looking for opportunities that will reshape the goals.

The fourth function is to *evaluate* plans and actions, to play out a scenario to see what will happen. If the evaluation is favorable, we carry out the action. We also can learn from the evaluation, perhaps discovering new gaps or opportunities, resulting in problem detection or in a new way to represent the problem, as when we would modify our goals.

The concept of problem solving appears incomplete without the aspect of discovering opportunities. There is an infinite set of instances in which problem solving should be initiated. We do not have all the money we want or all the vacation time. We are not driving cars that are as luxurious or sporty as we want, and so forth. So the potential for problem solving exists on a massive level. Yet we are not defining each of these as problems and wasting time worrying about these discrepancies. De Groot (1945) and Isenberg (1984) have suggested that what triggers active problem solving is the ability to recognize when a goal is reachable. In the standard view, this seems paradoxical, since it claims that a course of action that is generated after a goal is defined is evaluated for plausibility and used to determine whether to pursue that goal in the first place. There must be an experiential ability to judge the solvability of problems prior to working on them.

Experience lets us recognize the existence of opportunities. When the opportunity is recognized, the problem solver working out its implications is looking for a way to make good use of it, trying to shape it into a reasonable goal. At the same time, the opportunity is shaping the goal by raising the level of aspiration and identifying additional goal properties.

Example 9.1 shows how an organization shifted its goals because of the way it evaluated a business plan. In evaluating a course of action, officers of a company discovered an opportunity and leverage point. This information caused them to revise the goal and led to the synthesis of an expanded course of action.

Example 9.1
Learning to Love Telemarketing

The parent company organizes franchises for services. Each of the individual franchisees needs to use telemarketing to obtain customers, and each finds the task of hiring, training, and managing telemarketers to be burdensome. The marketing director for the parent company identifies this as a problem, but with an obvious solution: the parent company can centralize the telemarketing across the United States. The president of the parent company is lukewarm to this idea, since it requires a large investment. Then he realizes that with a centralized group of telemarketers, he can pursue his ideas about direct order sales. At that point he becomes even more enthusiastic about the project than the marketing director.

As the marketing director and the president mentally simulated the proposed telemarketing center, the president noticed a new and different possibility. This idea, to use telemarketers for catalog sales, increased the president's level of aspiration and changed the nature of the goal he wanted to pursue. The opportunity to use the telemarketers for direct order sales also suggested some fragmentary action sequences that could be easily blended with the original goal of helping the franchisees.

Traditional Models of Problem Solving

To get a better appreciation of the concept of leverage points and how they fit into a nonlinear account of problem solving, it is useful to contrast them to some more traditional models. Problem solving is a different phenomenon when we engage in it in natural settings from when we study it under laboratory conditions. Aspects of everyday cognition such as problem finding are usually not studied in the laboratory. We do not investigate problem-finding skills in studies where we present subjects with a problem or puzzle that is ready made. Certainly experimenters must restrict a phenomenon in order to study it. We run into trouble when we do not realize what our studies have been excluding.

Traditional approaches to problem solving treat the process as open to decomposition into component elements that are relatively independent of each other. Traditional approaches also view the process of problem solving as proceeding in a mechanistic fashion, from one stage to the next, using a set of operators as transformation rules.

First, we will examine the approach that relies on stage models, the most common treatment of problem solving. After that, we will look at the artificial intelligence approach, the most sophisticated treatment.

Stage Models

Stage models are the most common description of problem-solving activities. Raanan Lipshitz and Oma Bar-Ilan (1996) have found examples of researchers and theoreticians who have presented various models:

- Two-stage models: idea getting and idea evaluation.

- Three-stage models: problem finding, design of alternatives, and choice.

- Four-stage models: understanding the problem, devising a plan, carrying out the plan, and evaluating the results.

- Five-stage models: identifying the problem, defining it, evaluating possible solutions, acting, and evaluating success.

- Six-stage models: identifying the problem, obtaining necessary information to diagnose causes, generating possible solutions, evaluating the various solutions, selecting a strategy for performance, and performing and revising the solution.

- Seven-stage models: problem sensing, problem definition, alternative generation, alternative evaluation, choice, action planning, and implementation.

- An eight-stage model.

To simplify these variations, we can propose a generic four-stage model that comes reasonably dose to these varieties:

1. Define the problem.

2. Generate a course of action.

3. Evaluate the course of action.

4. Carry out the course of action.

This description generally makes sense. On logical grounds alone, it is hard to evaluate a course of action (step 3) before generating it (step 2).

We can run into trouble with this model by following the linear sequence of steps too strictly. For example, you would not want to start generating courses of action until you had a fairly good idea of what the problem was; however, for many common problems we will not be able to reach a good definition because they are ill defined. We cannot begin with a definition since there is none.

Think about a fireground commander racing to put out a fire. The goal seems well defined: extinguish the fire so it does not start again. However, as we saw in chapter 2, the commander has to judge whether to attack the fire or begin search and rescue, or do both. If the building is deserted and in poor shape, the commander may choose to let it burn rather than use resources to prevent its spread. Commanders are judged by whether they choose the right action in a situation, and sometimes their superiors and peers will disagree about what that right thing was.

The criterion for claiming that a goal is ill defined is that experienced people might not agree about how to satisfy the goal. Writing a good story has an ill-defined goal. Different English teachers could disagree in their judgments of whether a specific story satisfies the goal of being good. Solving a university's parking problem is ill defined; experts are certain to disagree about what a good outcome is.[7] One person might favor building large parking structures in the middle of campus to preserve space. Another would put all parking at the edges of campus and serve commuters with a bus system, to make the campus car free. Architects will have trouble agreeing on acceptable designs, in part because of the disagreement over goals.

In contrast, a mathematical equation (e.g., $x + 7 = 12$; solve for x) is an example of a problem with a well-defined goal. No one would disagree with the answer ($x = 5$) or with the intent of the problem. For many people, solving well-defined puzzles is satisfying because there is a right answer. There is pleasure in making the different strands tumble into place.

Most natural goals seem to be ill defined. Some are ill defined to a minor extent, like firefighting. Some are more strongly ill defined, like solving a parking problem. Some are extremely ill defined, like writing a good short story.

Most of the studies of problem solving and decision making have centered on well-defined goals—solving mathematical equations, physics problems, or syllogisms in deductive logic, for example. The appeal of these well-defined problems is that researchers can perform carefully designed experiments manipulating different variables to see if the manipulations change the proportion of correct answers. Because all the problems have correct answers, there is no ambiguity in these studies. Therefore, the field of problem solving has concentrated on tasks with well-defined goals.

Because it is so systematic, we are attracted to the standard advice of following the stages from problem definition to option generation and evaluation. Yet in dealing with an ill-defined goal, the advice is sure to fail. The first step, define the goal, can never be completed if the goal is ill defined, and that means the problem solver is not supposed to go further. Instead, the problem solver is trapped at that first step. The standard method for solving problems is worse than useless; it can interfere when people try to solve ill-defined problems (Klein & Weitzenfeld, 1978).

Consider the following quotation: "What do you want to do with your life? Where do you want to be in five years, ten, or even twenty? What kind of lifestyle do you want to have? All of these questions need to be answered BEFORE you start pursuing a career focus and even before you decide on an education." This advice came from a pamphlet designed for high school students *(Federal Jobs for College Graduates)*. I wonder how many readers with advanced degrees could answer the questions.

Problems can be unstructured in several ways, not just through vague goals. According to Reitman (1965), a problem can be ill structured if the initial state is not defined, the terminal state is undefined, or the procedure for transforming the initial state into the terminal state is undefined. For some problems, clarifying the initial state is the most important outcome. For example, diagnosing the disease causing a mysterious set of symptoms will usually enable a physician to determine the appropriate course of treatment. For other problems, such as rescuing people from a burning building, the diagnosis of how they got into the building is irrelevant. Next, let us consider the case in which the terminal state is ill defined. For some problems, clarifying the terminal state is critical. For example, a teenager searching for a job may not have a clear idea of the essential characteristics of a good job. For other problems, such as trying to cut the crime rate by half in a large city, the goal is well defined, and what is needed is to diagnose the prime causes of crime (e.g., unemployment, lenient judges, inconsistencies in legal codes, and so forth) and to find procedures for eliminating those causes. Finally, the transformation of initial into terminal state may be critical, as in constructing a complicated plan, or it may be trivial, as in the case of a physician who knows just what to do once an accurate diagnosis is made. Therefore, the focus of problem solving can be very different depending on the nature of the problem.

The four-stage model is incomplete and misleading. It does not tell us much that is useful about defining goals or how to generate courses of action. It merely states that these steps must be taken. It can include stages such as diagnosis that may be irrelevant for certain types of problems. It misleads by implying that the steps should follow a linear sequence. Most behavioral scientists studying problem solving now agree about the shortcomings of stage models (e.g., Mintzberg, Raisinghani, & Theoret, 1976; Smith, 1994; and Weick, 1983). The components of a stage model are themselves reasonable. The difficulty is not in the components of the stage models, but in the assumption of linearity. The account in figure 8.1 relies on similar components but organizes them to make them more applicable to ill-structured problems.

Artificial Intelligence Approach

Artificial intelligence researchers try to use computers to perform complex judgment and reasoning tasks. In the 1950s, Herbert Simon and others realized that computers could be used to manipulate symbols as well as numbers. By coding knowledge as symbols, Simon and his colleagues were able to make computers learn, draw inferences, and solve problems. In doing so, he made the study of thinking a respectable scientific endeavor. The proof of success in programming a computer to copy the thinking of human subjects could be tested by comparing the computer's performance with those of the human subjects it was supposed to imitate. Previously, psychologists in the United States had rejected the study of thinking as too unscientific. The dominant research paradigm was to study the learning behavior of lower organisms, such as rats and pigeons. Simon and his colleagues helped to change all that.

In 1972, Allen Newell and Herbert Simon published *Human Problem Solving*, describing their success in writing computer programs that could emulate human thought processes for tasks such as chess and puzzles. Example 9.2 shows a cryptarithmetic task that they used in their research.

Example 9.2
DONALD + GERALD = ROBERT

The cryptarithmetic task is to solve a problem, DONALD + GERALD = ROBERT, with only the due that D = 5. Each letter corresponds to a different number, and the task is to figure out the numerical value of each letter.

DONALD

+GERALD

ROBERT

Starting with the fact that D = 5, we can figure out that T is 0. Also, in the far left column we see that D (5) plus G is at least 6 and at most 9. We know R is an odd number, since in column 5, L + L = R, and we know there was a one carryover. So R is either 7 or 9. And so forth.[8]

The field of artificial intelligence has resulted in a number of important findings and applications but has not had the full impact that its original developers expected. The potential for this work is limited because artificial intelligence is primarily about well-defined problems. Puzzles such as the cryptarithmetic task in example 9.2 are well defined. In studying problems like this, Newell and Simon found that people use heuristics such as finding intermediate goals and solving them as a way to break up the whole problem.

The focus on well-defined problems is not the only limitation of the artificial intelligence approach. Although it claims to be describing how people solve problems, the approach is limited to the processes at which digital computers excel, such as setting up and searching through lists.

Now we are in a position to see what is missing from the artificial intelligence approach to problem solving. Here are some of the basic claims of the artificial intelligence approach:

1. The problem is represented as a closed problem space generated from a finite set of objects, relations, and properties.
2. Problem solving is the search through the problem space until the desired knowledge state is reached.
3. The search can be heuristic (means—ends analysis to set up subgoals and reduce differences).
4. Reformulating a goal means removing unnecessary constraints.

Artificial intelligence programs establish a problem space, consisting of all the descriptions and implications of the objects, their properties, and their relationships.[9] The job of the program is to discover at least one pathway that will work to connect the initial and the desired end state. The program can conduct a heuristic search so that it does not have to examine every alternative. For example, if the program hits a gap, that is, a difference between where it is and where it needs to be, then it can make the reducing of this gap a subgoal and focus its search on ways of reducing that difference. This is termed a means-ends analysis—the strategy of identifying a barrier to reaching an end state, making the new goal to overcome that barrier, and so on.

The artificial intelligence community can point to many impressive accomplishments, but we have to be wary of its claims. In fact, each of the individual claims runs into trouble, and the entire approach rests on questionable assumptions.

First, the idea of a problem space does not match anything we know of experience about human problem solving. I do not know of any evidence that shows that people generate problem spaces except in combinatorial, well-defined problems such as figuring out the probability of getting three heads if you throw four coins simultaneously. If you did not know the formula to use, you might just write out all the permutations and count up the frequencies. For situations that are more complex or less precise, we would usually not try to lay out the problem space of objects, relations, and properties.

Second, the idea of searching through a problem space misses the experience we have of noticing things we had not considered before, and discovering or synthesizing a new approach. If we have already set up the problem space, we are unlikely to make these discoveries as we work on the task.

Third, there are other strategies in addition to the means-ends analysis. Using means-ends analysis to reduce differences is not the same as noticing opportunities. When we solve problems, we are alert to opportunities that let us make progress, even if those opportunities do not correspond to the obstacles we are trying to eliminate.[10] In addition, Voss, Greene, Post, and Penner (1983) studied ill-structured social science problems and found little evidence for straightforward means-ends analysis.

Fourth, in solving problems we do not reformulate goals merely by removing constraints. We sometimes make radical shifts. Think again about the car rescue in example 5.1. The commander of the rescue team was not eliminating unnecessary constraints as much as he was changing the nature of the goal: lifting the victim through the roof instead of getting him out of one of the doors.[11]

The artificial intelligence program is not a technique for *generating* options. Instead, it is a procedure for setting up a search space and then using heuristics to achieve more efficient searches to *find* a good option. Conducting rapid searches is what digital computers do best. A computer does not have to do anything constructive to search through a space. It does not have to generate anything new. If the search space can be structured well enough, it can turn up findings that are novel. For example, if you give a computer a thousand different ice cream flavors, ten types of cones, and five hundred toppings, it will identify a range of options no one ever considered before.[12]

One of the primary mechanisms of artificial intelligence is to spread out the alternatives exhaustively and filter through them efficiently. This is the same strategy used in the analytical approaches to decision making. These approaches urge us to generate large numbers of options in order to be reasonably sure that the set will include a good option. Then we are supposed to search through these options, filtering out the inadequate ones, to find a successful one. Computational approaches try to reduce thinking to searching. Thus they show their greatest successes with tasks that can be transformed into searches.

To examine the ideas about problem solving represented in figure 9.1 more critically, it may be useful to consider an incident that placed high demands on both problem-solving and decision-making skills. The most interesting aspects of this incident were about detecting problems, representing the problems, and generating new courses of action.

The *Apollo 13* Mission: A Case Study of Problem Solving

The incident in question is the explosion of an oxygen tank following the launch of the spacecraft and the difficulties of bringing the astronauts safely back to earth. On the surface, it is a story about adventures in space, but at another level it is about problem solving and decision making: detecting problems, understanding the nature of the problems, improvising solutions, and selecting courses of action. Lovell and Kluger (1994) have described the *Apollo 13* mission, particularly the time-pressured workarounds to unexpected failures, under conditions of high uncertainty. I counted seventy-three problem-solving and decision-making episodes in the book.

This type of retrospective review can be helpful in tying issues together. It can also be misleading, since the *Apollo 13* mission is not representative of other types of problem-solving incidents and because the recollections of astronaut Jim Lovell may be inaccurate regarding the processes used to solve the various problems. One thing that makes me suspicious is that no one in the book ever makes a stupid mistake. Perhaps Lovell is blessed with gifted colleagues, perhaps he is a pure soul who is attuned to the good in people, or perhaps his memoirs have been sanitized to reduce friction. Therefore, we need to be careful in accepting Lovell and Kluger's account as reality. But that should not stop us from seeing what we can learn from it. (Cooper, 1973, has provided an accessible account of the accident that is consistent with the one offered by Lovell and Kluger.)

One easy thing to do is look for examples of the categories of figure 9.1: problem detection, problem representation, generation of a course of action, and evaluation.

Problem detection was usually not important because the problem was clear-cut and expertise was not required to notice the problem. For example, the initial loss of oxygen triggered all kinds of alarms. It would have taken a dedicated effort not to notice that a problem had arisen. The instruments showing a loss of oxygen also pointed to an obvious impending problem of keeping the astronauts alive. Other problem detections did require expertise. I estimated that problem detection played a key role in twenty of the seventy-three episodes. For example, using the lunar excursion module (LEM) as a lifeboat created a problem of eliminating carbon dioxide, since the LEM was not equipped to handle three astronauts for extended periods of time. This difficulty could have been missed, with critical consequences.

Problem representation was a primary process, playing a key role in thirty-one of the seventy-three episodes. In thirteen of the episodes, the problem representation directly led to the strategy or plan adopted. By knowing what type of problem they were facing, the mission controllers recognized how to react. From the outset, the mission controllers needed to make sense of all the unexpected instrument readings they were getting. They needed to get a big picture of what had suddenly happened to their spacecraft. Once they built their situation awareness, the nature of the problem shifted from performing the planned mission to the new mission of finding a way to save the astronauts. Problem representation was central in making sense of all the sudden demands: keeping antennas aligned, preventing the spaceship from developing thermal imbalance because it was no longer rotating systematically to protect it from the direct exposure to the sun, adjusting to losses of power and oxygen, and so forth.

There were about five instances of goal revision. The most dramatic was the shift in goals from trying to continue the mission while repairing the problem, to calling the mission off and concentrating on returning the astronauts safely. In hindsight, this seems like an obvious shift, but the mission controllers and the astronauts resisted it. In industrial settings, such as running a manufacturing or production process, supervisors have trouble with this type of breakpoint, where they have to abandon business as usual and move to an emergency mode. Sometimes they wait too long to make this shift.

The incident also required many subgoals, such as figuring out how to reduce power soon after the accident, or devising a plan to power up the command module in two hours, rather than the full day (using thousands of amp hours) that was typical. There were many examples of these, since each new challenge carried with it a new set of subgoals. These are the basis for means-ends analysis: finding a difference (e.g., it takes a day to power up the spacecraft and I have to do it in two hours) and making it the new goal to pursue. This incident demanded a great deal of means-ends analysis in the sense of identifying new subgoals.

I did not see the type of goal shift we would find with ill-defined goals. The *Apollo 13* mission may not have shown much goal revision because the goals were fairly well defined to begin with. Most of the changes in goals involved shifts in priorities, such as the uses of water. (Water was needed by the cooling system, to protect the equipment, and also by the crew.) Therefore, this may have been the wrong type of incident to study goal redefinition. Another possibility is that I am mistaken in my emphasis on goal redefinition.

The *Apollo 13* incident did not require as much diagnosis as I had expected. I found only ten examples of diagnosis plus another two after the mission was over (to find out why the explosion had occurred and to find out why the trajectory of the spacecraft was shifting during its return to Earth). For problems such as finding ways to eliminate the buildup of carbon dioxide, reduce electrical power consumption, and conserve water use, diagnosis was irrelevant. The problem representation was clear, and the mission controllers needed to find a novel course of action. This illustrates why the process of diagnosis is portrayed as optional in figure 9.1.

For those episodes where diagnosis was needed, it played a critical role. For instance, during the return to Earth, battery 2 started to falter. There were only four batteries available. If the spacecraft was to develop battery problems on top of all the other failures, the chances of success would go even lower, and more workarounds would be needed. One of the mission controllers tried to diagnose the cause of the problem and determined that it was a low-probability malfunction that had existed in all the batteries of every LEM. The odds of other batteries failing were very low. In other words, the malfunction was not part of the unique crises afflicting *Apollo 13* or part of the other system failures. Based on this diagnosis, the mission controllers were able to ignore the problem with battery 2 and proceed with their plans.

The level of detail for carrying out the diagnosis is important. The astronauts and the mission controllers would have liked to have a diagnosis of the cause of the original malfunction (which turned out to be an explosion of one of the two oxygen tanks). However, it was more important to find out the nature of the damage than to learn why it occurred. The mission controllers performed an initial diagnosis to learn what was causing the bizarre sensor readings. The diagnosis was that the spacecraft had lost one of its two oxygen tanks and was quickly losing the oxygen in the second tank. That explained the sensor readouts and provided a dear problem representation. They did not have a diagnosis of what caused the loss of the oxygen tanks. Only at the end of the mission did the astronauts see the extent of the destruction to the oxygen tanks. And only after several months did the investigation team learn how the maintenance and design process had created the hazard in the first place, leading to a condition where an unshielded wire in the oxygen tank generated a spark after a routine action to turn on the fan to stir the contents of the oxygen tanks. This level of diagnosis would have had no value during the emergency.

Some of the most compelling episodes in this incident were about constructing new courses of action. These stood out because so much of the mission was designed to be carefully scripted, yet when the script had to be abandoned, the mission controllers showed themselves capable of wonderful improvisation. I counted eighteen instances in which new courses of action were invented, along with many additional instances in which a course of action was recognized but without a need to do anything inventive.

For the cases where actions had to be constructed, the accounts did not have enough detail for me to judge the extent to which means-ends analyses and leverage points were used, or other strategies or combinations of strategies. Several episodes suggested means-ends analyses, such as when the controllers discovered that the reentry battery was 20 amp-hours below what was needed. The problem was a difference between what existed and what was needed. The controllers searched for a way to reduce this difference and found that the LEM had excess capacity, so the new course of action was to transfer LEM power up to the command module.

Other episodes suggested the use of leverage points, and in many of the instances in which new courses of action were generated, both means-ends analyses and leverage points appeared to be used. The means-ends analyses identified new subgoals, and the leverage points identified the promising starting points for constructing the courses of action. For example, the mission controllers needed a way to align the reentry of the ship. The typical procedure was to use the horizon of the earth as it moved across a window, sweeping past hash marks etched on the window for this purpose. However, *Apollo 13* was returning from the nighttime side of earth; the astronauts could not check their alignment against a horizon they could not see. One of the team leaders realized that the moon would be visible as it set against the earth's horizon during the critical reentry time. He planned a course of action to develop calculations about when the moon should disappear, so the crew could determine if they had the correct entry mark.

One of the most unexpected things I learned from reviewing the *Apollo 13* episodes was the importance of forecasting. In my tally, fifteen of the episodes required forecasting. In four of these, the forecasts resulted in a revised problem representation, and in another three episodes the forecasting produced problem detection. Forecasting was needed to calculate when the spacecraft would run out of oxygen and water. The forecasts showed that the mission controllers could not retain the planned course, because the oxygen would not last long enough. They would have to work out a new course. This surfaced a new problem to be solved. Forecasting also came into play at the end of the mission, when the observed trajectory began to deviate from the expected trajectory, which meant that a new problem was detected. The mission controllers had to figure out whether the deviation was going to get worse and, if so, how to handle it. They were not able to diagnose the cause of the deviation until after the mission.

The mission controllers did perform evaluations of the different courses of action that were proposed, to assure themselves that the various workarounds would succeed. Thus, in recommending a new procedure for changing the course of the crippled ship, the suggested action was studied in a simulator to verify that the action would work and that the timing parameters were accurate. The mission controllers were using actual simulations along with mental simulations to test the actions.

I counted only four instances of decision making that involved selecting between alternative courses of action. One was the decision to shut the reactant valves. The second was to use a direct abort (i.e., turn the ship around) or let it continue around the moon. The third was whether to have the crew sleep before attempting the difficult task of powering down the spacecraft (letting the crew sleep would reduce the chances of error, but it also would waste power while they were sleeping). The fourth was selecting the type of burn strategy for returning the spacecraft to earth.

The first decision, to shut the reactant valves, was an attempt to stop the oxygen loss, because no one knew where the leak was. The decision meant that the mission to land on the moon would have to be abandoned, because the reactant valves could not be reopened by the crew. The mission controllers and the crew resisted this course of action; they did not want to terminate the mission. However, the action was clearly necessary, so there was no formal comparison between options.

The second decision was to select a course of action for returning the ship. The choices were to use a direct abort (turn the ship around) or an indirect abort (continue to fly the orbit around the moon but eliminate the landing). Since the explosion had possibly damaged the main engine and had caused the loss of the electricity needed to fire the engine, the direct abort option was judged not to be feasible. What appeared to be a decision turned out to be straightforward.

The third decision was about letting the crew sleep before powering down the spacecraft. The mission director chose to have the crew power the ship down before sleeping. Based on the account by Cooper, this decision was made by imagining the consequences of losing power during the six hours of sleep time, versus the consequences of having a sleepy crew do the complicated task.[13] The mission director did not appear to compare the two options on the same set of criteria but mentally simulated the outcomes for each and chose the outcome that made him less uncomfortable.

The fourth decision was to select the type of burn for returning the spacecraft after it orbited the moon. Option 1 was a super-fast burn that would return the ship to earth thirty-six hours later. One penalty was that the return would be to a part of the Atlantic where the U.S. Navy did not have any ships. A second penalty was that this option required the crew to jettison the service module that would normally protect the heat shield, and the mission controllers worried that the heat shield might have been damaged by the explosion. They also worried that even a normal heat shield might not survive a sudden shift from deep freeze to reentry, since no one had ever conducted that type of test. Option 2 was to use a slower burn that would add a few hours but land the ship in the Pacific. The disadvantage was the same need to jettison the service module. Option 3 was to use a short burn, land in the Pacific, but keep the service module. This option would have the ship land more than twenty-four hours later than the super-fast burn. The crew was short on consumables such as oxygen and water. This decision was hotly debated, and option 3 was selected. According to Lovell and Kluger, the decision was made on the basis of perceived worst case. The difficulties with consumables were large, but the mission controllers believed they were manageable. The risks of jettisoning the service module were unknown and could be catastrophic. Framed in this way, the comparison was between a course of action that was painful but manageable and a course of action with a risk that was plausible and catastrophic.

The problem solving that went on during the *Apollo 13* mission was intended for a number of purposes:

- Generate new actions.
- Provide forecasts.
- Formulate plans.
- Derive diagnoses.
- Make decisions.
- Revise goals.

In reviewing the problem-solving activities that went on during the rescue, we can see that they did not require a standard sequence of steps, and most of the problem solving did not require either diagnoses or the generation of a novel course of action. Forming an accurate problem representation was the most common activity for this incident. Other incidents will show different patterns.

Problem Solving and Decision Making

Many researchers agree that the distinctions between problem solving and decision making blur in natural settings. Some prefer to treat problem solving as a subclass of decision making (called upon when the person needs to formulate a new course of action). Some prefer to see decision making as a subclass of problem solving (called upon when the person has to compare several courses of action). There is more overlap than difference.

Consider the case of an undergraduate finishing her first year of college. Because she misses her friends, she may be tempted to transfer to a school that is closer to home. It appears that she has a decision to make: stay at the original college or transfer. Nevertheless, in many cases the student will not make a choice. Instead, she will shift into a problem-solving mode. She will check on how many credits will be lost in the transfer, gather more information about the quality of the professors in her major field of study, reconsider whether she should join a sorority, imagine how her grades might fall if she were living closer to home, check on the availability of rides to make it easier to return. She may plan to use her earnings for the summer to buy a car so she feels less trapped at her current university. These are as much problem-solving as decision-making activities.

In order to define problems and generate novel courses of action, we need to draw on our experience to make judgments about:

- Reasonable goals and their attributes.
- The appearance of an anomaly.
- The urgency of solving a problem (whether to take anomalies seriously or treat them as transients that will go away).
- What constitutes an opportunity worth pursuing.
- Which analogues best fit the situation, and how to apply them.
- The solvability of a problem.

Each of these judgments is its own source of power. The sources of power in this list overlap considerably with the ones covered in the discussion of decision making. It seems as if there are two primary sources of power for individual decision making and problem solving:

- Pattern matching (the power of intuition).
- Mental simulation.

Pattern matching provides us with a sense of reasonable goals and their attributes. It gives a basis for detecting anomalies and treating them with appropriate seriousness. It helps us to notice opportunities and leverage points, discover relevant analogues, and get a sense of how solvable a problem is. The judgment of solvability is also responsible for letting us recognize when we are unlikely to make more progress and that it is time to stop.

Mental simulation is the engine for diagnosing the causes of the problem, along with their trends. It plays a role in coalescing fragmentary actions to find a way to put them together. And it is the basis for evaluating courses of action. The themes covered thus far in reviewing problem solving and decision making are the core components for my perspective on naturalistic decision making. The development and use of these sources of power are elaborated in the following chapters.

Applications

One application is to be less enthusiastic about rational planning approaches. Certainly there is value in trying to envision goals more clearly in planning and preparation. Nevertheless, we must accept the limitations of our ability to make plans for complex situations. We can prepare to improvise as we redefine the goals midway through a project.

Most so-called rational methods of problem solving are variants of the stage models presented earlier. These approaches are taught in many different settings: business schools, engineering departments, organizational development courses, and in special seminars and workshops. The simplicity of the methods makes them attractive and easy to remember. For example, Kepner and Tregoe (1965, 1981) presented a systematic and general method for problem solving in their book *The Rational Manager.* According to Kepner and Tregoe, you first need to determine what the values of different parameters ought to be. Then you determine what the values are. Then you figure out when the values changed. Then you find out what else changed around that time, and, presto, you have uncovered the cause of the problem. This approach works as long as you are dealing with well-defined goals and fairly static work settings.

Of course, it is a good idea to try to define the goal as clearly as possible before proceeding. Robert Mager (1972) has described several useful methods for clarifying goals. I agree with him that goal clarification is important, especially at the beginning of a task. My skepticism about rational problem-solving methods is that they do not prepare you to improvise, act without all of the relevant information, or cope with unreliable data or shifting conditions. They do not prepare you to learn about the goals throughout the problem-solving process.

A second application is to be less enthusiastic about creativity programs. A range of different creativity methods has been proposed: brainstorming, synectics, and permutations of elements. The permutation of elements, for example, involves specifying all the different possibilities for each variable and then combining them to create an assortment of alternatives. Let us return to the illustration of making new types of ice cream sundaes. You can have the flavors themselves (coffee, pistachio, licorice, peach, etc.), the added ingredients (cookie crumbs, berries, walnuts, etc.), the toppings (whipped cream, bananas, fudge, tiny meatballs), and so forth. By combining these, you have a large number of possibilities. Most of these possibilities are new (pineapple ice cream with coconut chunks, topped with bacon flakes), and many are truly awful (pistachio ice cream, mini meatballs, and caramel topping). These procedures seem like desperate attempts to use systematic procedures as a substitute for imagination. In most domains, we need not off-the-wall creative options but a clear understanding of the goals. The creativity methods may sometimes look promising for identifying new possibilities, but the cost is having to plow through all the poor ideas. Even brainstorming, a method that has been around for decades, seems primarily a social activity. If the participants generate their ideas individually, the resulting set of suggestions is usually longer and more varied than when everyone works together. Mullen, Johnson, and Salas (1991) have documented the finding that brainstorming reduces productivity.

Another application of the concepts of leverage points and nonlinear problem solving is to gain a better understanding of planning. Tom Miller and I (1997) have studied planning teams in several different settings and have formulated a number of conclusions about planning, teamwork, and problem solving. (This effort was sponsored by the Office of Naval Research, in conjunction with the Naval Research Laboratory.) Our primary data source was a series of three field observations of planning exercises for combined (army, navy, air force and marines) and integrated planning for the use of aircraft. The first exercise, Roving Sands, was conducted in New Mexico and Texas, and our observer was Tom Miller. The second exercise was conducted in the Pacific, and our observers, Tom Miller and Laura Militello, were stationed on the USS *Kittyhawk*. The third exercise was conducted in the Atlantic, with Tom Miller stationed on the USS *Mt. Whitney*. We collected observations about strains in the planning process, about procedures that were formalized, procedures that were informal, and procedures that were ignored. We collected data about planning strategies that had to be abandoned and strategies that were improvised out of necessity. We also reviewed data from studies we had previously performed in other domains (Patriot missile batteries, U.S. Marine Corps regimental command posts, medical evacuation planning teams). These studies covered seven different observations and more than one hundred interviews.

We learned that planning is not a simple, unified activity. We need to distinguish the functions of the plans and the types of environments in which the planning and execution will take place.

Plans can differ with regard to the functions they serve. These functions include:

- Directing and coordinating the actions of team members.
- Developing shared situation awareness.
- Generating expectancies.
- Supporting improvisation.
- Detecting inconsistencies.
- Establishing time horizons.
- Shaping the thinking of the planners.

This last function, to promote individual and team learning, can overshadow the others. Sometimes planners engage in lengthy, detailed preparations that quickly become obsolete, yet they continue with the same process, again and again; it appears that the function is to help them all learn more about the situation and to calibrate their understanding, rather than to produce plans that will be carried out more successfully.

In our sample of planning environments, we found that plans differed along some key dimensions: how precise the plan was made, whether the plan was modular (elements that were relatively independent) or integrated (coordinating all the elements), and the level of complexity. Sometimes precision can be useful; at other times it reaches unnecessary levels. There are times for using modular elements (that are loosely coupled with each other) and times to build integrated strategies that are more efficient but less robust. Complexity can be a sign of sophistication—or a sign that the plan is likely to break down.

We also learned that forcing functions in the environment played a major role in determining the type of plan adopted. A stable environment permitted more precise and complex plans. A rapidly changing environment favored modular plans because these permitted rapid improvisation. A resource-limited environment favored integrated plans that were more efficient. Time pressure and uncertainty made it more difficult to construct integrated plans.

Our work on nonlinear problem solving helped us to notice events that were not occurring. In one high-level command and control setting, we realized that goals were not being widely disseminated, leverage points were not being identified, and evaluations were not being conducted. We were able to study how the forcing functions were contributing to the omissions of these processes. Goals were not being disseminated because the planning team was distributed, consisting of experienced members who shaped the priorities, and less experienced members who compiled the detailed orders. The experienced planning cell did not want to communicate the rationale for priorities because they did not want the compilers to interpret the goals. As a result, leverage points were not being identified. This might have reduced efficiency, but the planners were not concerned with efficiency. Evaluations were not being conducted because the compiled plans were so modular that the planners had difficulty differentiating good from poor plans. This system resulted in modular rather than integrated plans. One advantage of this system was that if a plan needed to be changed at the last minute, it was fairly easy to make the shift without disrupting the rest of the units. We have seen in domains where the plans were highly integrated that changes in just one portion resulted in a ripple effect, and therefore discouraged improvisation.

By viewing planning as a type of problem solving and taking into account nonlinear aspects of problem solving, it should be possible to gain a richer appreciation of the planning process. Cognitive scientists have not given as much attention to planning as to problem solving, and there seems to be a good opportunity for research here. In particular, the functioning of distributed planning cells would appear to be worth examining in more depth.

Another topic to consider is strategic planning. Mintzberg (1994) has written a comprehensive account of the failures of strategic planning and of its inherent limitations. These limitations are consistent with the naturalistic decision-making perspective to support expertise and to be wary of how decomposing tasks and performing context-free analyses can degrade intuition.

Key Points

- Most problems are ill defined. Most studies of problem solving use well-defined goals.

- To solve an ill-defined problem, we have to clarify the goal even as we are trying to achieve it, rather than keeping the goal constant.

- Experience is needed to make a variety of judgments, ranging from identifying opportunities to gauging the solvability of a problem.

- Artificial tasks do not require domain experience to arrive at solutions, and classical accounts usually ignore opportunities.

- Experienced problem solvers can distinguish genuine anomalies from transients. Artificial tasks give the problem to subjects, thereby ignoring the process of problem finding.

- Structuring a problem is using a barrier or leverage point to construct a course of action, not organizing a problem into a space that can be searched efficiently.

- Standard advice on problem solving is aimed at well-defined goals and can interfere with solving ill-defined problems.

- Problem solving is a constructive process. Computational approaches to problem solving rely on procedures, such as searching through problem spaces, that have little psychological reality.

10

The Power to See the Invisible

This chapter is about expertise.[1] One view of experts is that they have accumulated lots of knowledge. While this is undoubtedly true, it conveys an image of people whose brains are filled with facts, heavy with memories, weighed down with wisdom. In many fields, the time needed to develop expertise is up to ten years. Thus, we see a relationship between expertise and age. This reinforces the image of experts as slow-moving creatures who may talk and think slowly because they must search through so much information.

This chapter presents a different image of experts, based on the highly skilled people we have observed, interviewed, and studied in different domains. The accumulation of experience does not weigh people down; it lightens them up.

Experts see the world differently. They see things the rest of us cannot. Often experts do not realize that the rest of us are unable to detect what seems obvious to them.

An analogy may help to illustrate this point. Many years ago I had the following experience. After a long day of work, I got ready for bed. While I was waiting for my wife to finish work on an article she was writing, I dozed off. I must have been lying there on my side for about twenty or twenty-five minutes, with one eye pressed down into the pillow and the other exposed to the overhead light. My wife came in and turned off the light, so that the room was dark. This woke me, and when I sat up, I had the distinct feeling that one of my eyeballs had fallen out of my face. (Try the demonstration. Cover up one eye, with a heavy patch, a scarf, or the palm of a hand [covering it only with your fingers lets in too much light] for about twenty minutes. Then go into a windowless room, turn off the light, close the door, and then uncover your eye. Experience the difference. It will help you feel the contrasts described in this chapter.) What happened to me was that while I was lying on the bed, the eye that was pressed into the pillow was shielded from the light. Rhodopsin, the chemical responsible for night vision, was regenerating in that eye. By the time my wife came in, the chemical was up to its maximum, and that eye could detect objects under even very low illumination. The other eye had been exposed to the light, and the rhodopsin in it was continuing to be depleted. The sensitivity of the chemical makes it effective in the dark, just as it makes it vulnerable to being bleached out by light. When my wife turned out the light and I sat up, I had one eye that could see fairly well (the one pressed into the pillow) and one that was useless. The contrast was so strong that I had the sensation that there was a decent amount of light in the room, but that one of my eyes had ceased to work. I rubbed the eye to see if that would help, but it did not. I felt around on the blankets to see if it had rolled out somewhere. Not finding it, I jumped out of bed and stumbled into the bathroom. I turned on the light and looked in the mirror. Happily, my eye was still sitting there next to my nose, where it had always been. I could now see with that eye. Very bizarre, I thought. With trepidation I turned out the light and found that now I could not see well out of either eye. Then I figured out what had happened.

I have gone into this incident at length to reinforce that image of the contrast between being able to see versus being totally in the dark. Because of their experience, experts have learned to see all kinds of things that are invisible to others. That is why they can move freely in their domains while novices must pick their way carefully through the same terrain.

The incident also shows that the light-exposed eye does not know what it is missing. It cannot sense what it is like to see inside those dark shadows.

There are many things experts can see that are invisible to everyone else:

- Patterns that novices do not notice.
- Anomalies—events that did not happen and other violations of expectancies.
- The big picture (situation awareness).
- The way things work.
- Opportunities and improvisations.

- Events that either already happened (the past) or are going to happen (the future).
- Differences that are too small for novices to detect.
- Their own limitations.

These aspects of expertise can be tied to the two primary sources of power we have been examining: pattern matching and mental simulation. Pattern matching (intuition) refers to the ability of the expert to detect typicality and to notice events that did not happen and other anomalies that violate the pattern. Mental simulation covers the ability to see events that happened previously and events that are likely to happen in the future.

We also encounter some additional sources of power. The ability to make fine discriminations must involve some sort of perceptual learning; not a great deal is known about this type of learning, and it does seem to be different from pattern matching. In addition, the ability to see one's own limitations and to manage around these seems distinct from the other functions under discussion.

The following sections describe these eight aspects of expertise.[2]

Patterns

The secretary problem illustrates what it means to recognize typicality. Consider a case where the new managers of an organization need to hire their first secretary. They may go through a lengthy process to define the job requirements and criteria and then interview many secretaries. They are novice secretary selectors. In contrast, office managers who have been in charge of large secretary pools for a long time would not have to interview many people. They are experienced secretary selectors. They might interview the first candidate on a list and recognize that he or she is much better than average. They do not need to look any further. The novices who need to interview many applicants are developing a sense of how secretaries differ, how much variability there is between them, and what a strong candidate, one who is better than average, looks like. The experienced office managers would have a good sense of typicality and could recognize a superior candidate without having to go through the learning process.

Novices have difficulty seeing relationships that are obvious to experts. We found that fireground commanders could look at a burning building and know what was happening inside. They could envision stairways, elevator shafts, and roof supports and how each was being affected by the fire. Chapter 4, on the power of intuition, discussed how our ability to see patterns gives us situation awareness, which helps us recognize appropriate goals and relevant cues. People who are not experts will have trouble detecting typical patterns.

Example 10.1
The Instructors Who Couldn't Save Their Own Lives

In 1981 my wife, Helen, and I conducted a study of cardiopulmonary resuscitation (CPR) (Klein & Klein, 1981). We prepared six videotapes of people performing CPR on a red-haired lifesaving dummy called Resusci-Annie. Five of the videotapes showed relative novices—people who had completed an eight-hour course on CPR. The sixth videotape showed a paramedic.

We played these videotapes to three audiences: ten novices who had just finished an eight-hour CPR course, ten CPR instructors who were experienced teachers but had never performed CPR on an actual victim and ten paramedics who had used CPR many times. The study called for the participants to make a series of judgments. The last one was perhaps the most interesting. We asked each participant to imagine that it was his or her own life on the line. They had to identify one of six people in the videotapes who they would want to do CPR on them.

The paramedics recognized expertise when they saw it. Nine of the ten picked the actual paramedic. When asked why, they could not point to any one thing. It was the entire pattern of his behavior, the smoothness with which he worked, that they liked. He seemed to know what he was doing.

The novices too generally chose the paramedic. He got five of their ten votes. The instructors did not do as well. The paramedic in the tape was not following the rules they taught so carefully to their students. He wasn't carefully measuring where to put his hands for example. Only three of the instructors chose him to save their lives.

Anomalies

Novices are confused by much that happens to them because they have so much trouble forming expectancies. They keep encountering events they did not anticipate. As they begin to form expectancies, they also begin to get surprised each time an expectancy is violated. One critical type of cue that surprises experts, but not novices, is the *absence* of a key event. Since novices do not know what is supposed to happen, they are slow to appreciate the significance of something's not happening. Experts pick this up right away.

Here is an example of the importance of experience in noticing a missing event. Several years ago, a new researcher joined my staff. After a few months, she commented on how we always worked on the edge, barely making deadlines. That was not my perception at all. I thought we had made great progress in becoming more orderly and less crisis driven. In talking with her, I realized that while she had been with us, there had been a report and a proposal that went out pretty close to the wire. We had also submitted ten other proposals that had gone out smoothly. I knew that because the previous year a set of ten proposals had almost overwhelmed our office staff, so I noticed how calmly the work had gone recently. The new senior researcher did not have that background. She did not notice the absence of frenzy when the ten proposals went out. That type of cue, a missing event, is invisible to novices.

These missing events can be described as negative cues.[3] Experience is important for allowing decision makers to form and use expectancies. Only through expectancies can someone notice that something did not happen. One of Arthur Conan Doyle's stories shows how Sherlock Holmes solved a case using his ability to notice what did not happen. In "Silver Blaze," the vital due was a dog that did not bark at night. The dog usually barked when strangers came by. The fact that the murderer passed the dog in silence meant that the dog recognized him (Doyle, 1905).

In the recognition-primed decision model, proficient decision makers are described as being able to detect patterns and typicality. They can size up a situation in a glance and realize that they have seen it, or variants of it, dozens or hundreds of times before. Their experience buys them the ability to recognize that a situation is a typical case. The opposite side of this coin is noticing when a pattern is broken or an expectancy is violated. In the RPD model, this triggers diagnostic efforts, including efforts to take advantage of an unexpected opportunity.

The Big Picture: Situation Awareness

Experts appear to have an overall sense of what is happening in a situation—an ability to judge prototypicality. Whereas novices may be confused by all the data elements, experts see the big picture, and they appear to be less likely to fall victim to information overload.

The phenomenon of situation awareness is receiving increasing attention. Endsley and Garland (2000) present a variety of perspectives on ways to measure situation awareness.[4]

The RPD model offers an account of situation awareness. It presents several aspects of situation awareness that emerge once a person recognizes a situation. These are the relevant cues that need to be monitored, the plausible goals to pursue and actions to consider, and the expectancies. The discussion of problem solving in chapter 8 suggests another aspect of situation awareness: the leverage points. When an expert describes a situation to someone else, he or she may highlight these leverage points as the central aspect of the dynamics of the situation.

The Way Things Work

Experts see inside events and objects. They have mental models of how tasks are supposed to be performed, teams are supposed to coordinate, equipment is supposed to function. This model lets them know what to expect and lets them notice when the expectancies are violated. These two aspects of expertise are based, in part, on the experts' mental models.[5]

Since the experts have a mental model of the task, they know how the subtasks fit together and can adapt the way they perform individual subtasks to blend in with the others. This makes their performance so smooth. They do not even feel that they are performing subtasks because the integration is so strong. If they have to explain what they are doing to novices, they may have to stop and artificially break it down into subtasks. Often they feel uncomfortable teaching the separate steps because they know they are teaching some bad habits. They are teaching the novices to do the task in a choppy way. In the short run, though, this task decomposition makes it easier for the novices since they do not have to worry about the big picture. They just have to remember the steps. As part of their mental model of the task, experts know various tricks of the trade, along with the conditions for using them.

The mental model of the team coordination lets the expert anticipate what the other team members will need and will be doing. Think about a rookie soccer player, perhaps a striker. She may have the speed and coordination to score goals, but she often will be in the wrong place, trailing a play rather than leading it. As she gains a sense of how the game flows and how her teammates react to different situations, she can put herself in more favorable positions to score goals.

Experts also have mental models of equipment. They are not just pressing buttons and receiving messages. They know enough about how their equipment works to interpret what the system is telling them. They know when their equipment may mislead them. One navy electronic warfare technician referred to his console as "a liar." He knew that it might report airplanes that were not there, under certain conditions, and he had worked out strategies for double checking. He knew why these spurious signals might arise (because of the hardware and the algorithms), and he did not hold it against the equipment. In contrast, a novice would be likely to believe everything the console reported, and be fooled, and then regard the equipment with distrust for being unreliable. The experts understood that the equipment is reliable and also limited in predictable ways.

An industrial designer once described to me how he viewed ordinary equipment such as car doors and radios. Earlier in his career, he would feel irritation when he encountered something that was poorly designed. Eventually he learned enough about how things were manufactured to appreciate the reasons for the poor designs. He did not excuse the designs but had reached a point where he could look at most common appliances and devices, recognize the mechanisms inside them, and imagine how the design engineers had chosen to have the equipment constructed.

Opportunities and Improvisations

Chapter 8 discussed the importance of spotting leverage points—seeing opportunities and being able to make adjustments to take advantage of them. These leverage points maybe visible to experts but invisible to novices.

One aspect of being able to improvise that was not discussed in chapter 8 is the ability of experts to generate counterfactuals: explanations and predictions that are inconsistent with the data. Perhaps they have this ability because they have learned not to place too heavy a reliance on data. Novices, in contrast, have difficulty imagining a world different from the one they are seeing.

We recently studied weather forecasters, to try to learn how they predict changes in ceiling that allow aircraft to take off and land at airports. (Ceiling refers to the lowest layer of clouds on an overcast day.) One observation was made on a day when the ceiling was too low for aircraft operations. One forecaster, who was not identified as having much expertise, was asked when he thought the ceiling would lift. He said his prediction was for the ceiling to lift above 1,000 feet by 2:00 P.M. that afternoon. (It was then about 10:00 A.M.) Probing for counterfactual thinking, we asked what sequence of events might occur that would result in the ceiling lifting earlier than that, by noon. He was unable to imagine such a possibility. He had followed a set of rules to generate his prediction and could not conceive of a different world. To us, this signaled the fact that he was not an expert. We received some confirmation when we returned after lunch, at 1:00 P.M., and learned that the ceiling had already lifted above 1,000 feet.

In the RPD model, one pathway in the decision cycle is to seek additional information. This may seem like a routine activity, but it also requires expertise. (A mindless information-gathering strategy is not likely to be useful.) Experienced decision makers appear to be able to spot opportunities where the information that can be helpful can be readily obtained. For example, a weather forecaster trying to predict when a ceiling will lift may notice that the ground temperature is not rising as rapidly as usual during the morning. The critical cue here is the trend in temperature increase, and the interpretation of this trend in relationship to the typical pattern of increase. Moreover, this trend can be easily tracked using one of the available displays. Skilled decision makers may be able to seek information more effectively than novices. This skill in information seeking would result in a more efficient search for data that clarify the status of the situation.

The Past and the Future

The past and the future are part of experts' experiences. They grow out of the ability to run mental simulations. A skilled kindergarten teacher can look at a worried five-year-old in September and anticipate how the child is going to look in June. A parent bringing a child in for the first day of school may be devastated by the way the child clings. Thoughts of disaster fill the parent's head. Is the whole year going to be like this? Will my child develop school phobia? Will my child's educational career be blighted from the very start? This type of thinking is typical of new parents and is immature in its unreasoning dread that this moment of difficulty will persist forever. In some ways, the parent's immaturity mirrors that of the child, certain that this initial feeling of panic and abandonment will be his or her own eternal fate. Only the teacher knows that by the end of the week, the same child will be bouncing out of the car and refusing to let the parent come into the classroom. The teacher has seen this hundreds of times before and can mentally simulate the way the year will progress.

In aviation, there is a term to describe people who are so wrapped up in what they are doing that they are insensitive to what lies ahead: *flying behind the plane*. It describes people who are either so novice or so overworked or have such poor situation awareness that they are not generating expectancies; they are not preparing themselves properly. Jacobs and Jaques (1991) use the term *time horizon*. Different tasks require different time horizons, referring to the amount of look-ahead needed. In driving a car at 60 mph, you would be foolish to open the door and look down at the lines to make sure you are in your lane, since at that speed your ability to make adjustments is compromised by your reaction time. You would need to look ahead by many yards in order to steer a smooth course. In driving at night, you can vary your time horizon simply by adjusting your headlights. If you turn them off, you dare not go very fast. If you put on the parking lights, you can speed up a little. If you turn on your headlights, you can travel at the speed limit. You may have difficulty if the road is poorly marked and winding. If you put on your brights, you can maintain speed on difficult roads because you have bought yourself more reaction time.

Jacobs and Jaques have suggested that as people move up the organizational ladder in industry, they need to look further ahead. Managers may be anticipating events weeks ahead. Senior managers may be preparing for events a year or two away. The president of a large company should be seeing into the future five or ten years or more. In part, this is because of the difficulty of responding at different levels in the organization. A president of a company who wants to make some change should be looking years out into the future. If he or she tried to get a change made at lower levels within a few hours, mayhem might result. In contrast, the line manager can make changes within minutes. The appropriate time horizon depends on the reaction time of the system at different levels.[6]

Experts also experience the past. As we saw, a skilled designer can look at a part and perceive how it must have been manufactured and how the decisions were made to form it one way rather than another. Skilled chess players claim that they can tell which opening in a game had been used. They even assert that they can recreate the game up to that point. People who troubleshoot system malfunctions try to imagine how the fault might create the mix of observed symptoms.

Experts perceive a situation as the patterns and relationships that grew out of the past and will grow into the future, not just the cues that exist at the moment. All these are perceived at the same time; all are part of their situation awareness.

The ability to see the past and the future rests on an understanding of the primary causes in a domain and the ability to apply these causes to run mental simulations. This is one way to distinguish true experts from people who pretend to be experts. The pretenders have mastered many procedures and tricks of the trade; their actions are smooth. They show many of the characteristics of expertise. However, if they are pushed outside the standard patterns, they cannot improvise. They lack a sense of the dynamics of the situation. They have trouble explaining how the current state of affairs came about and how it will play out. They also have trouble mentally simulating how a different future state from the one they predicted might evolve.

Another aspect of mental simulation is to be able to decenter, to see the world through the eyes of others. This has been especially apparent in our study of tank platoon leaders, who needed to anticipate their adversaries. Both trainee tank platoon leaders and the instructors noticed the same cues. However, the instructors were also considering cues that were not present. For example, they imagined how the adversary was approaching from the other side of the hill, what the adversary was seeing, and where the adversary was going to look for signs of an opposing force. The new trainees, when asked to form a defensive position, spread out the prescribed number of meters and took cover at the places that felt right to them. The instructors immediately noticed all kinds of flaws in their defenses. The trainees had never been in the position of storming a position such as the one they were trying to create. They did not have any way of viewing it from other eyes—this despite the fact that the trainees were all officers and college graduates, and some were from West Point. The instructors were enlisted men, none with college degrees. This was not a matter of intelligence. It was a matter of experience.[7]

Fine Discriminations

Experts can detect differences that novices cannot see, cannot even force themselves to see. Wine tasters can tell one type of grape from another and even one year of wine from another. To novices, wines are generic: they all taste the same. If you are just starting to drink wine, no matter how much attention you pay, how much you swirl the fluid around in your mouth, you don't get it. That's because "it" is not a fact (the Civil War began in 1861) or an insight (dividing one number into another is like subtracting it several times). You cannot learn just by being told or learn it all of a sudden. It takes lots of experience, and lots of variety in that experience, to notice differences.

Alan Lesgold at the University of Pittsburgh studied the way radiologists interpret X-rays and found a clear difference in what an experienced radiologist notices versus what a new student finds (Lesgold et al., 1988). Some physicians have tried to explore the limits of a radiologist's ability to make discriminations. Several years ago, the organizers of a radiology conference held a contest to see who could do the best job at interpreting difficult X-rays. For fun, they slipped in a slide that had a double exposure of two different lungs superimposed on each other. The champions were not deterred. They were able to detect that the slide had been doctored and even hypothesized that it was a double exposure.

Managing Our Own Limitations

There is another direction that experts can see, and that is inward. They can see inside their own thought processes—the process of metacognition, which means thinking about thinking. An experienced student taking a time-pressured exam might come across a complex mathematics problem and judge that it will take a long time to figure out. Perhaps it is an area the student had not given much preparation, or maybe the student knows he or she is likely to get confused in the equations, or some other reason. If the student decides to skim the question in order to work on it subconsciously but to move on to other problems to finish more of the test before coming back, that is an example of metacognition.

Four components of metacognition seem most important: memory limitations, having the big picture, self-critiques, and strategy selection.[8]

Experts are often sensitive to their own memory limitations, including their working memory for holding something like a telephone number and their long-term memory for anticipating that they will not be able to recall where they hid that birthday present several months into the future. As a result, they can adopt subtle procedures to avoid the difficulty. They can also factor in their level of alertness, their ability to sustain concentration, and so forth.

Experts are not only better at forming situation awareness and seeing the big picture, but they can detect when they are starting to lose the big picture. Rather than waiting until they have become hopelessly confused, experts sense any slippage early and make the necessary adaptations.

Experts can critique themselves. Since their performance is less variable than that of novices, they can more easily notice when they do a poor job, and they can usually figure out why, in order to make corrections. Experts also seem more likely to critique their judgments and their plans, since they can use their experience to see where the judgments might be wrong and their plans weak.

Using these abilities, experts can think about their own thinking to change their strategies. Regardless of whether they want to avoid memory limitations, loss of the big picture, continued performance difficulties, or poor judgments and plans, experts try to find more robust strategies. These can be decision strategies, strategies for where they should focus their attention, or strategies for reducing workload. They can include strategies for practicing to overcome some of the limitations.

For some obvious reasons, novices have difficulty in situations requiring metacognition. Everyone needs some experience with a task before they can anticipate where they will run into trouble. They need to have some experience with different strategies for handling a task in order to learn about their own abilities, both strengths and weaknesses, so they can take these into account.

There are many other characteristics of expertise, besides the ones already noted, that present the features of expertise most linked to naturalistic decision making. Included here are factors such as how experts can more smoothly carry out a sequence of actions and how experts integrate their reactions. As novices learn tasks well enough and those tasks become more automated, they gain the freedom to look ahead. You see this in new drivers. At first they worry about whether they will reliably hit the gas and brake pedals. They do not dare to go very fast. They are also not paying much attention to the road. As they become comfortable with their ability to manage all the tasks of driving, such as hitting the right pedals quickly and turning the steering wheel accurately, they can start to look farther ahead and then speed up. Another performance change is that individual acts and judgments become integrated into overall strategies. Instead of doing two or three separate movements, they all become part of the same movement. A good example is the behavior of a sixteen-month-old trying to throw a ball. Standing up is still not natural to the child, and throwing a ball while sitting is difficult. Doing the two at the same time is virtually impossible for many children of this age. A few years later, the two actions have been integrated into one.

The concepts of expertise can be linked to each other using an example of cooking a meal.

Example 10.2
Recipe for Disaster

I am going to have to cook a special dish for some guests, and I don't know what to make. A friend offers me a recipe for an outstanding dish. It is important to impress my guests, but it is also important not to fail as a cook. Should I make the dish? The answer depends on my expertise. I have little experience in cooking. I'm not even such a hot shopper. My family still recalls the time I was sent to the supermarket to buy a head of lettuce and returned with a cabbage.

Example 10.2 (continued)

For someone like me, it would be a mistake to use the recipe. A recipe, we all know, is a set of procedures. It includes a list of ingredients and a list of operations to perform on these ingredients. None of this is as simple as it seems.

Let's say I have decided to use the recipe. I start cooking away a few hours before the guests arrive. The recipe calls for a red pepper, and I don't have one. Can I use a green pepper as a substitute? The recipe calls for raisins. I don't have raisins. Can I use grapes and add sugar? The recipe calls for two potatoes. I dig out two and notice they look small. Should I add another one or two? In short, how do I improvise? How do I know the size of a typical potato? I am in trouble even before I have started cooking.

I realize I need to prepare side dishes, so I look in the refrigerator to see what there is. I must ignore the issue of how the dishes will taste together since I do not have the experience to imagine how my new recipe will taste. I can stare at its ingredients and directions and not be able to anticipate its final flavor. I look at an ingredient like "flour" and wonder what taste the flour is going to add. An experienced cook would know that the flour is in there to thicken the dish, and by adding too much flour I have just made sure it was going to congeal. The experienced cook could imagine how the originators tried it without flour, and decided to thicken it. I just see the word *flour*.

Now I am cooking the dish, grating the potatoes. But the work is taking too long, and the potatoes are turning an unappetizing brown. I was supposed to add these potatoes fifteen minutes ago, but it is hard to grate such small potatoes, and my fingers are getting tired. I lack the metacognitive skills to take into account the time it takes me to perform the operations. Should I turn the heat down under the pan while I am finishing the potatoes, or will that spoil some chemical process?

Speaking of finishing, what is the dish supposed to look like when it is finished? I've never made it before so I can't tell. The recipe says to bake it at 350 degrees for one hour, or until brown on top. I don't know what to make of "brown on top," so I better stick to the one hour. Is my oven calibrated accurately? It already looks done on top, but will it still be mushy inside? Even worse, my guests won't arrive for another twenty minutes. If I turn the oven off now, will it get too cold? Should I leave the heat on low, or will that dry the dish out?

An experienced cook would notice that the dish wasn't bubbling around the edges, so it wasn't done. The reason it was getting dark so quickly was that I had left the rack too dose to the heating coil. I don't see the missing event—the failure to achieve bubbling.

The point of this exercise is to show how much perceptual experience is needed to carry out tasks that may seem simple because they can be reduced to rules and procedures. We are often fooled into thinking that the procedures are going to be carried out easily. In fact, procedures often take much experience to interpret. Rules tell you that when a certain condition occurs, initiate a certain action. The trick is knowing when the first condition has occurred. The recipe can state, "When it is brown on top, take it out of the oven," but brown on top is not so obvious. Brown on top stretches from "just starting to change color" all the way to "beginning to smoke."

Expertise and Decision Making

How good are skilled decision makers under conditions such as time pressure? This section describes two experiments that we did to show the effect of expertise. Both used chess as the domain to study because expertise is nicely scaled by the United States Chess Federation. Based on their performance in tournaments, chess players are given point ratings that are calibrated so that a player whose strength is 200 points higher than another should beat that other player 75 percent of the time.

Chess players are rated as international grand masters (above 2,500 points), masters (2,200–2,500), experts (2,000–2,200), class A players (1,800–2,000), class B (1,600–1,800), class C (1,400–1,600), and class D players (below 1,400). The best players, like Bobby Fischer, Gary Kasparov, and Judit Polgar, are all grand masters. Most medium-size American cities are lucky to have a player at the level of master.

Roberta Calderwood, Beth Crandall, and I (Calderwood, Klein, & Crandall, 1988) examined how good chess players are under extreme time pressure. (This study was sponsored by the Air Force Office of Scientific Research and the Army Research Institute.) After all, many natural settings place severe time restrictions on decision makers. We developed the RPD model to explain how skilled decision makers cope with time pressure. Still, our field studies never showed whether the fireground commanders were making good decisions. Perhaps skilled decision makers fall apart under time pressure.

In the sequence of our studies, the chess experiment was one of our earlier projects. To find out what time pressure did to skilled players, we studied the quality of the moves that chess players made under regulation time and under blitz conditions. Regulation conditions require forty moves in a ninety-minute period, or about two minutes, fifteen seconds per move. Under blitz conditions, each player sets his or her chess clock for five minutes, and then the action starts. Your clock runs from the time your opponent moves and hits his or her timer button until you complete your move and hit your own button. If your flag drops or if you are checkmated, you lose. We estimated that in the blitz games, the players had an average of six seconds per move. Even if they did some thinking while it was their opponent's turn, they still did not have much time.

To gather our data, we arranged for three masters and three class B players to play games (one tournament for the masters and another for the class B players so strengths would be equal.) Each tournament was really two tournaments—one for regulation time and one for blitz time. Each pair of players engaged in four games, taking the white pieces (which go first) in one game and the black pieces in the other, for both regulation and blitz. We offered cash prizes for the winners of the tournaments, along with payments for serving in the experiment. In addition, the results counted toward the players' ratings, and that was probably more incentive for them to do well than the money.

We chose masters and class B players to ensure a fairly large difference in strengths. The grand masters who were consulting with us prefer not to rate the moves of weak players. Someone can make a brilliant move, and the grand master is not sure if the player sees the implications.

We did not bother to rate the moves at the beginning of the games, since openings are fairly ritualized and would not reveal much about improvisational decision making. We concentrated on the tough moves— the points where there were real choices (as identified by the grand masters), rather than the obvious moves where there is a forced sequence that anyone could see.

The experts rated each of these decision points on a five-point scale, where 5 is outstanding, and 1 is a blunder. Figure 10.1 shows the results. The most important finding in the figure is how high the quality of moves was, even under blitz conditions. The time pressure did not slow the

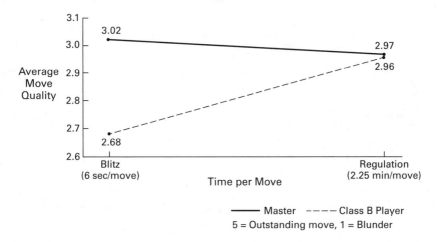

Figure 10.1

Average move quality of masters and class B players, regulation and blitz rules

masters down. Six seconds a move, one after another, facing a strong opponent, and the move quality hardly changed at all. When we talk about the importance of experience for naturalistic decision making, this is what we mean. There is no time to generate lots of options and compare them. There is barely enough time to pick up the piece, move it, release it, and hit the clock.

That the two groups did about the same under regulation time suggests that either our sample was too small or our rating scale was not sufficiently sensitive. But under the blitz conditions, the masters held their own, whereas the class B players dropped sharply. This shift was statistically significant.

Next we looked at the proportion of moves rated as blunders—a rating of 1 or 2 (see figure 10.2). Only a few moves fell into this category, but we did find a difference between masters and class B players. Remarkably, the masters kept the ratio of blunders constant around 7 to 8 percent, even under the blitz conditions. The class B players became ragged. For the regulation games, their rate of blunders was 11 percent. Under time pressure, this rate increased to 25 percent, a statistically significant finding (and a satisfying one to us). The class B players could not match the masters' steady play under time pressure. Still, the class

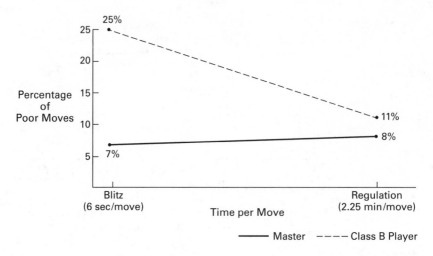

Figure 10.2

Poor moves for masters and class B players, regulation and blitz rules

B players made 75 percent of their time-pressured decisions without blundering.

This first experiment was successful in showing that skilled decision makers can perform at very high levels despite time pressure. The second chess experiment (Klein, Wolf, Militello, & Zsambok, 1995) examined a more detailed question, designed to test the RPD model itself.[9] The model claims that skilled decision makers can generate feasible courses of action as the first ones they consider, so there is no need to generate lots of options. Can skilled decision makers do this? If not, then the rationale for the RPD model disappears.

The design of the experiment was simple. We presented some mid-game positions to players and asked them to think aloud while they studied each one, up to the point where they had selected a move. We asked them to tell us everything they were thinking about, every move they considered, even the poor ones, and especially the first move they considered.[10]

Using the services of a chess master in southern Ohio, we had selected four board positions, from mid-game or early end-game positions. We used sixteen chess players: eight strong ones (rating of 1,700–2,150) and eight weaker ones (ratings of 1,150–1,600). Each player worked alone. After each one had finished all four boards, we asked him to give his rating for each of the legal moves available in each position. We wanted to understand which moves the players themselves thought were good ones and poor ones. The results are shown in figure 10.3. According to the players' ratings, there were a great many poor moves that were legally permissible, and only a small number of good ones. If the players were drawing randomly from the set of legal moves, their ratings for the first moves they thought of should show the same shape. The curve for the actual first moves considered is just the reverse: the players awarded high marks to the first moves they considered. They were playable and in many cases received the highest ratings. The results are statistically significant. When we examined the strong and the weaker players separately, even the weaker players gave high ratings to their first moves.

The data in figure 10.3 are based on subjective ratings. Maybe the players were thinking they generated good moves but really generated poor moves. We needed an objective measure of the move quality. We had selected the board positions from games that had been objectively rated by a panel of grand masters, who awarded points to the different moves.

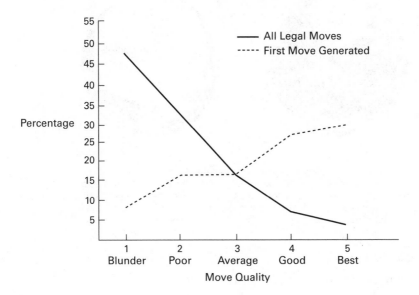

Figure 10.3

Quality ratings of first moves and all legal moves

The best move got ten points, a move that was not as good might get eight points, or five points, perhaps a few were worth two or three points, and the rest of the moves were not awarded any points at all. We had planned the experiment this way because we wanted an independent measure of move quality. To analyze the results, we were not interested in how many points a move received. A move that received any points at all was a plausible one. Any move that got no points was not worth considering. All we had to do was tally how often a first move got any points. These results are shown in figure 10.4. For all 124 legal moves, only 20 had been given points by the panel of grand masters. (There were 124 legal first moves in the four board positions we used—around 31 per board.) If the players in the experiment had been sampling randomly from the possible legal moves, they would have shown the same ratio; about one sixth of their first moves would have received points. The actual ratio was four out of six. Most of the moves they considered had received points from the

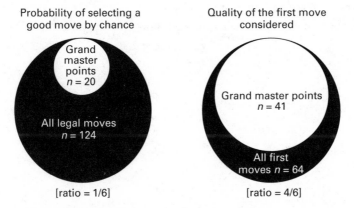

Probability of selecting a
good move by chance

Grand
master
points
$n = 20$

All legal moves
$n = 124$

[ratio = 1/6]

Quality of the first move
considered

Grand master points
$n = 41$

All first
moves $n = 64$

[ratio = 4/6]

Note: A move was rated acceptable if it received points from a panel of grand masters and unacceptable if it did not. The 16 subjects each used four boards, for a total of 64 first moves. There were approximately 31 legal first moves in each of the four board positions, for a total of 124 legal moves.

Figure 10.4

Objective evaluation of the first chess move generated

grand masters, and again the results were statistically significant. And again, the weaker players still showed the effect, almost as strongly as the better players. Even weaker players generated reasonable options as the first ones they thought of.

The data confirmed the prediction made by the RPD model: skilled decision makers generate feasible options as the first ones they think of. Therefore, there is little to be gained by generating and then evaluating lots of options. In chess, it is important to find the best move, not just a good one, so players do continue to search for the best options. Yet we also found that for the most part, they settled on the first option they had thought of, even after considering some others.[11]

There are two major objections to this experiment. The first is that our findings are obvious. Everyone knows people can generate reasonable options as the first they consider. The second objection is that the players may have thought of really bad moves that they never told us. Maybe they were thinking of all the options, randomly, at some subconscious level, and filtering them out before they got to the level of consciousness. If this was true, we had not proved anything.

These objections contradict each other; one or the other, but not both, can be held. If you feel we have not really confirmed our hypothesis, and it still makes sense to believe that people generate large sets of options without being aware of it, then our findings are not obvious at all.

The first objection is that our findings are obvious. They are not obvious to professional trainers who teach problem-solving skills by insisting that people generate large sets of options to do a good job. Perhaps this advice is useful under some conditions, such as very low experience levels. Yet if our results were so obvious, the instructors in these courses would not be presenting their seminars.

The second objection is that people might still be generating the full set of options at a subconscious level. I agree that the think-aloud method we used is subjective, and this could affect our findings. But what is this objection claiming? That people subconsciously generate a full set of options at each choice point? Consider what happens if you take this seriously.[12] What is a full set of options? It is all the legal moves, plus the illegal ones, plus nonmoves. For example, you move your queen up a square, and I throw my glass of water in your face or call you an unpleasant name. The number of different actions available to me is infinite. If I have to generate all of them subconsciously each time I come to a choice point, then I will not have time to make many decisions each day. So we cannot take seriously the idea that we start with all the options and filter down to the final winner. There has to be some mechanism for generating only reasonable options, a mechanism that does not depend on filtering out bad ones.

These two experiments show that experience does shape decision making. Experienced people have an impressive ability to withstand time pressure and generate plausible options so they do not have to waste effort and attention by comparing lots of options. Rather than trying to wipe experience out of the studies because it can bias the results, we can try to design studies to understand its many aspects.

Applications

The most important application is to train people to achieve expertise more quickly. The perspective we use to understand expertise will govern the approach. The most typical perspective is that experts know more; they have more facts and rules at their disposal. In this chapter I have taken a different perspective: expertise is learning how to perceive. The knowledge and rules are incidental.

To date, the field of technical training has been dominated by efforts to teach rules, facts, and procedures. Technical training had been unex- amined and unstructured through the 1960s, and many technical train- ing programs from those years were poorly organized and conducted. In the 1960s and 1970s in the United States, there was a great interest in systematic approaches to training. These methods treated the skills and knowledge to be imparted during training as a set of procedures and rules that could be decomposed and systematically taught.

This strategy makes sense for simple, procedural tasks. Especially in high-turnover jobs, with minimally educated workers, the strategy allows for efficient instructional programs. Systems approaches to training were an improvement over anarchy. Nonetheless, they were not designed to teach people to gain higher levels of expertise or to make better judg- ments and decisions.

Hubert Dreyfus and Stuart Dreyfus (1986) have described how peo- ple move from the level of novices to experts. They claim that novices follow rules, whereas the experts do not. We would be mistaken to think that the experts had learned the rules so well they did not have to refer to them. Hubert Dreyfus uses the example of learning to ride a bicycle by using training wheels. As adults, we do not believe we learned to use those training wheels so well that they became an ingrained part of our bicycle riding perspective. We outgrew the need for training wheels. We developed a sense of bicycle dynamics.[13]

Presenting the procedures to trainees gives them a false sense of progress. This confidence dissipates when novices realize that applying the procedures depends on context and that no one can tell them what context is. Judgment and decision tasks in natural settings are rarely straightforward. If we want people to think like the experts, we have to be able to understand how the experts are thinking. We have to clarify their strategies and their ways of perceiving the situation. We have to elaborate on each aspect of expertise so that expertise becomes the guidepost for the training. In chapter 7, I discussed a project for the U.S. Marine Corps to help squad leaders learn like experts, rather than trying to teach them to think like experts. In that setting, we did not have the conditions for identifying critical cues, patterns, and so forth. In other settings, however, it is possible to do the knowledge elicitation to find out how skilled decision makers think and to make some of these findings available to trainees. Methods of cognitive task analysis have been developed for this purpose.

Cognitive task analysis is the description of the expertise needed to perform complex tasks. The steps of cognitive task analysis are to locate sources of expertise (and acquire background knowledge in the process), evaluate the quality of the expertise, perform knowledge elicitation to get inside the head of the skilled decision makers, process the findings so they can be interpreted to others, and apply the findings. Traditional task analyses have concentrated on the procedures to be followed and have had relatively little to say about perception, judgment, and decision-making skills. As we move to more complex jobs, especially as information technologies place more demands on workers and their supervisors, we have to go beyond the traditional task analyses.

In organizations, much of the knowledge is held within the heads of the workers and is never shared. This is tacit knowledge. In most organizations, the culture seems to ignore the expertise that already exists, to take it for granted. If a skilled worker retired after thirty years on the job and tried to leave with a favorite personal computer, some programs, or a set of tools, he or she would be stopped. The organization knows the value of the equipment. But the organization lets the worker walk out with all of that expertise, which is worth far more than some minor equipment, and never says a word, never even notices the loss.

Yet in an organization, knowledge is a resource and should be treated as such.[14] We can draw a parallel between knowledge and petroleum.

In the early 1800s, petroleum was a nuisance. It fouled the drinking water and got on farmers' boots. Then in 1854 a Canadian geologist figured out how to extract kerosene from petroleum, and the headlines read, "Good News for Whales." All of a sudden, petroleum was a resource. Today we have a variety of petroleum engineering disciplines for making use of petroleum. We have ways to locate the petroleum, assay its quality, extract it, process it, and use it (see table 10.1).

We can form a similar list for knowledge as a resource. We can identify sources of expertise, assay the quality and value of the knowledge, extract the knowledge, codify it, and apply it as well. Therefore, we can talk about a discipline of knowledge engineering. Organizations interested in taking advantage of their own expertise could use knowledge engineering to create a culture of expertise. We can use cognitive task analysis to perform knowledge engineering.[15] The first step is to *identify sources of expertise*. People who have been in an organization for a while will have accumulated some experiences worth capturing. We usually find that there is not one expert. Rather, different people know

Table 10.1
Aspects of Knowledge Engineering

Process	Petroleum	Knowledge
Search	Where to drill	Where the expertise is
Evaluate	Whether to drill	Value of knowledge
Extract	Drilling rigs	Knowledge elicitation
Process	Refine the petroleum	Codify knowledge
Apply	Use for heat/power	Use for training and design

worthwhile things in different areas. The job of cognitive task analysis is to focus on the expertise, not the experts. The aim is to find individuals whose experience is respected in the organization, in order to learn how they see their job.

Step 2 is to *assay the knowledge*. Cognitive task analysis takes time and effort. No one would start such a project if there was not a compelling need or benefit in the first place. Once we have identified the sources of expertise, we can again evaluate the value of the project. Following the parallel to petroleum engineering, just because we have found oil does not mean we should start drilling. We have to examine the difficulty and cost of the drilling against the quality of the oil. If it is low grade and difficult to extract, we leave it in the ground.

The importance of the knowledge has to be balanced against the costs of extracting it. The cost of extracting knowledge can be considerable: interviews, transcriptions, analyses, methods for representing the knowledge, and then the cost of distributing the lessons learned. What is the payoff of the project? Who will gain, and by how much?

In some settings, cognitive task analysis is a good investment. Several years ago, AT&T started a project to build a course to train software developers to become more proficient at debugging and troubleshooting. AT&T spends a lot of money each year on software development and troubleshooting, so the course had definite benefits. Because the corporation planned to present the course to many software engineers, it decided that investing in making the course as strong as possible was worthwhile. Under these circumstances, knowledge engineering was cost effective. AT&T hired us to interview fifteen skilled technical people and to use these interviews as a basis for the two-day program. The reaction to the effort was quite positive. Some of the training developers believed that this was the strategy they should use in preparing future courses: going back into the company and taking advantage of internal expertise.

The third step is to *extract the knowledge*. Cognitive task analysis methods have been developed for getting inside the heads of experts.[16] These methods include structured interviews, interviews about actual events that were challenging, interviews about the concepts experts use to think about a task, and simulated tasks that require the expert to think aloud during performance or respond to interview questions after completion.

In the next chapter I describe one of these methods in greater detail: the use of stories about challenging events to elicit knowledge from experts.

Step 4 is to *codify the knowledge*. We have seen and used many different ways to represent the knowledge elicited. Applied researchers use diagrams, charts, lists of critical cues, computer simulations of the experts' thought processes, annotated stories, transcripts of interviews, even videotapes of interviews.

In the project for AT&T, the course developers used the stories as part of the materials for the new course. For the neonatal intensive care unit project, some instructional materials were developed to train the detection of sepsis. They presented the incident accounts—the stories—and noted the critical cues. In this way, the cues were presented within a context, making them easier to understand and to use. When we tested the ability of nursing students to remember the cues to sepsis, we found a high level of recall even after several weeks.

It is often useful to identify the decision requirements (the key decisions and how they are made) of the task. For each decision requirement, we show why it is difficult, and the cues and strategies that experts use to get around the difficulty. These decision requirements can be crossreferenced to actual incidents. Anyone wanting more detail can follow an audit trail back to the interviews and incidents that were used to identify the decision requirements.

The final step is to *apply the knowledge*. We have already covered a range of examples of how cognitive task analysis can be applied. The stories, diagrams, tables, and lists of critical cues have all played a role in one project or another. They have been used to identify key cues for diagnoses of sepsis, to train nurses to recognize these cues, to provide cognitive modeling[17] of the troubleshooting strategies of expert programmers, and to show system designers what essential decisions have to be supported by interfaces.

Cognitive task analysis is a method for capturing expertise and making it accessible for training and system design. Other forms of application may be better selection methods and better methods for building a corporate memory.

One type of application we have not covered is the use of cognitive task analysis to provide guidance for organizations that want to cut down on expensive schoolhouse training. Formal training does not always transfer to the workplace.

Many organizations rely on direct experience, on-the-job training (OJT), as the primary vehicle for instruction. However, little is known about the way skilled coworkers and managers actually provide OJT. Beth Crandall and Caroline Zsambok have completed several studies of OJT.[18] In examining the way people teach perceptual skills rather than merely procedures for operating equipment, they found that the skilled coaches and OJT providers work very differently from classroom instructors in terms of how they watch the novices, assess what the novices are seeing, and introspect to show the novices the way they are looking at the task (Crandall, Kyne, Militello, & Klein, 1992; Zsambok, Crandall, & Militello, 1994). Beth found that the tutoring for nurses in a hospital intensive care unit centered on procedures and equipment operation. The tutoring was very spotty regarding the perceptual aspects of expertise. As a result, the trainees felt ill prepared, and this feeling of inadequacy may have contributed to the high turnover rates. Because recruitment and training are so expensive, turnover is a problem in hospitals. However, the nurses identified as tutors were never trained themselves to describe perceptual skills or to enhance the development of perceptual expertise in the trainees. By looking at the opportunities for perceptual training, Beth and Caroline have developed a strategy for teaching skilled workers to do a better job of providing OJT. We have had good success in setting up OJT programs, particularly for the Los Angeles County Fire Department, to help prepare captains to bring new firefighters quickly up to speed.

Caroline Zsambok and Rebecca Pliske set up an OJT program for an international franchise company of small retail stores. The problem was that product quality and customer service were uneven. After the program was set up, the store managers and staff members reported that performance of the new employees had improved. In addition, for the seven months following training, the stores with the OJT program increased their sales per month by an average of $24,500 per store compared to the same period in the previous year. In a matched set of stores that had not established the OJT program, the monthly increase in sales averaged only $10,300 per store.

Another area of application for cognitive task analysis is market research. We do not think of consumers as experts but we can still use cognitive task analysis to understand the way consumers make judgments and decisions. Market researchers prefer to use structured questionnaires and interviews, sampling respondents from different market segments. The research, based on laboratory methods, is sound. Unfortunately, the results of these surveys provide limited insight into how the consumers are making their decisions. Another approach to market research is to run focus groups: collections of consumers who are invited to talk and respond informally. This approach is more useful for gaining a sense of the consumer's thinking processes, but it still does not allow the researcher to probe deeply.

We have had several opportunities to use cognitive task analysis to identify consumers' decision strategies. Laura Militello has led these projects. In one market research project, we were told that the company already had all the answers it needed, including a satisfactory model of the consumer's decision making. The sponsor did not expect us to add anything new, especially since we had not been working in the area of interest. The only reason to enlist our help was that the project was so important that she wanted to make sure her group had not missed anything. Two weeks later, Laura's team conducted two days of in-depth cognitive task analysis interviews with individual consumers. At the end of the two days, the sponsors, who watched behind one-way mirrors, had learned more than they had expected. These detailed descriptions of how, when, and why purchase decisions are made could not be obtained via questionnaire data. The sponsor convened her team, described the results of our interviews, and began to formulate an action plan based on our findings.

Cognitive task analysis will not always be this successful, but it is an important supplement and alternative to the quantitative methods used in the field of market research.

Key Points

- Experts can perceive things that are invisible to novices: fine discriminations, patterns, alternate perspectives, missing events, the past and the future, and the process of managing decision-making activities.

- Skilled chess players show high-quality moves, even under extreme time pressure, and high-quality moves as the first ones they consider.
- Training to high-skill levels should emphasize perceptual skills, along with mastery of procedures.

11

The Power of Stories

We would be dazzled if we had to treat everything we saw, every visual input, as a separate element, and had to figure out the connections anew each time we opened our eyes or moved them from one fixation point to another. Fortunately, that is not necessary. We see the world as patterns. Many of these patterns seem to be built into the way our eyes work. We have detectors to notice lines and boundaries. The world is organized in our eyes to highlight contrasts, before any information reaches our brains. We have other powerful organizers to frame the visual world into Gestalts, so we naturally group things together that are close to each other. If a flock of birds flies overhead, we see it as one flock, sharing a common fate. Each time the flock shifts direction, we do not have to track the trajectories of each bird individually. If one bird flies off on its own, that is the bird we notice. It has broken the pattern of common fate, and it commands our attention. Infants see the world in this way. Show four-month-old infants several dots moving together, and they treat them as one unit. Send one dot off by itself, and the infant is surprised. We know it is surprised because it stops drinking its milk at that instant. It shows a startle reflex. Even infants organize the visual world through patterns.

My claim in this chapter is that we similarly organize the cognitive world—the world of ideas, concepts, objects, and relationships. We link these up into stories. By understanding how this happens, we can learn to make better use of the power of stories.

A story is a blend of several ingredients:[1]

- Agents—the people who figure in the story.
- Predicament—the problem the agents are trying to solve.

- Intentions—what the agents plan to do.
- Actions—what the agents do to achieve their intentions.
- Objects—tools the agents will use.
- Causality—the effects (both intended and unintended) of carrying out actions.
- Context—the many details surrounding the agents and actions.
- Surprises—the unexpected things that happen in the story.

In a simple form, a story ties these and other ingredients together. Here is a story we heard during the project Beth Crandall did with nurses.

Example 11.1
The Case of the Infant Whose Heart Wasn't Beating Eighty Times a Minute

A nurse in a neonatal intensive care unit has been providing primary care for a baby in the isolette next to the baby described here. She has noticed this other baby having subtle color changes over a period of several hours. He fades out a bit, then comes back to a healthy pink on his own. She remarks on it to his primary nurse, who has noticed these variations too. Then in a matter of seconds, the baby turns deep blue-black. The monitor shows that his blood pressure has bottomed out completely; his heart rate drops but then levels out and holds steady at eighty beats per minute.

She knows immediately that he has suffered a pneumopericardium. Air has filled the sac that surrounds the heart and turned it into a balloon; the air pressure around the heart prevents it from moving blood through the heart into the baby's body. His heart is essentially paralyzed. She knows he will die within minutes if the air around his heart is not reieased. She knows this because she has seen it happen once before, to a baby who was her patient. That baby had died.

Meanwhile, the baby's primary nurse is yelling for X-ray, and a doctor to come and puncture the baby's chest wall. She figures that the baby's lung has collapsed, a common event for babies who are on ventilators, and, besides, the heart monitor continues to show a steady eighty beats per minute. The nurse who first spotted the problem tries to correct her—"It's the heart; there's no heartbeat"—while the team around her continues to point to the heart monitor. She pushes their hands away from the baby and screams for quiet as she listens through her stethoscope for a heartbeat. There is none, and she begins doing compressions on the baby's chest. The chief neonatologist appears, and she turns to him, slaps a syringe in his hand, and says, "It's a pneumopericardium. I know it. Stick the heart." The X-ray technician calls from across the room that she is right: the baby's

> **Example 11.1** (continued)
>
> pericardium is filled with air. The physician releases the air, and the baby's life is saved.
>
> Afterward, the team talks about why the monitor had fooled them. They realize that the monitor is designed to record electrical events, and it continued to pick up the electrical impulses generated by the heart. The monitor can record the electrical impulse but cannot show whether the heart is actually beating to circulate blood through the body.

This story is a warning not to trust machines because they can mislead. It is a warning that lifesaving methods, such as air tubes, can kill the infants they are supposed to sustain. It is a story about expertise. The nurse who had seen a baby die of pneumopericardium could recognize the symptoms better than the other nurse. This is also a permission story. It tells when it is all right to make a fuss, to refuse to be reassured even if you have to risk a friendship. It tells about the culture of the hospital, where the boundaries are, and what it takes to convince others. You may find additional lessons in the story.

Stories like this contain many different lessons and are useful as a form of vicarious experience for people who did not witness the incident. They also help to preserve values, by showing newcomers the kind of environment they are entering. For our purposes as researchers, these kinds of stories also help us understand situations and relationships.

We like to hear good stories retold. What is more interesting is our need to *tell* stories, again and again. Each telling helps us understand more about the lessons embedded in the story. I suspect that this need to tell stories starts very early, even before the beginning of language. I have even seen storytelling in a child who had not yet started to talk—my nephew Alexander.

When Alexander was sixteen months old, before he had uttered a single word, not even *Mama*, he told a story, based on an incident that occurred in his home. He had always been fascinated by the family dog, Casey, a Samoyed, and loved to pull on Casey's white fur. Casey suffered these attacks, trying to stay away from Alexander. One day Alexander cornered Casey and pulled a little too vigorously. Casey yelped and gave Alexander a slight nip on the hand to teach him to be more careful. Alexander was traumatized by this attack. When his mother, Sandie, got home a few hours later, Alexander rushed up to her and thrust out his hand to show the bandage, the evidence of his wound. Then he told her what happened. He made a "heh, heh" breathing sound to imitate Casey, followed by a "Grrrrrrr" to show Casey's response to Alexander's presence. Then he pulled his hand sharply away, to mimic his response to the bite. Next, he cradled his one hand in the other to show that it had been hurt, accompanied by pretend crying sounds and expressions, and ending with a display of the bandage. There you have it. The complete story.

When his mother showed the proper sympathy, Alexander repeated the story. He repeated it again to his father, my brother, Mitchell, a few more times. For weeks after that, Alexander told his story. He told it repeatedly to his parents, to me, and to the members of my family. In a shopping mall, if someone bent down to him and made polite conversation, Alexander would tell his story. The bandage came off, leaving a small mark that Alexander incorporated into the story. As he gained some words, he dropped the "heh, heh" breathing sound and said "Casey" to identify his assailant. (Alexander later added a second story to his repertoire, a report of a magical trip through a car wash. It had a weaker plot but a better set of sound effects.)

Features of Good Stories

A story about the infant whose heart almost strangled is effective for several reasons. It is dramatic. A child almost died; only a last-minute intervention saved him. It allows empathy. We can imagine ourselves being the nurse who ignored the warning, so if there are lessons to be learned, we want to learn them. It is instructive. We sense wisdom in this story, even if we are not sure of all the messages. Therefore, we want to keep it in the back of our heads as an analogue in case we ever wind up in a similar situation. Drama, empathy, and wisdom are key. Stories are remembered because they are dramatic. They are used because we can identify with one or more of the actors. They are told and retold because of the wisdom they contain—the lessons that keep emerging with each telling.

A good story usually has some element of surprise; that is the dramatic part. People sometimes tell us chronologies, series of events, and we may listen politely, wondering what the point is. My nephew

Alexander's story was a chronology. Now that he is older, he is learning to tell better stories.

A good story is a package of different causal relationships—what factors resulted in what effects. The more complexity and subtlety, the more there is to be learned. If the story gets too confusing, though, it stops working. It has to draw together different components clearly and memorably and show their connection. Researchers try to figure out causal relationships by running experiments. We will run twenty subjects to see if we reliably get a result. However, to control the conditions, we may have to restrict the background context. For that reason, we are never sure of getting the same result outside the laboratory. In contrast, a story records an event that happened within a natural context. It documents that under these conditions, these causes operating simultaneously produce this result. In its way, a story is also a report of an experiment, linking cause and effect. It says, "Under these conditions, this is what happens."

Even the request for more details can be seen as an attempt to pin down the conditions more carefully, to understand after the fact what the causes really were.

In a scientific experiment, we usually identify one cause and vary its levels to see how it affects some outcome. For instance, in the first chess study described in chapter 10, we wanted to see how time pressure affected the proportion of blunders in a chess game, so we varied time pressure and measured blunders. We found that time pressure has a small effect on blunders. Actually, we wanted to look at two causes at the same time: time pressure and skill level. By varying both, we found that each cause separately has a small effect on blunders, but together they have a large effect. Time pressure strongly increases blunders for class B players but not for masters. We can call this an interaction, because the effects of the time pressure variable differ, depending on the second variable, the skill level. Sometimes experiments vary three or four things at once, but if the results show a triple order interaction, even the original experimenters have trouble keeping everything straight. Therefore, our experiments study only a few causal factors at a time. As a result, we do not gain a good picture of how the different causes affect each other. Compare this to a story, where the outcome is affected by many important variables or causal factors, each of which needs to be described and to have its influence traced. The story is a package for describing the important causes and allowing the listener to think of other possible causes for the events.

Perhaps we value stories because they are like reports of research projects, only easier to understand, remember, and use. The limitation of a story, which makes it nonscientific, is that no one has controlled the conditions. If you hear a story, you do not know if you have been given all of the relevant causal factors. You do not know exactly how the causal factors would interact if the conditions were slightly different. In the pneumopericardium story, if the baby had turned slightly less blue, would the nurse have responded? If the heart rate had fluctuated more, would the second nurse have intervened? We do not know. We just know that under this constellation of conditions, this is what happened. We have lost precision, the ability to trace each factor, in order to gain richness, the full set of interacting conditions. For most purposes, the trade-off is worthwhile. We know that at some point, if the change in the baby's color had been too small or had been masked by some other condition, the first nurse would not have noticed. If the heart rate had fluctuated too much, the second nurse would have noticed. So we know the variables; we just cannot pin down the exact thresholds where each nurse would react.

Stories have to have endings, as do experiments. If I describe an experiment I ran and admitted that I had never found the time to analyze the data, you would ask why I bothered running the experiment. You need the findings to trace the impact of the factors studied. In a story, the ending shows how the main themes were resolved. We have been in many situations where people made complex plans, but handed these off and never learned if they were carried out, or what happened. As a result, the planners never got the feedback to learn how to do better. When we asked them for stories, they had none to tell, because they did not have the Gestalt of a plan plus outcome.

Besides drama, empathy, and wisdom, good stories have a number of more mundane but still necessary features:

- Plausibility. The elements are believable. We have to be able to accept each step and action, or should expect an explanation if elements do not seem plausible. These anomalies have to be explained away.[2]

- Consistency. The elements fit with each other.
- Economy. The range of details is complete without getting too inclusive.
- Uniqueness. We prefer stories that are not open to alternate explanations.

These criteria are similar to the ones mentioned for mental simulation in chapter 5. There is a definite overlap between stories and mental simulation. Both are causal chains. Both share the same need for plausibility, consistency, economy, and uniqueness. The major difference is that mental simulations are stories we run inside our head, where there is less room for complexity. Therefore, we cannot have as many agents or transformations. Also, we are making up the mental simulation, whereas the stories we tell are usually about events that really happened, so it is easier to add details and elaborations. Mental simulations are constructed in working memory, so they have to be streamlined. Another difference is that stories are about people and their intentions, whereas mental simulations can address sequences of events for inanimate objects as well as for people.[3]

Using Stories to Make Sense of Events

One of the most common uses of stories is to understand. After a day of flying, military pilots gather to discuss their adventures. Perhaps a radar system was malfunctioning and after several tries, the pilot figured out a workaround, to bypass the usual procedures. So he or she tells that story because it is the type of story you want to tell a few times while its implications are sinking in, and the other pilots want to listen because it might happen to them sometime. They want to gain a vicarious experience.

We see the same thing happening with mothers in a park. One woman might describe how her daughter fought against having to go to bed for weeks, until the mother tried some new idea, maybe reading, being careful to start with the exciting books and working back to the familiar and soothing ones. The other mothers listen, trying to pick up some more tricks of the trade and maybe also to fathom the mysteries of why a child who gets too sleepy will not go to bed without a major tantrum. In the storytelling of the pilots and the mothers, experiences are being crystal-lized into expertise. Tricks of the trade are being discovered.[4]

Pennington and Hastie (1993) studied the way people make sense of legal evidence presented during a trial. (This work was discussed earlier in chapter 7.) They found that the decision makers try to assemble the evidence into a story. The task of jurors, to hold all the evidence in their heads, is too difficult. By organizing the evidence into a story, the task of recalling and understanding the evidence becomes easier. A juror who has built a story compares it to the stories presented by the prosecutor and the defense attorney. Pennington and Hastie found that the mock jurors in the experiment accepted the claim that more closely matched the story they themselves had constructed. The jurors were using their stories to evaluate the stories that the attorneys were trying to tell.

We may gain some insight by using a case where it did not work—a case where the story the defense lawyers put forward was not believed by the jurors. In 1991 the heavyweight champion of the world, Mike Tyson, was convicted of raping a young woman in a hotel. Tyson's lawyers had learned that in getting ready to go out with Tyson, the young woman had been excited and had made an offhand comment to a roommate about her chances of using Tyson to become wealthy. Tyson had recently been divorced and had given his ex-wife a settlement of several million dollars. The defense lawyers felt that they had the makings of a good story in which a woman tried to use her time with Mike Tyson to her advantage; when the relationship did not extend past the first evening, she tried to extort the money by claiming rape. In support of the defense story, the woman had not gone to the police immediately after the rape. She had waited a few days, which fit in with the idea that she claimed rape only when her original scheme (perhaps to marry Tyson, divorce him, and become rich) did not work out. As with any other story, there were some weaknesses that had to be patched up. For example, the woman had been physically injured during intercourse with Tyson, but the defense felt it could explain these injuries away: the woman was petite, and Tyson was a heavyweight boxer.

This story was not successful. The physical injuries the woman suf-fered were predominantly those found in rape victims. Moreover, the woman's behavior for the days after the rape, before going to the police, showed shock and depression, typical of rape, rather than anger, revenge, and plotting. Her testimony in front of the jury showed her to be well brought up, innocent, and trusting, not scheming, as the story claimed. At that point, the victim had not sought monetary gain by filing for damages. The jury had to figure out why a nice-looking young woman would subject herself to the ordeal of a rape trial simply to punish Tyson, if her goal was riches and fame. The criminal trial would not make her rich, and she had refused to reveal her identity. Was it anger? She had a lot of time to cool off, and she did not seem angry. The story failed to explain too many facts and observations. The jury rejected it, and found Tyson guilty. While the trial was going on, I asked an attorney if lawyers receive much training in story building. He said there is virtually no such training. Law school concentrates on legal arguments, precedents, rules of evidence, and other matters, not on training what makes people accept or reject stories.

It seems to me that Tyson's lawyers had a better story they could have told. Instead of trying to convince the jury that the victim was a scheming villain instead of an innocent victim, I wondered if the defense might have done better accepting the woman as sympathetic. They could have accepted her naiveté and her trusting attitude. They could have argued that the events that evening had gone further than the victim had expected. She had been manipulated (but not coerced) into having intercourse and had been physically hurt as well. Afterward, she was confused and depressed, as everyone described, and feeling guilty. She had not wanted the evening to end that way, and she might have reconstructed events to believe that she had actually been raped, that she had protested more vigorously at the time than was the case. Therefore, her claim that she was raped would have been sincere but mistaken.

This story still might not have worked, but it seems like a better story—more consistent with the evidence, more plausible, more coherent—than the one offered by Tyson's lawyers. It might have created sufficient ambiguity to sway some jurors from concluding that guilt was established beyond a reasonable doubt.

Let us look at another example of story building as a way of making sense of events. The example is the assassination of John F. Kennedy. The purpose of the example is to show how stories can be used to interpret claims.

Example 11.2
The Magic Bullet

The Warren Commission, in its official report of the assassination, claimed that a single bullet struck both President Kennedy and Texas governor John Connally. According to the report, the bullet entered Kennedy's back, exited through his neck, entered Connally's body, shattered his rib, exited his chest, reentered Connally's right wrist, shattered the radius bone, exited the wrist, reentered Connally a third time, and buried itself in Connally's thigh. After Connally was brought to Parkland Hospital, the bullet fell out and was found next to his stretcher.

That is a lot of work for a single bullet. Some conspiracy theorists, including Oliver Stone in his movie *JFK*, claimed that the assassination plotters sent someone to deposit the bullet next to Connally, to cover up their tracks. They claim that the bullet found next to Connally was a fake. Its purpose was to suggest that the many different wounds were caused by only a few bullets, in keeping with the pretense of a single gunman, Lee Harvey Oswald. According to this conspiracy theory, if the world knew how many bullets had actually been fired and from how many directions, everyone would realize that there was more than one assassin. Therefore, the conspirators needed to cover their tracks.

Jacob Cohen (1992) has reviewed the autopsy and ballistics tests that support the idea of a "magic bullet" that did all the things described above. The part of Cohen's analysis in which I am interested is his attempt to take the conspiracy theory seriously. He asks us to imagine that there was a plot, with several assassins firing simultaneously, and that there was a cover-up plan to drop the bullet next to Connally's stretcher. How did the plotters know that they needed to drop off a bullet in the first place? If their job was to make it seem as if there had been fewer bullets, why add one more? Surely this would be more likely to add suspicion rather than alleviate it. If Connally was wounded (and why would he be on a stretcher otherwise?), presumably the bullet that wounded him was still in his body, where it would be found by his physicians.

The only reason for the extra bullet is that the plotters were trying to make the magic bullet theory credible and divert suspicion. They must have been thinking that as long as people believed the Warren Commission report (which was perhaps also a part of the scheme), the conspirators were safe. A weak link in that report was going to be the idea of the magic bullet, so they had to plant it next to Connally.

The idea of a magic bullet emerged only months later, after analysis of films, autopsies, and X-rays. To make this story work, we have to imagine (mentally simulate) how the plotters dreamed it all up in advance, down to the exact course that the bullet was supposed to take. Let's derive a story of how the plotters might have reacted when they realized that their scheme included the weak element that the same bullet, fired from the

---

Example 11.2 (continued)

Texas Book Depository, was supposed to hit both Kennedy (once) and Connally (three times).

"Uh oh," one of the plotters would have said. "That's going to look unusual."

"No problem," another plotter would have answered: "We'll just get all the physicians and X-ray technicians to fake the physical evidence. And if they won't go along, we'll just hide JFK's body for around forty minutes and alter all his wounds so they match the X-rays. You'll see, everything will fit in with the idea of a single bullet."

"But aren't there going to be a lot of people firing at Kennedy? I mean, how are we going to know in advance who's going to hit him, and where they're going to be positioned, so we can tell everybody how to fake all the X-rays just right?"

"Pish posh. Sonny, you're dealing with the CIA. Sure, we bungle our share of foreign plots. This time we'll get everything perfect. Don't worry."

"What if a bullet from the grassy knoll team hits the side of the limousine, the side facing away from Oswald? Won't that be a problem?"

"Always with the what-ifs. It's a disease with you. Listen, these are sharpshooters, not terrorists. And if a bullet does go wrong, we just confiscate everyone's film, all the eyewitnesses, and do it without being traced. Or we take over the media so that no one finds out. Lots of ways to make it happen."

A conspiracy theory has its own problems. As long as the idea of plotters is left murky (e.g., "The CIA can do anything and get away with it"), then a conspiracy may seem plausible. But when we try to build a story of how the conspiracy might have proceeded, we run into trouble. The idea of plotters dropping off an extra bullet, which originally seemed to explain so much, now raises more questions than it resolves. Each of these complications (e.g., why put the bullet next to Connally, how to anticipate the magic bullet theory, how to fake the evidence) is a strain on the plausibility of the conspiracy theory. We are prepared to explain away one or two exceptions, but as they keep mounting up and they get more difficult to account for, we lose confidence in the story. This part of the conspiracy story fails to meet standards of plausibility and consistency.

In chapter 5 we discussed how a mental simulation could be used to diagnose a situation by recreating the chain of events that led up to it. Story building can generate a diagnosis. In troubleshooting a piece of equipment, a technician is building a story of what might have gone wrong to explain the set of observed symptoms. If we view troubleshooting and diagnosis in this way, then we can apply the criteria of good stories to get a sense of how troubleshooting proceeds. The troubleshooter is trying to construct a causal chain that leads from the initial conditions to the fault. The links in the chain have to be plausible. For example, wires do not suddenly snap; there is no reason for them to do so, and it rarely happens. So troubleshooters like the one in the following story do not consider wire failures as possible causes unless there is a good reason.

Example 11.3
The Case of the Seasonal Short

The house is old and not in good condition. Its electrical system, for example, is a constant source of problems. One is that a fuse keeps blowing. The home owner is finding these interruptions frustrating. Electricians have been called in and learned that the fuse blows in the summer, not in the winter. The electricians find no problems.

Finally an old master troubleshooter is brought in. He talks with the home owner, and they conduct an inspection together. In the basement, they go into a storage room. The master electrician asks about the way the room is used. The home owner explains that in the summer, they have the room rearranged because they use it to create a walkway. During the winter, they just pile up the equipment and keep the door closed. The master troubleshooter asks the home owner to rearrange everything as it would be in the summer. He looks at a carpet that marks the main pathway. He gets down on his hands and knees and feels the length of the carpet. He finally locates a protruding nail that happened to puncture one of the key electrical wires. In the summer, each time someone stepped on the nail, the system would short out. In the winter, no one had a chance to step on the nail.

The troubleshooter explains that he didn't waste his time with the major components of the electrical system, since these had been checked. He knew that intermittent shorts are hard to find without tearing up the entire wiring system.

The strategy he used was to find a key change between the two seasons, to get a clue about where to find the culprit.[5]

Several years ago we interviewed some of AT&T's best software programmers to find out what made them such effective troubleshooters. We found that they followed a common strategy of building successive stories. The initial reports of the failure suggested a likely problem, and this story directed them to inspect certain components. Sometimes the initial search worked. If it did not, it at least told them something more about what was working and what was not. It helped them come up with a better story, which aimed their inspection in a different direction. The troubleshooters were simultaneously building a better story and using the stories to gather more information. This process matches the nonlinear account of problem solving we covered in chapter 9. There was a simultaneous use of the current state of knowledge to move forward and of failures to add to the current state of knowledge. Story building and story modification play a central role in diagnosis.

Applications

The method we have found most powerful for eliciting knowledge is to use stories. If you ask experts what makes them so good, they are likely to give general answers that do not reveal much. But if you can get them to tell you about tough cases, nonroutine events where their skills made the difference, then you have a pathway into their perspective, into the way they are seeing the world. We call this the critical decision method, because it focuses attention on the key judgments and decisions that were made during the incident being described.[6]

In her project with the neonatal intensive care unit, Beth Crandall had asked the experienced nurses how they detected the early signs of sepsis. They told her it was experience and intuition. They did not know what they knew, because what they knew was perceptual—how to see. The only way Beth was going to find out anything useful was to have the nurses tell their stories of specific instances, each tied to a different set of perceptual cues. At the end of the interviews, Beth could draw all the stories together and compile a master list of cues to sepsis.

During the years that we have used stories to elicit knowledge, we have evolved a strategy. First, we try to find a good story, one with lots of expertise, perceptual skills, and judgment. Sometimes an expert will try to tell a story that is dramatic but has little value for us. In our first study of fireground commanders, people often wanted to tell us about incidents where someone had died, because they remembered these incidents vividly. We soon found that most of these stories had no point; no difficult decisions had been made. We had to give better instructions, asking for stories about events that were nonroutine, where a novice might have faltered. We gradually evolved a strategy for conducting the interview and typically now make four passes through the incident.

The first pass is to hear a brief version of the story, to see if it has good possibilities, and to prepare ourselves to probe the important parts, and not waste time at the beginning on trivial issues.

The second pass is for the full telling of the story. We try to get the details pinned down to a time line so we can get a better sense of what happened and to visualize when and how long things took. Sometimes the time line helps us catch inconsistencies. If possible, we diagram the story, showing how one state of knowledge transformed into another, and noting the situation awareness at each stage.

The third pass is to probe the thought processes. We usually ask what a person noticed when changing an assessment of the situation and what alternate goals might have existed at a certain point. If a course of action was selected, we ask what other actions were possible, whether the person considered any of them, and if so, what were some factors that favored the option chosen. We like to ask about hypotheticals. For instance, if a piece of information had not arrived, what would the person have most likely done? If that option was blocked, what would the reaction be? Marvin Cohen has his own way of probing critical incidents. He will fasten on an essential part of the story and tell the person, "Now imagine that that *didn't* happen. Why not? What could explain such a thing?" Both of these probes help uncover some of the hidden assumptions that experts make without thinking and without letting others know about them.

If time permits, we make a fourth pass through the incident. At each choice point—whether about interpreting the events or choosing a course of action—we ask if a novice could get confused. "If I were the one making the decision, if by some fluke of events I got pressed into service during this emergency, would I see this the same way you did? What mistakes could I make? Why would I make them?" This probe has generally elicited good information about what an expert notices that a novice might not.

Example 11.4
The Misleading Manuals

The software engineer uses a program to print out some reports. He is under time pressure to complete those reports. He notices that the short ones go through fine, but the longer ones are cut off. For some reason, the system prints only half of each. He asks someone about the problem and is told that the reports are kept short for efficiency. He reads through the manual and does not see anything to indicate that the reports must be kept short.

Now he is suspicious. He realizes that carefully reading the code that makes up the computer program will take too long. After lunch he decides to skim through the program code. He notices the number 255 again and again. Even without going through the details of the program, he recognizes that 256 bytes represents a natural constraint used very often. He imagines that the 255 might be a way of cutting off a job just before it reached this limit. Now he has some firm evidence. He brings the program code to one of the developers, who confirms that there is a limit on the allowable size of the reports. No one had bothered putting this instruction into the manual.

Figure 11.1 diagrams the incident. In the interview, we asked where someone might have made a mistake. The software engineer replied that the most likely error was to assume a bug in the system rather than an undocumented limit. A novice looking for a bug could have wasted hours playing around with debugging programs and getting nowhere. Another mistake would have been to go running for help too early because the culture of the company discourages these types of unjustified requests; a person who asks for help too quickly loses credibility. A third error would have been to conclude it was an undocumented limit and to search for the problem by reading through the source code. This would have taken too long. The evidence of the 255s was enough to legitimately ask for help.

This story is about the experience needed to form the right initial diagnosis. It is also a permission story, as was the pneumopericardium example. It tells how people are supposed to seek assistance in this culture.

Conducting these interviews is not easy. In my company, we train people for months. We start with workshops and exercises, then usually a project to code interviews someone else conducted. Next the trainee

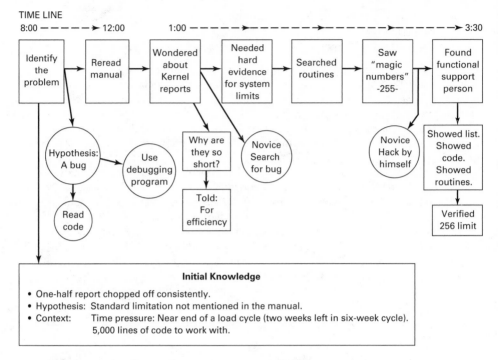

Figure 11.1

Finding the hidden restriction in the misleading manuals

assists in interviews by taking notes. Finally the trainee leads an interview, with an experienced interviewer watching. Conducting a useful interview takes more than merely following procedures. Interviewers have to be able to recognize where in an incident expertise comes into play, so they can spend most of the time probing the right areas. They have to judge which probes are likely to bring out the most useful information and how long to spend on any topic. They typically have access to experts for a limited amount of time, usually a few hours, and they want to hear as many incidents as possible. We try to select probes in advance, to fit the objectives of the interview, but we have to make adjustments depending on the context of the incident. Interviewers also need a sense of what is a good story. Some people do not seem to have this sense. They will conduct an interview and tell us about the incident, and our reaction is, "So what? What's the point?"

Therefore, it is misleading to say we just ask people to tell us stories. A lot more has to go on than just swapping war stories with experts. Finding a good story is difficult enough; it is even harder to use the story as a wedge into the expertise of the interviewee. The cognitive probes we use and the follow-up questions we ask go far beyond a process of passively listening to a story for forty minutes.

Additionally, we try to talk as little as possible, leaving the expert to do the work. That means that if an expert has finished with one topic and is naturally moving into another, we might go along if the topic was something we planned to cover, even if it is not the one we want to cover next. We can come back to the missed topic; usually, in fact the expert comes around to it later. Keeping track of the item that did not get covered adds to the mental workload, but it is worth it to keep the discussion going smoothly rather than lurching from one topic to another. Once someone observed us interviewing F-15 pilots and later commented that there was not a method; we were just having a conversation with the people. We were amused by this comment since it was made on the third day of the project. On each of the first two days, after finishing a full day of interviews, Marvin Thordsen, Laura Militello, and I had spent an additional two or three hours figuring out what had worked, what had not, and what changes we were going to have to make in our strategy. It took a lot of work to get the interviews to flow smoothly and give us what we needed.

Without a set of strategies for learning about expertise, it can be easy to ask simplistic questions and obtain uninformative responses. Many of the televised interviews with professional athletes fall into this trap. Solomon (1996) provides an example of how not to elicit expertise, in reporting interviews with Evgeny Kissin, a highly acclaimed pianist:

Though Kissin can speak of music with intellectual clarity, he can no more verbalize how he has arrived at his way of playing the piano than the leopard can explain how he got his spots. "How do you choose your encores?" I asked him when we first met, in London in the early spring, the day after a recital. "They come to me," he said. "How do you judge an audience?" "I feel something in the air." "How do you decide when you are ready for a piece?" "This is always very clear to me." "How do you decide which concerts to attend?" "I attend the ones I'm interested in." It must have been like this to interview the early saints (p. 114).

Solomon may want to conclude that he is confronted with a saintly figure, but another interpretation is that the questions themselves resulted in the inarticulate responses.

Just as the story form helps us probe for the expertise, the story also helps to communicate the expertise. In the project for AT&T, the course developers used the stories as part of the materials for the new course. They even included some videotapes from the interviews, to provide the trainees a fuller sense of how experts approach a troubleshooting task. For the neonatal intensive care unit project, we developed some instructional materials to train the detection of sepsis. These materials presented the incident accounts, the stories, and noted where the critical cues were to be found. In this way, the cues were presented within a context, making them easier to understand and to use.

Because a cognitive task analysis can be fairly labor intensive and requires well-trained interviewers to do knowledge elicitation, it may not always be possible to conduct such a study when needed. In a project sponsored by the Navy Personnel Research and Development Center, we developed a streamlined method for doing cognitive task analysis that people with less experience could use (Militello & Hutton, 1998). This strategy has evolved from research on the different aspects of expertise.

Not every knowledge engineering project works out. I will end this chapter with an example of one of our more memorable failures, many years ago.

Example 11.5
The Case of the Mangled Proceedings

A friend is organizing a large conference and asks if my company can help. She had put on a previous conference and had gone to the effort of preparing a volume of proceedings. All the presenters had submitted abstracts of their talks. The document was tedious to read and not very useful. Now as she prepares for another conference, she asks if we can attend the sessions, listen to the stories, and compile them as a record of the conference. It sounds interesting, so even though we will not be interviewing anyone, we agree to do it. Five of us go over to the center where the conference is taking place, one for each of the five concurrent sessions. Each time

Example 11.5 (continued)

a presenter puts on a slide about the major ideas, everyone in the room starts writing furiously, but we observers just sit back. Every time a presenter gives an example or tells a story, we are writing furiously and the others sit back.

By the end of the two days, we have accumulated a wonderful set of stories. We know that all the official viewgraphs listing the five key steps to do this or the seven ways to do that are fairly useless. You can exchange these slides from one session to the next, and no one would notice. Their slides are filled with useful tidbits like, "Keep the lines of communication open," and "Don't wait too long when problems are building up." Presumably these bits of wisdom are going to help those who keep trying to close lines of communication and who insist on waiting too long whenever a problem is detected. We are confident that in recording the stories of line experience during organizational crises, we have captured the real expertise.

I gather all the stories and incident accounts and write them up into a short, thirty-page conference "proceedings." The incidents the presenters have described are funny, and tragic, and exciting, with many useful ideas, lessons learned, and cognitive modeling. The other people in my company who see the document are also enthusiastic. We send it to the conference organizer, and she is even more enthusiastic than we are. She wants to get some additional funds so we can expand this into a book. As a formality, the conference organizer sends a copy of the document to each presenter to make sure each are comfortable with the way he or she is represented.

That's when everything falls apart. Most of the presenters are disappointed. Some are furious. The problem is that each presenter wants to be remembered for the dry viewgraphs on "twelve essential keys to a happier relationship between management and labor." They had worked hard on these presentations and are shocked that the official record won't show any of their thinking, any of their viewgraphs, any of the important conclusions they had presented. Instead, they are going to be remembered as people who just swapped stories and anecdotes.

We want to explain to them how meaningless these slogans are in contrast to stories, such as the one showing how they had kept the lines of communication open during a difficult incident in which a plant was shut down. We had included some introductory material for each story to identify the main points, but that is not enough for the presenters. It is going to be a losing battle. We withdraw the document, and add it to the set of stories we tell.

Key Points

- Stories organize events into a meaningful framework.
- Stories serve as natural experiments, linking a network of causes to their effects.
- Stories are similar to mental simulations; they are evaluated using many of the same criteria.
- Stories can be used to extract and communicate subtle aspects of expertise.

12

The Power of Metaphors and Analogues

After the attack on Pearl Harbor in 1941, the Japanese commander, Mit-suo Fuchido, was surprised by its success. He asked, "Had these Americans never heard of Port Arthur?" That event, which was famous in Japan, had preceded the Russo-Japanese War of 1904. The Japanese tactic was to destroy the Russian Pacific fleet at anchor at Port Arthur in a surprise attack. The tactic worked, and to the amazement of the world, the Japanese won the war (Wohlstetter, 1962).

People use analogues and metaphors to perform a variety of difficult tasks: understanding situations, generating predictions, solving problems, anticipating events, designing equipment, and making plans. An analogue is an event or example drawn from the same or a related domain as the task at hand; a metaphor comes from a markedly different domain. Each experience we have, whether it is our own or one we have heard about from someone else, can serve as an analogue or a metaphor. Each time we take on a task, we can draw on this vast knowledge base, this bank of experiences and stories and images. We may overlook an analogue, select a misleading one, or fail to interpret one correctly. Usually our experience bank works smoothly, providing us with structure and interpretation even for tasks we have not been faced with before.

In the early 1980s, engineers given the task of estimating how long auxiliary power unit of a B-1 aircraft would last before it had to be repaired looked up the data for the same unit on a C-5A airplane to get a ballpark figure. The C-SA auxiliary power unit was an *analogue* they used for prediction.

Around the same time, Stephen Jobs and Steve Wozniak were designing the Macintosh computer, using ideas they had seen at the Xerox Palo Alto Research Center, Hewlett-Packard, and other places. They adopted the idea of making the interface of the Macintosh work like a desktop. Users could see folders, maneuver a mouse to pick up one folder and put it in another, and so forth. The concept of a desktop was a *metaphor* for using the Macintosh interface.[1]

The Logic of Metaphorical Reasoning

Once, metaphors were treated simply as adornments to language. An English teacher would cite a favorite example from Shakespeare, perhaps, "My love is like a red rose," and we were all supposed to lean back in our seats, giddy with the fragrance of the metaphor. (This is actually a simile because it uses *like,* but we need not worry here about these types of details.) However, researchers have been trying to understand the way metaphors affect our thinking, as well as our emotional reactions.[2] They have found that metaphors affect what we see and how we interpret it. Lakoff and Johnson (1980), in their book *Metaphors We Live By,* showed that metaphors govern the way we think about issues. The metaphor ARGUMENTS ARE LIKE WAR tells us we should be attacking each other's positions, particularly the weak points, and defending our own weaknesses. If we used the metaphor ARGUMENTS ARE LIKE MUSIC PRACTICE, we would be using arguments as an opportunity to find out how we are each contributing to disharmonies.

Lakoff (1986) has shown that a woman who complains to her boyfriend that "this relationship isn't going anywhere" is using the metaphor of a journey for assessing the relationship. A journey has a beginning, a clear ending, and an expectation of continual progress. If progress ceases, then it is no longer a journey—or in this case, a worthwhile relationship. A different metaphor, that a relationship is an arch, would convey that the pieces achieve more together than they could individually. They transcend themselves, and success is seen as stability rather than change and progress.

Lakoff and Johnson and other researchers have made us aware of the metaphors that guide our thinking. A metaphor uses a base domain, a familiar domain, to achieve situation awareness, that is, to interpret and understand a new domain. Political debate can be seen as a struggle for the defining metaphors. In the United States, when there is an opportunity or need to help a small country in the midst of a civil war, the metaphor of a schoolyard may be introduced. One of the stronger students steps between two smaller children having a scrap, letting them cool off before they can do too much damage. This is a heroic image. The countermetaphor is usually the tar baby image from the Uncle Remus stories—an image of trying to help but getting stuck further and further in the tar, until it is impossible to be extracted. This is a frightening and vivid metaphor, usually tied to the Vietnam experience.

Metaphor does more than adorn our thinking. It structures our thinking. It conditions our sympathies and emotional reactions. It helps us achieve situation awareness. It governs the evidence we consider salient and the outcomes we elect to pursue.

If this framework makes sense, then it should produce some useful implications. To find out, Dent-Read, Klein, and Eggleston (1994) conducted a study to understand how we might use metaphor to design equipment.[3] We began by interviewing the leading metaphor researchers to see what suggestions they might make. None of them had any helpful ideas, and some were discouraging, arguing that metaphors cannot be put to work in this way.

Then we shifted to designers themselves, visiting and interviewing people identified as producing innovative systems and interfaces. Here we got the opposite answer: that metaphor was at the core of these designers' work. Some designers explained that every time they considered an interface, they had to consider the metaphors that would be uppermost in the users' minds. For the first word processors, the metaphor was the typewriter, and the job of the interface designer was to build on that metaphor while avoiding dissimilarities. The keyboard was the same, but users did not have to hit the carriage return at the end of each line, and that was going to take some getting used to. They also had to issue warnings about periodically saving a file so it would not be lost in case the system crashed. This was not a problem with typewriters.

One designer, John Reising of the U.S. Air Force's Flight Dynamics Laboratory, showed us different schemes for helping pilots navigate a safe path through a dangerous airspace. The planners could often determine an effective route in advance, so the task was to help the pilots follow it. One approach Reising showed us was to use the metaphor of a highway in the sky. His displays portrayed a highway on the screen, and the pilots guided their airplanes to fly on this highway. A U.S. Navy approach was to present a phantom airplane on the screen, flying the selected route. Here the pilots flew in formation with this phantom, following it wherever it went. If they were going to have to start speeding up, the phantom's afterburners would light up. If the pilot was going too fast, the phantom would deploy its drag chute, ordinarily used on landing to slow down.

We learned that effective metaphors were the ones helping to organize action. They were trading in on well-learned behaviors, such as flying formation, driving on a highway, or moving folders on a desktop, so that the new task could be performed smoothly using coordination skills that had already been developed.

We also found metaphors that did not help very much, such as a hospital metaphor to show pilots which subsystem of their aircraft was sick. For these ineffective metaphors, the organization was conceptual, not coordinating actions. By noting that the hydraulic system was "sick," the interface was not offering anything useful to pilots. The pilots do not have the well-learned reactions to sickness they do to flying in formation. We can also see that metaphor can be used for training. On an airplane trip, I was once sitting next to a woman studying a tennis book. The book specified the proper form for each stroke. For hitting the ball at the net, the legs were supposed to be so many inches apart, shown in an illustration as the length of a racket. The arms should be at the proper height, elbows flexed at the proper angle (the illustration showed a protractor overlaid on the elbow), racket head facing the proper direction, and so forth. I could not imagine how anyone could ever swing at the ball, trying to remember so many rules. I compared that approach to the advice I once heard from an experienced instructor that "hitting a ball at the net is like pushing a pie into someone's face." In short, it was not like stroking the ball, hitting a forehand. It was a choppy motion. Although few of the students actually had pushed a pie into anyone's face, the metaphor was compelling. It achieved its effect of coordinating arms, legs, body, and timing for a difficult shot that most of the students had previously been hitting poorly. The instructor also taught the students that to hit a backhand in tennis they should try to imagine they were throwing a Frisbee.

Again, the metaphor provided an overall for body flow in performing the action. When an action is decomposed into its elements, the chore of coordinating those elements comes at the end. With a metaphor, the overall coordination *was* the starting point.

The Logic of Analogical Reasoning

In trying to understand how people solve ill-defined problems, one strategy is to try to reach a goal while simultaneously trying to define the goal, using failures to specify the goal more clearly. There is a second strategy: to find an analogy that suggested features of the goal. For instance, if my car will not start, my goal is to get the engine running. If I recall a time when I left the lights on by mistake and killed the battery, I might figure out that the lights run directly off the battery. Therefore, I could test whether the battery is okay by turning on the lights to see if they work. If they do not, then my problem is not the vague one of getting the engine started but the specific one of overcoming a dead battery. Analogical reasoning can also suggest options. If I drive a car with a manual transmission, perhaps I recall a time when I saw someone start such a car by letting it roll downhill, to get the engine started even without a working battery. But there are no hills near me. Perhaps I can have my passengers push the car to create the necessary force.

There are several hypotheses about how analogical reasoning works. One approach was the work of Robert Sternberg (1977), who studied the components of solving analogue problems a:b::c:d—for example, dog is to flea as shark is to flea as shark is to (whale, remora, eel, squid). The correct answer would be remora, since it attaches itself to the shark, rides along with it, and depends on it for food. Sternberg's research was carefully done and interesting, but this model of the components is not very helpful, for two reasons. One was that he was working on fairly artificial types of problems, with limited context. Even worse, Sternberg gave his subjects the second term of the analogue. He told them what analogue to use. In contrast, problem solvers have to find an appropriate analogy to use. In most cases, finding a good analogy is the hardest part of the job.

Another approach was offered by Amos Tvtrsky (1977), who had proposed a method for defining similarity in terms of the number of elements two items shared in common. This method could explain how people judged degree of similarity and satisfied themselves that a similar case was worth using. The difficulty is that every pair of items shares an infinite number of features in common. Take this book and your left shoe. They are both closer to the moon than the sun, both closer to the sun than to the center of the Milky Way, both lighter than your car, both larger than your mouth, and so on, forever. Merely counting common features would not work either. The features in common had to be important ones. They had to be features that had the same cause-and-effect relationships.

Julian Weitzenfeld (1984) determined that similarity does not make sense without purpose.[4] If your purpose is to start a car with a dead battery, letting it roll downhill and pushing it on a level stretch of highway are similar actions. If your purpose is to start a car that is out of gasoline, letting it roll down a hill to a nearby telephone booth is not the same as pushing it on a level stretch of highway. You cannot just look at the two actions—letting the car roll and actively pushing it—and determine if they are similar. It depends on what you want to do. A coffee can and an inner tube are both similar as containers for transporting gasoline. They are dissimilar as ways of maintaining an even pressure on the tires of a bicycle.

Weitzenfeld and I studied the way people actually used analogies.[5] We had discovered a community of engineers at Wright-Patterson Air Force Base who make extensive use of analogies to solve difficult problems. While Julian and I were thinking about how people apply analogues, this community was doing it every day.

The engineers we studied were faced with an important and difficult task: predicting the repair rates of the component parts of new airplanes before the airplanes were ever built. If the engineers overestimated the reliability, the air force would not stock up on enough spare parts; the airplanes might have to stop flying while manufacturers made more spares. If the engineers underestimated reliability, then the air force would have warehouses filled with unnecessary spare parts and waste taxpayers' money. It was important to make accurate predictions.

The engineers would have preferred to use an analytical method to figure out the reliability, but there were no good analytical methods for making the predictions. In 1971, two people figured out a strategy for the engineers to use. One was Major Don Tetmeyer, working in the U.S. Air Force's Directorate of Engineering at Wright-Patterson Air Force Base. The other was Frank Maher, a psychologist working for a private company near the base. The strategy they came up with was to use data on similar pieces of equipment. They called their method comparability analysis. It works in this way:

1. Define as well as you can the system whose reliability you want to predict.
2. Find the closest example possible of a similar system being used by the Defense Department.
3. Explain the rationale for selecting that system.
4. Gather the data on the reliability of that system.
5. Adjust the reliability data to reflect differences between that system and the one in which you are interested.
6. Explain the rationale for the adjustment.
7. Present the prediction for the planners to use.

Since comparability analysis was developed, it has been applied in the air force for a variety of new aircraft, and it is also widely used in the navy and the army.

Julian and I realized this was a good example of analogical reasoning. In studying the way comparability analysis had been used in predicting the reliability of the subsystems on a bomber, the B-1 aircraft, we found straightforward applications and some interesting twists. Here is an example of a straightforward case.

Example 12.1
Sizing Up the Ducts

The B-1 duct system is similar to the duct system of the FB-111 aircraft, except that the B-1 is larger and needs more ducting. Therefore the FB-111 numbers are adjusted upward by the right proportion. (In this example, "FB" stands for "fighter-bomber.")

Here is a slightly more complex case.

Example 12.2
Pressurizing the Hydraulic System

To estimate the reliability of the hydraulic system on the B-1 airplane, an engineer chooses as his comparison case the hydraulic system on the B-52, the airplane the B-1 is supposed to replace. However, the B-1 hydraulic is going to use 4,000 pounds per square inch of pressure, versus 3,000 psi for the B-52. The engineer recognizes that the higher pressure will cause increased wear and lower reliability, so he takes the reliability data for the B-52 hydraulic and reduces it by a third. He does not think the B-1 hydraulic system will be as reliable as the B-52.

Others might disagree with his estimate. They might claim that the new materials used in the B-1 would help things out. Even if they disagreed, they could see the rationale for his prediction, and they could add their own adjustments.

These predictions work in the following way. A set of factors affects the reliability of a hydraulic system. We know many of them, but not all of them, and we do not know how they interact with each other. If we can find an analogy with which we feel comfortable, we can use it because it reflects the full set of causal factors, even the ones we cannot yet identify. The analogy also reflects the interactions between causal factors, interactions we cannot specify, so it lets us make a prediction that reflects factors whose existence we do not know and whose properties we do not know. That is the power of analogical reasoning.

If we did not want to use analogical reasoning for tasks like these, we would be stuck. We would not know enough to construct formulas or to use them or have enough hard information to proceed. By using analogues, we are tapping into the same source of power for stories. We are applying an informal experiment, using a prior case with a known outcome and a semi-known set of causes to make predictions about a new case.

Example 12.3
Rejecting an Analogue That Is Identical

An engineer finds that the auxiliary power unit on the B-1 will be identical to the auxiliary power unit used on a cargo plane, the C-5A. The engineer judges that the demands on an auxiliary power unit from a bomber like the B-1 are going to be so different and so much greater than on a cargo plane that he throws out the C-5A data.

Bombers may have to scramble, which means starting up and taking off in a hurry without waiting for everything to warm up gradually. Unlike a cargo plane, all sorts of systems are started up at once, placing great burdens on the auxiliary power system. In addition, bombers may have to conduct sharp maneuvers to avoid enemy fighters and antiaircraft missiles. Cargo planes are not subjected to these types of forces. Because of the difference in the working environment, the engineer concluded that the data from cargo operations would not help him.

From these examples, Julian and I learned a great deal about how people use analogical reasoning in a natural setting.

First, we learned that they do not select analogues just based on similarity. If you are buying a green car, you do not try to find the reliability records for green cars. You would select an analogue that shares the same dynamics, the same factors that affect what you are trying to predict. If you do not have enough experience to take causal factors into account, you can get into trouble. The engineers we studied were all knowledgeable.

Later, when Chris Brezovic, Marvin Thordsen, and I studied the decision making of new tank platoon leaders, we found that analogical reasoning was about as likely to hurt them as to help them. For example, during one mission, the tank platoon leader decided to use a certain route because he had used it three days earlier, when the exercise had been in the same area. However, he was inexperienced. He did not consider the fact that it had rained heavily the night before. This time when he sent his tanks down that route, the first two got stuck in the mud, and the whole mission fell apart. He thought he had a perfect analogue for selecting a route that would work, but he missed a key difference.

Second, we learned that some causal factors are easy to adjust for, and others are not. If pressure affects the reliability of a hydraulic system, then even if I pick an analogue with a different pressurization, I can just multiply to get an estimate. That is easy. On the other hand, if the pattern of use affects the reliability of an auxiliary power unit because the strains of a bombing run are vastly different from the smooth profile of a cargo flight, then I do not know how to make this adjustment. As a result, I must throw the analogue out altogether, even if the equipment is identical. If the difference can be captured as a proportion, then the causal factor can be adjusted for. If it cannot be reduced to a proportion, then we would only try to guess at the adjustment if we were desperate. Julian concluded that we select analogues on the "mysterious" features (the qualitative categories that we cannot easily adjust) and adjust on the more straightforward features. We would select an analogue airplane that flew the same type of mission and adjust on a size dimension; we would not select an analogue that matched on size and adjust on type of mission.

Third, we learned that the logic of reasoning by analogy is similar to the logic of an experiment: to draw a conclusion without having to know all of the important factors operating. Imagine that someone comes back from the Brazilian rain forest with a new drug, derived from the leaves that grow above the canopy of vines and branches, and claims that the drug will cure AIDS. We might test it in an experiment by identifying AIDS victims to serve as subjects, randomly assigning them to an experimental group that gets the drug and a control group that does not. We would see if the AIDS patients in the experimental group improve, compared to the control group. If they do improve, we conclude that the drug had an effect. Notice that we draw this conclusion even though we do not know all the causes of AIDS, and we do not know how the causes we have identified interact. By randomly assigning the subjects, we could feel confident that the same causal factors were at work in the two groups, although we did not know what they were.

Similarly, when we use an analogy, we are trying to set up a condition where the same causal factors are at work, even though we do not know what they are. The analogue is selected to match on the causal variables as closely as possible, and we adjust the data to take into account aspects where we know the matching is inadequate. Sometimes we do not take into account variables that are important because we do not know about them. That is why we have less confidence in analogical reasoning than in the results of an experiment. Analogical reasoning is intended to be a guide in cases where we cannot set up experiments, cases where we do not know enough to work out the equations.

There is a delicate balance to using analogues. If we know a great amount, we do not need the analogues; we can just figure out the formulas. If we know very little, analogical reasoning may be as likely to get us into trouble as to help us. Analogical reasoning seems to help most when we are in between: we know something about the area but not enough for a satisfactory analysis. Just as we discussed in the previous chapter on the power of stories, an analogue represents a set of causal variables interacting with each other. By using and adjusting the analogue, we are making predictions that incorporate factors that we cannot identify.

The next question to investigate was how accurate these predictions are. To find out, I collected a set of predictions that had been made on the A-10 aircraft. I obtained the comparability analysis predictions made during the design of the A-10 and compared them to the actual reliability data. In the hands of experienced engineers, predictions made from analogies matched up fairly well with the actual data (Klein, 1986). The correlation between the A-10 predictions and the A-10 data on the mean time between failures was statistically significant at +.76. For another measure, mean maintenance hours per flying hour, the correlation was even higher, +.84.

Some predictions were not accurate. The correlation between predicted and actual repair time was only +.36. I found that these were cases where the engineers lacked solid data for the analogues chosen and had generated their own estimates. This lesson seems important. The method of using analogues uses so much subjective estimation that it needs to be grounded in hard data. If we make up the data that we then adjust, the accuracy drops.

Example 12.4
Predicting the Attendance at a Movie Theater

I live in a village, Yellow Springs, Ohio, with a population of less than 4,000. It has some pleasant restaurants and shops where artisans sell pottery, clothing, and paintings. And it has a wonderful movie theater, the Little Art, which plays movies that never come to multiplex theaters in malls.

Example 12.4 (continued)

Antioch College is aware of how important the theater is to the community, so when the theater is about to close, the college purchases it. The college does not want to lose money on the deal, so it requires the people running it to at least break even.

Jennie Cowperthwaite, the long-term manager of the theater, can no longer just show movies that are important or receive critical acclaim regardless of their popular appeal, like Orion's Belt. She needs to figure out which movies are going to attract large audiences. To help her out, Dan Friedman, in the Psychology Department at Antioch College (and also a movie fan), arranges for a student who needs an honors project to go through the Little Art database. The student assembles all the information the Little Art has gathered on all the movies they had shown in the previous ten years. Dan and the student and I figure out a set of categories for coding each movie: action/romance/political, American/British/subtitled, cartoon/documentary/revival, and so forth. The student enters these data into a database, and we analyze the trends. We can identify the types of movies that seem to draw the largest crowds and the ones that should never be booked again. When we are done, we have a chance for a study, using this database to make predictions about the attendance at future movies. The Little Art shows two movies a week. We select an upcoming eighteen-week span during which the theater is going to play thirty-five movies (one plays for a full week). For each movie, Dan and I try to find an analogue—a movie close to it—that had already played at the Little Art and is in the database. We retrieve the data on that movie, look at its characteristics, make the adjustments, and generate a prediction. We do this for all thirty-five movies. Next, we go to a control group of seventeen people who live or work in Yellow Springs and ask each to predict the attendance at each of the upcoming thirty-five movies.

We also collect one more data point. We ask Jennie, the manager, to make her predictions without using the database. Then Dan and I wait for the thirty-five movies to be shown to tally up the outcomes.

The control group predicts slightly better than chance. The correlation between their median (typical) predictions and the actual attendance is +.17—not very high. Jennie does much better. Her predictions correlate +.31 with the actual numbers. Dan and I are two amateurs who have never booked a movie in our lives. Our predictions correlate +.45, the highest of all. This is a tribute not to our experience or our math abilities, but to the fact that we used the database filled with analogues.

People regularly use analogical reasoning. If you want to sell your house, the realtor estimates its market value by calling up a database of houses that have recently been sold, to capture the current demand for houses in your area. The realtor looks for houses like yours—same neighborhood, same style. These are difficult variables to adjust for; it is easier to match on them and adjust for number of square feet and size of lot. If the house you are selling has a swimming pool but none of the good matches has one, the realtor may estimate the value of swimming pool separately by looking through the database for two houses that are virtually identical except for a swimming pool. The difference between them is the value of the pool, and the realtor can factor this into your home. The logic and the procedures are virtually identical to what the engineers were doing in estimating reliability, and to what Dan and I did to predict movie attendance.

This section has concentrated on one use of analogical reasoning— making predictions—as a way to illustrate how analogues are retrieved and modified. There are several other important ways that we use analogues: to generate expectancies, and solve problems.

Generating Expectancies

Analogues can be extended to help project what is going to happen in a new situation. Refer back to example 12.1, concerning the threat of a falling billboard at the scene of a fire. The commander looked up and saw a billboard on the top of the building. He remembered a previous fire, an analogue, in which the flames had burned through the wooden supports for a billboard, sending the billboard crashing down. The commander then ordered that the crowds of onlookers be moved back a safe distance in case the same thing should happen. The analogue provided him with an expectancy that he used to anticipate and avoid a potential problem. Analogues and metaphors also provide scientists with new hypotheses (Hesse, 1966) in some of the same ways that they provide decision maker with expectancies.

Solving Problems

Analogues provide the problem solver with a recommendation about what to do. In doing a homework assignment in mathematics, a student will look back through the notes to find any exercises that the teacher did can be used as a template, to follow the same strategy. The logic of this process is the same as the logic for making predictions: recall a previous case that had the same dynamics as the current one, identify the strategy used, modify it to meet the current requirements, and carry it out. Even if you do not have a chance to think it all through, you trust that the causal factors are roughly the same so the procedure should work; you have selected the analogue in the first place because it matches on the causal factors.

As we saw earlier, you need a certain amount of experience to use analogical reasoning reliably. Novices run the risk of missing important causal factors and therefore choosing the wrong example as a model or misapplying that example. If we want to help train novices, we might provide them with annotated examples. For example, a mathematics teacher might present a core set of examples to serve as analogues. For each example, the teacher could describe the choice points in the solution where someone might have taken the wrong path or chosen the wrong formula. The teacher could explain the cues the expert used in avoiding these traps. In that way, learners get the advantage of the examples along with guidance on the principles they have to learn to safely apply the examples.

System designers make frequent use of analogues. They draw on previous projects that they did or on other people's projects with which they are familiar. In studying the types of evidence and information on which designers rely, Klein and Brezovic (1986) found that design engineers prefer to gather firsthand evidence by running little demonstrations using mockups. When demonstrations are impractical, the design engineers looked for previous systems to serve as analogues. They used these analogues to tell them what tolerances to use, what configurations, and so forth.

We have also seen designers run into trouble by misusing analogues. In the following example, the designers ignored important causal factors and believed they had a match when they should have rejected the analogue.

Example 12.5
A Case Where AWACS Was the Wrong Analogue

The joint surveillance target attack radar system (JSTARS) is a new aircraft designed to fly close to battle lines and look down at the adversary's movements. JSTARS is going to be flying as close to the battle lines as possible, putting it in the range of anti-aircraft weapons. Because of the risk, JSTARS needs to have a dedicated workstation to manage its own defense. The designers try to understand what needs to go into this self-defense suite and use the AWACS aircraft as an analogue.

The designers conclude that self-defense will not be much of a problem, because it has not been a problem for AWACS. Both aircraft are slow moving and not very maneuverable. AWACS has a large number of weapons directors at radar scopes to keep an eye out for trouble, and JSTARS will also have a number of people at radar scopes. It seems like a good analogue, transferring the AWACS experience to JSTARS—except that JSTARS will not have dedicated air support, interceptors whose primary task is to protect it, the way AWACS does. Also, the people on the radar scopes will be searching the ground for enemy movement. In AWACS, the weapons directors are looking at the air picture. JSTARS has very little capability for looking out for airplanes that might be attacking it, whereas AWACS can see for hundreds of miles away. AWACS is a secure platform, whereas JSTARS is a giant kick-me sign in the sky. It will be flying a slow and predictable course, generating lots of electrical signals for an enemy to home in on. In our judgment, the AWACS analogue misled the original design team so they did not give the self-defense function sufficient attention.

During Operation Desert Storm, the U.S. Air Force did use JSTARS. However, it made sure that there were no enemy fighters or anti-aircraft batteries around, and they provided escorts of friendly fighters to protect JSTARS.

Applications

Two types of application stand out: using analogues in comparability analysis, and using them in advanced computer reasoning systems.[6]

The technique of comparability analysis has been used for many different functions during the past twenty years. It has also been misused, most notably by careless technicians who did not bother making adjustments. For instance, in one case the reliability data for a piece of naval equipment were simply plugged into an army project, ignoring the fact that ships tend to float smoothly, whereas tanks and trucks bounce around.

The predictions were not accurate. Failures such as this will reduce the credibility of the method even though the failure was in the application of the method. The method was misused because the people applying it did not understand the logic behind it.

In our own work on analogical reasoning, we found scant opportunity to use comparability analysis. Most people are fully capable of reasoning by analogy themselves. We cannot do much except to give a technical name to what they are already doing. We prepared a description of how to do a more thorough job of using analogues in making predictions. We found that most people are fairly satisfied and do not want to go to the extra effort.

One type of assistance is to build a computer-based system for helping people retrieve and use analogues, or prior cases. Computer scientists have been exploring the use of systems based on analogical reasoning to overcome the weaknesses of the rule-based expert systems. Roger Schank (now at Northwestern University) was one of the leaders of this movement, along with Janet Kolodner (Georgia Tech University) and Kris Hammond (University of Chicago). Edwina Rissland (University of Massachusetts) has studied the use of case-based reasoning for providing legal advice. Several case-based reasoning shells are currently available.[7] Here is an example of one of the case-based reasoning projects on which we worked. This project, sponsored by the Air Force Materials Laboratory, was intended to demonstrate how analogical reasoning could be applied in the area of manufacturing.

Example 12.6
Bidder's Associate

Most manufacturing companies keep records of previous work, and these records could be a valuable database for making bids on future work. However, the data are kept by part number, and when time is short, the marketing department may not be able to find the right case. Maybe someone will remember, "Hey, didn't we make something like that three years ago?" and then, with luck they may track down the part number and find out what it had cost. More often, the reply will be, "You may be right, but I have no idea how to dig that out," so they will start from scratch in preparing their bid.

We set up a working relationship with a manufacturing company near us, Enginetics, a job shop that makes jet engine parts to order. In contrast

Example 12.6 (continued)

to companies that turn out the same part again and again, firms like Enginetics are called on to make the unique parts of which people need only a few copies. With each new job, they are challenged to determine if they can make it, and, if so, what process they will use. They have to trade off the costs of the processes (e.g., bore the holes on this machine, then shape it on that machine, and so forth), against the time needed for each step and even the scrap materials. It may be easier to make it one way, but they will wind up with too much scrap, so it is better to use a different strategy. They even have to take their own learning curve into account. There may be a clever new approach, but they know it might take them four to five runs before they get it right, and they do not have enough time or profit margin to gamble. Each job is a new problem to be solved.

Our agreement is to build a system to help the marketing staff find and use prior cases. This is a case-based reasoning system, although the system does not do much reasoning; its primary value is helping the planners find relevant cases and use the information contained in them. We help them assemble their corporate history, the jobs they bid (including the ones they lost), and the history of manufacturing the parts for the jobs they won. Buzz Reed, the CEO of my company, and David Klinger performed this project. Their system is called Bidder's Associate.

Bidder's Associate uses the existing database. In preparing a bid on a new part, it lets the staff rapidly search through their files to see if they had made anything like it in the past. Sometimes they find a previous instance with the same part number, which is great, unless the costs of materials or something like that have changed. More often, there are no simple matches, and the system has to find similar cases. We code the previous cases on several features, such as size, type of material, and even popular names. For example, a round part that has slots cut into it was given the nickname "turkey feather assembly." That is how everyone refers to it, so that gets put into its file to help in retrieval.

Bidder's Associate finds a number of similar cases and lets the operator pick which one(s) to work with, to adjust. The output is a documented bid with the cost categories so that everyone will know the reasoning behind the bid. The output includes a concept of how the part will be made if Enginetics wins the bid. The system allows bids to be prepared with less time and effort, and the company also has more confidence in these bids.

Bidder's Associate is delivered in 1989. The first time a process engineer uses Bidder's Associate, the first case that pops up on the screen is nearly a perfect match, a part they made two years ago. He had not worked on the earlier project, but be recognizes that it is a mirror image of the one he is bidding on. He reads that the earlier part had a 30 percent scrap rate, so he goes to the shop floor and finds that the scrap rate can now be drastically reduced. He is able to prepare a bid with a dear idea of how the company will manufacture the item.

Key Points

- Metaphors and analogues direct thinking by framing situation awareness, identifying appropriate goals, and flagging relevant pieces of information.
- Analogues provide a structure for making predictions when there are many unknown factors.
- Analogues function like experiments, linking interactive sets of causes to outcomes.
- By taking into account the difference between the analogue and the current case, we can adjust the analogue data to derive a prediction.
- Analogical predictions are most helpful when there is a good database but not enough information to apply more rigorous analyses.
- Analogues are useful for generating expectancies and solving problems.

13

The Power to Read Minds

It happens too many times. You send someone on an errand, a simple one, and the person gets it wrong. Maybe you are trying to repair a coffee mug, and you ask your spouse to add glue to the shopping list. Your spouse comes back with a glue that does not work on ceramic, and when you try to explain why it is not satisfactory, he or she answers, "You didn't say anything about a mug. You asked for glue, and that's what I bought. Was I supposed to read your mind?" Or you ask a child to clean up a room, and he picks up everything that was on the floor so it can be vacuumed. You return and complain that you have company coming in five minutes and the room is a mess; there isn't even a chair to sit on, and he says, "I did what you asked. You didn't say anything about company. Was I supposed to read your mind?"

The answer is yes. Whenever we make a request—ask for an errand or give a command—we need the person to read our mind. To make this possible, both parties have to extend themselves. The person making the request can help by specifying the intent behind the request. The person trying to carry out the request has to imagine what the other person really wants, to handle all the details that did not get explained.

"Please pick up some glue at the hardware store since you'll be going to shop next door anyway" does not sound like a difficult request. But when you walk into the hardware store, you find that there are different types of glues: for wood, for glass, for metal. Some are advertised as superglues that will never fail. Is that good or bad? Might I want to dissolve the glue later? So I really should tell you why I wanted the glue: to repair a ceramic mug, my favorite one. The handle has come off, and it has a small crack, but I believe it can be salvaged as a home for a small plant and stay around like an old friend. You are moved by my devotion to pottery, and agree. Now that you know my intent, you can select the right type of glue and the right amount—the smallest tube the store sells. But wait. Is that economical? How much ceramic glue would I need in the coming months, and what are the chances that this tube will dry up or get lost? You would have to know me and my glue-using habits to make this choice. Perhaps I should have told you the size, but it never occurred to me, and besides, I do not know what sizes the tubes come in.

Then you run into another choice: quick drying or not? That depends on how the mug was broken, and if it was a clean break, whether I have a vise for clamping the pieces together. Is it better to leave me holding the pieces together for hours? Yet if you get me the quick-drying kind and I clamp the pieces together incorrectly, it could be very hard, or impossible, to pull them apart and reconnect them. You also need to know something about my manual dexterity. This is a tougher job than it seemed. You may find yourself using mental simulation to imagine my using the different kinds of glues. The better you know me, the better you will be able to carry out the errand successfully, because you will be able to read my mind and take into account all the things I did not say.

Usually we cannot specify all these details in advance. If you are doing a favor for me, I have to rely on your ability to read my mind and imagine how I would have made all the choices. I do not believe I could anticipate all the relevant details to tell you. There are some people I do not trust, and I do not give them difficult errands.

Being able to read someone's mind is an important ability for working with others. In example 13.1, the decision makers chose to follow their orders literally, without trying to read the mind of the person who issued the orders.[1]

Example 13.1
The Escape of the *Goeben*

The *Goeben* was a German battleship stationed in the Mediterranean Sea at the start of World War I. The British Navy was supposed to find and destroy it once war was officially declared. The British failed; they had the *Goeben* surrounded but became confused about the intentions of the admiralty, so they let the *Goeben* escape through the Dardanelles and into the Black Sea, where it forced the Ottoman government to enter the war on the side of Germany (which resulted in the loss of its empire and the creation

Example 13.1 (continued)

of the British Mandate in the Near East). The *Goeben* also bottled up 95 percent of the Russian shipping (since their only warm water ports were on the Black Sea), helping to create the hardships that led to the Russian Revolution.

In the days preceding the war, Britain knew that it would have to eliminate the *Goeben*, the only German threat in the Mediterranean. The British ships kept a continual search for it and trailed it as much as possible. They were waiting for the beginning of the war, when they would be permitted to sink the *Goeben*.

Once war was declared by England, at 11:00 P.M. August 4, 1914, the *Goeben* managed to stay out of sight for a few days. Eventually it was located and surrounded by a dozen British ships. Unfortunately, the commander of these forces was unsure how to interpret the directions sent on July 31 by Winston Churchill, the head of the Admiralty. The instructions to hunt down the *Goeben* included the direction, "... do not at this stage be brought to action against superior forces."

Churchill wanted the *Goeben* destroyed. He also was aware of the heavy Austrian battle wagons and wanted the British to be careful with these, hence the warning not to become engaged against superior forces. Churchill's intent in this warning was for his ships to steer clear of the Austrians. However, Rear Admiral Sir Ernest Troubridge, the commander of the ships surrounding the *Goeben*, felt that the sentence could also be applied to his own situation. Technically, the *Goeben* was larger than any single one of his own ships and had larger cannon. He debated what to do and decided that the safest course was to regroup rather than run any risks. By letting the *Goeben* pass, it escaped east, into the Black Sea.

When Churchill heard about what had happened, he was staggered. He had never intended for his message to be interpreted the way that it was.

The commander was unable to read Winston Churchill's mind, to fathom the intent behind the sentence requesting care in engaging superior forces. In hindsight, Churchill could have avoided the error if he had added more information about the Austrian ships. His eagerness to attack the *Goeben* should have been sufficient. If he had tried to clarify every point in every order, to prevent any ambiguity, the job would have been impossible. The resulting documentation would have tied up the communications lines, and the important points would have been submerged in the flood of details and clarifications.

The answer is not to pile on the details. That takes too long, and it has its own costs. We may want to pretend that rules and procedures are simple and but they are not. For example, if you give someone the direction to press a button when a green light comes on and the person asks, "What is green?" there is no way to respond. You could explain "green" is light at a wavelength of 530 to 570 millimicrons, but that information is unlikely to be helpful. We assume that living in a shared culture will provide us a basis of common referents. If we have to labor at breaking out all of the assumptions behind requests, teamwork and cooperation would become almost impossible.

One place where we can see the importance of giving and understanding requests is in flying airplanes. When each member of an aircrew does not have the same understanding of what is intended, the results can be tragic. Many taped conversations recovered after crashes document the failure of different members of the aircrew to understand what others want to do. We had a chance to observe this ourselves in a study we did for NASA, using actual aircrews flying missions in the NASA 727 full flight simulator. This was a project to observe team coordination and decision making during difficult conditions. Marvin Thordsen and I watched several aircrews react to simulated malfunctions. The crews were composed of a captain, copilot, and flight engineer.

Example 13.2
Combat Inside the Cockpit

One of the malfunctions is an unusual fuel leak from the number 3 tank, in the right wing. We watch three crews, and in two of them the captain and the flight engineer disagree.

In addition to the obvious problem of not being able to fly as far because of fuel loss, the captains are concerned about a secondary implication, loss of balance. Since the tank is in the right wing, that wing will get lighter as the fuel leaks out. Therefore, the plane will be difficult to control during landing. In fact, this is the more serious problem since the airplane has sufficient fuel to divert to nearby airports.

In each case, the captains tell the flight engineers to reconfigure the fuel flow so that all engines are fed from the good tank, in the left wing. The intent is to draw down this fuel supply, lighten up the other wing, and restore balance. Nevertheless, in each case, the flight engineers resist or misunderstand the request. Since the flight engineers are responsible only for monitoring and managing the fuel flow and not for handling the controls, they are more worried about a shortage of fuel. In one case, the captain has to swivel completely around in his chair (giving up the task of flying the plane

Example 13.2 (continued)

to the copilot) to check on what the flight engineer is doing. He sees that the flight engineer had not carried out his request and is still using the fuel from the number 3 tank. This configuration is not what he wants. The flight engineer explains how this will make sure they do not waste any fuel. The captain is unable to persuade the flight engineer to make the changes until the copilot comes to his rescue. Finally, the flight engineer bows to their wishes. When the airplane lands, the imbalance in weight is 2,000 pounds between the two wings. In a second flight, with a different crew, the captain is never able to explain his wishes to the flight engineer. This airplane lands with a 5,000 pound imbalance. The recommended maximum imbalance for safe flying is officially set at 1,000 pounds.

The problem was not that the flight engineers were simply mishearing what the captains were requesting. Rather, they were not grasping what the captains wanted to do. The captains asked for a reconfiguration and thought the reason would be obvious. The flight engineers reinterpreted the request into something that made more sense to them. If the one captain had not turned to look back, he may never have known what the flight engineer was doing and would not have realized he was being misunderstood. The flight engineer was unable to figure out that the captain was asking for an unusual reconfiguration; he could not read the captain's mind.

If we can work with people who understand the culture, the task, and what we are trying to accomplish, then we can trust them to read our minds and fill in unspecified details. A team that has much experience working together can outperform a newly assembled team.

A study was once done for NASA (Foushee, Lauber, Baetge, & Acomb, 1986) to investigate the effect of fatigue on performance. Flight crews were asked to fly eight-hour missions in a high-fidelity simulator. The researchers presented the same malfunctions at the beginning of the flights for some crews and at the end for others. They expected that the crews would react better at the beginning, when they were fresh. The results were the opposite: the crew members did better at the end of their missions. Their advantage was all they had learned about working together. They learned to anticipate how each member would react, and they became adept at reading each other's mind.

Flight crews are not the only teams to wrestle with the problem of guessing intent.[2]

Example 13.3
The Fatal Tug-of-War

During an operation, the surgeon decides to lower the patient's blood pressure. He directs the anesthesiologist to give the patient a drug that will have this effect, but does not explain what he is trying to accomplish. The anesthesiologist gives the drug, notes that the patient's blood pressure goes down, and boosts the level of another drug that will increase the blood pressure. To the anesthesiologist, this is standard operating procedure to keep the patient's vital signs stable. The surgeon notes that the blood pressure is higher than he wants and directs the anesthesiologist to increase the dosage of the first drug. The anesthesiologist follows the request, watches for the blood pressure to reduce, and then boosts the drug that will return the blood pressure to its normal level. This cycle continues until the patient ends the game by dying.

When I am at work, no one does a better job of reading my mind than Barbara Law, who has worked with me since 1979, longer than any of my other colleagues. No matter who else has reviewed an article or manuscript, I am uneasy unless she has had a chance to go through it.

Example 13.4
My Safety Net

I complete a draft of a paper on how to communicate intent and give it to Barbara to edit before we send it out. She notices that I am citing some data from another study we have recently finished. Just to be safe, she goes into the files to make sure all the numbers match. She finds one or two discrepancies, and since I am not around, she brings them to George Kaempf, the lead author of that study, to clarify. She knows that I want to send the draft to Jim Banks, one of our sponsors at the Army Research Institute Field Unit in Monterey. She also knows that Jim had recently seen George Kaempf's paper. She wants to make sure Jim does not find any mismatches between the two. When George cannot resolve one of the discrepancies, Barbara takes the initiative of holding up the draft. She reasons that it is more important to get the details straight than to rush out my manuscript.

Now compare this example to another incident that took place in my company.

Example 13.5
Marvin's Mouse

One of Marvin Thordsen's jobs is to keep our computer systems working. One day there is a malfunction in the mouse used to operate one of our more powerful systems, and it cannot be repaired. Marvin sends in a request to purchase a replacement. To make sure the request is perfectly clear, he tracks down when the original mouse had been ordered and writes that he wants the exact same mouse, and he even includes the date on the earlier purchase order for reference. He believes he has covered all bases. He has done a careful and thorough job. There should be no ambiguity.

To Marvin's surprise, the replacement mouse doesn't work; it doesn't even fit. Somehow the front office has ordered the wrong one. In tracking down the reason, Marvin finds that the hardware company no longer makes the original mouse.

The front office had assumed that Marvin was trying to indicate the company he preferred to order from. It contacted that company and ordered the mouse that was closest in price to the original. They were not aware that there was a compatibility problem, that not all mice fit all machines. Besides, Marvin was traveling when they ordered the mouse, so they couldn't ask him, and he seemed to want the replacement quickly. They wanted to show how responsive they were.

Here the front office tried to read Marvin's mind, and failed. They thought they knew what he was after: an inexpensive model from the same company. They did not have the experience to know about hardware compatibility issues. Marvin knew they lacked computer hardware experience, and that was why he tried to make the task easy by digging up the old invoice with the part number. In hindsight, he realized that he should have explicitly told them he needed an inexpensive mouse that he could use on that specific computer model. That way they would have known more about his intent. They could have improvised better when the original mouse was unavailable. By telling the front office exactly what to do but not giving the rationale, he was leaving them vulnerable when the original plan fell apart.

In contrast, look at example 13.4. I gave Barbara Law virtually no instructions other than to review my manuscript. Because of her experience, she could detect a potential problem (the mismatch in numbers), see the bigger picture (a friend and sponsor might also notice the mismatch), anticipate the impact (slight loss of credibility), balance the priorities (fixing the problem versus getting the draft out quickly), and take the initiative to decide on holding up the draft. She could do all these things because she knows my priorities and the things that have bothered me in the past. She could therefore anticipate what I really wanted here.

Intent

On a team, a number of things can happen when there is a shared understanding of what the team is intending to do. Table 13.1 lists some outcomes we have seen when the people on the team understand its intent, in contrast to situations where people are told what to do without understanding why. When you communicate intent, you are letting the other team members operate more independently and improvise as necessary. You are giving them a basis for reading your mind more accurately.

One important function is to increase independence so that team members need less attention and monitoring. They can evaluate whether they are making progress. If you just tell me a sequence of steps to carry out, I am always wondering if I am doing them right ("Is this what you wanted?") and waiting for permission to start the next step. When you have asked me to do something and we both know the goal, I should be able to perform at a higher level. I should be better able to tell if I am making a mistake. Additionally, I can make better use of my

Table 13.1
Functions of Communicating Intent

Promote independence
Improve team performance by reducing need for clarifications
Detect deviations from the assumptions made by the leader
Catch errors in advance and anticipate problems
Promote improvisation
React to local conditions without having to wait for permission
Recognize opportunities that were not part of the plan
Set priorities in order to make trade-off decisions
Continue beyond the outcome without having to wait for the next order

experience to notice errors in your planning, along with problems that might arise.

If I run into problems while carrying out the task, I may warn you that the goals were wrong.

The other primary function of communicating intent is to allow better improvisation. We do not want everyone on a team freelancing. That becomes chaotic. Remember how the front office improvised and ordered the wrong mouse. Still, we must accept that few of us can think out all the contingencies in advance, and unless we want to direct every step our teammates take, we are going to have to cede responsibilities, including judgments about how and when to carry out critical tasks. When team members understand the intent and reasoning behind a task, they will be better able to improvise. They will adjust to the field conditions that the planners cannot know about, by finding ways to jury-rig solutions when the plan starts to run into trouble. They will recognize opportunities no one expected. They should be able to understand the goals well enough to set and revise priorities, to decide when to grasp an opportunity and when to let it go. And if they complete a task before receiving more instructions, they will be able to proceed on to the next task rather than wait.

Larry Shattuck (1995), a U. S. Army Lieutenant Colonel currently heading the human factors program at West Point, did a study on Commander's Intent statements, used to explain the purpose for carrying out a plan. He presented military operations plans to battalion commanders serving in the field. Each battalion commander read and interpreted the plan and communicated his intent to his own company commanders using a variety of methods, including a Commander's Intent statement, operations orders, and briefings. They relied on the standard procedures that they had been using together for months. Then Shattuck interviewed the battalion commanders to find out how they wanted their company commanders to react to an unexpected development in the scenario. Next, Shattuck videotaped company commanders as they described how they would react. The company commanders' responses matched those of their battalion commander only 34 percent of the time. When Shattuck told the battalion commanders how their subordinates had adjusted, a common response was, "Why did he do that?"

There have been some documented examples of organizations that have worked to create independence and improvisation. According to the military historian Trevor Dupuy (1977), the Prussian Army created such an organization following their lackluster showings against Napoleon. They regrouped and established a professional force that showed its superiority in war during the next century. Despite what we have heard about German officers excusing themselves by claiming they were only following orders, the reality is quite different. German officers were expected to use independent thinking. The culture of the German Army is illustrated by a famous story described by Dupuy, about the strategy of mission tactics used by Prussian military leaders in the late nineteenth century.

Example 13.6
The Soldiers Who Were Trained Not to Follow Orders

A major, receiving a tongue lashing from Prince Frederick Charles for a tactical blunder, offered the excuse that he had been obeying orders. He reminded the prince that a Prussian officer was taught that an order from a superior was tantamount to an order from the king. Frederick Charles promptly responded, "His Majesty made you a major because he believed you would know when *not* to obey his orders."

It is easy to say we want to encourage improvisation and initiative and to make sure that people understand why they have been given certain assignments. In reality, this practice turns out to be difficult, because it means that the people at the higher echelons must give up some of their control. The U.S. Army has sought to accomplish this, with mixed results.

A technique the U.S. Army has tried is to issue Commander's Intent statements along with its mission orders, or operations orders, which give the details of the plan for the next day. The Commander's Intent statement helps the soldiers read the commander's mind if they run into uncertainty about how to carry out the orders under field conditions.

Some research on how well the Commander's Intent statements work has centered on the National Training Center in the high desert of California. Here, the U.S. Army mounts realistic training exercises using sophisticated laser and computer systems to keep track of opposing forces during battle. A brigade commander might drill his troops for months to prepare them for the National Training Center. Once they arrive, they face a nonstop series of battles for almost two weeks straight, learning to function despite fatigue and stress. Some observers have attributed the army's success in Operation Desert Storm to experiences gained at the National Training Center.

In one study of field exercises at the center, William Crain (1990) found that only 19 percent of the Commander's Intent statements said anything about the purpose of the mission and that communication of intent was mediocre. We have found the same thing. George Kaempf's study investigating the Commander's Intent statements at the National Training Center found great variation.[3] The shortest statement was all of 21 words, and the longest in our sample was 484 words. We asked domain experts to evaluate the effectiveness of a set of thirty-five statements. The average rating was below the midpoint of the scale, closer to very ineffective than to very effective.

A large part of this problem stems from the mysterious nature of intent itself. What does it mean to understand someone else's intent? If you could interrogate the person giving the orders, what would you ask? What knowledge do we need to understand what someone else wants?[4]

Considerations in Communicating Intent

In observing teams and reviewing their attempts to communicate goals, I have identified a few types of information that are important for describing intent (Klein, 1994). There are seven types of information that a person could present to help the people receiving the request to understand what to do:

1. The purpose of the task (the higher-level goals).
2. The objective of the task (an image of the desired outcome).
3. The sequence of steps in the plan.
4. The rationale for the plan.
5. The key decisions that may have to be made.
6. Antigoals (unwanted outcomes).
7. Constraints and other considerations.

All seven types of information are not always necessary. Instead, this list can be used as a checklist, to determine if there are any more details to add. In my company, whenever we begin a new project, we go through the relevant items in the checklist. We try to make sure that everyone working on the project has the same understanding of what we are after.

The first facet is the most obvious: to provide the big picture of why the task is being performed in the first place. When I reviewed the thirty-five Commander's Intent statements that George Kaempf and I had analyzed, this facet appeared in only fourteen of the statements, usually with just a single comment. This was the facet Crain found only 19 percent of the time. This was the facet Marvin Thordsen did not provide in example 13.5, when he received the wrong mouse. This was the facet Winston Churchill did not offer when he said that British ships were to avoid superior forces.

The second facet presents an image of what the successfully completed request will look like. This is almost always included. In my review of the thirty-five Commander's Intent statements, it was missing only once. But in about a third of the statements, the facet was described with the bare minimum, for example, "This is a defensive mission to defend at Phase Line Cigar." It would be like my sending you to the hardware store with the goal of buying me some glue. Your chances of success will go up if I give you a better picture of success: "I expect you to return with a small tube of ceramic glue sometime this afternoon." This image, together with the contents of the first facet, "so I can repair my coffee mug this evening," should do the trick.

The third facet is the plan—another place where people run into trouble. They try to pile on the details of how to carry out the assignment rather than giving the big picture. This was where Marvin went wrong in ordering the mouse. In the thirty-five Commander's Intent statements I reviewed, this facet got the most attention. It was included in thirty-two of the thirty-five statements and was the subject of about 40 percent of the comments. The commanders were telling their troops what steps to take rather than letting the troops understand what was in the minds of the commanders and the planning staff officers. Colonel Hanan Schwartz of the Israeli Defense Forces has argued that the plan should be left to the discretion of the unit carrying it out. Let them figure out how to achieve the mission. If you do not trust them, get others or do a better job of training. Just do not fall into the trap of choreographing each of their movements.

The fourth facet is the reasoning behind the plan. Here is where you can explain the rationale for the plan and even describe the thinking behind drawing up the plan. This is another opportunity to let someone see inside your head, to carry that knowledge along when putting the plan into action. In the formal Commander's Intent statements, this information was given thirty-one times in the thirty-five examples, usually in combination with 3, the plan itself. If I am sending you to the store for glue, I might explain that my plan is for you to save effort by first doing your grocery shopping since you might find the glue in the hardware section of the supermarket. If that does not work, you can go to the hardware store. Notice that by telling you the rationale, I am giving you a chance to suggest a different plan. You might prefer to pick up the glue first, since it is light and nonperishable, and then go buy your groceries. It does not make sense to buy the groceries first and then carry all the sacks and the frozen items with you into the hardware store.

The fifth facet gets you ready to make key decisions. There might be contingencies to expect: "Sometimes the hardware store gets crowded; if that happens, go to the supermarket first." There might be priorities to set: "If the hardware store is still jammed when you come out of the supermarket and it looks as if you'll have to wait fifteen or twenty minutes, skip it. It's no big deal. I'll run over there myself tonight." I found that thirteen of the thirty-five Commander's Intent statement included some information about key decisions and priorities. Colonel Schwartz has suggested that this could also describe known weaknesses in the plan, to help subordinates know the thinking of the planners and recognize when the plan might be breaking down. None of the statements I reviewed mentioned any weaknesses in the plans.

The sixth facet refers to antigoals, outcomes you do not want to happen. Information is meaningful only in the context of alternatives. If I tell you my intent is to win this battle, that does not add any real information.

Antigoals come in when there are meaningful alternatives to clarify.[5] In one of the Commander's Intent statements, the mission was to delay an enemy advance. The plan was to use artillery to slow the enemy down, and the commander added, "Do not become decisively engaged." He realized that during a defensive mission, it is easy to take a stand and get into direct combat, and he did not want that to happen. He felt that there was enough of a chance of his troops getting into a battle that it was worth telling them what he did not want. We cannot detail every outcome we do not want to see. Nevertheless, there are times when it can pay off to clarify what is intended by saying what is not intended. The facet of antigoals was added in five of the thirty-five statements.

The seventh facet includes constraints that should be taken into account and extra information—little observations such as "watch out for this" and "you might try to use that." In sending off a rookie driver on an errand, we might add, "There is a chance it will start raining. We haven't had rain in awhile, so the roads might get slippery. Be careful." In the Commander's Intent statements, these observations were usually about the terrain and about weather.

Besides these seven facets, I was tempted to add some more to cover time and resources. It seemed that a good description of intent should include an instruction about when the task should be completed and at what cost (e.g., dollars, hours, casualties). Hanan Schwartz convinced me to abandon this idea. He explained that a commander or leader who specifies time and resources is micromanaging. The effective commander needs to provide a sufficiently clear picture of the overall mission, including the potential follow-up. This information lets the subordinates make their own decisions about how best to achieve the task and the higher-level goals. There may be times to adhere to strict timetables and budgets. More often, in chaotic natural settings, schedules will slide, and resources will shrink or expand over the life of a project or mission. Decision makers who believe they can pursue the goals within the initial constraints are too inflexible. You want them listening to what is happening all over so they can adapt, slow down or speed up as is needed. Since one purpose of a Commander's Intent statement is to allow flexibility and improvisation, you do not want to restrict flexibility to adapt to changing conditions.

Karl Weick (1983) has described a streamlined version of a Commander's Intent statement. In Weick's version, these are five facets:

- Here's what I think we face.
- Here's what I think we should do.

- Here's why.
- Here's what we should keep our eye on.
- Now, talk to me.

The Commander's Intent statement is representative of any organizational setting where someone has to describe to others what they are supposed to be doing. Industry, educational settings, health care—all depend on the ability to communicate goals to others and to request clarification of goals where needed.

The art of describing your intent is to give as little information as you can. The more details you pack in, the more you obscure your main points. However, if you leave out an important consideration, you run the risk that the person will become confused at a critical decision point.

In framing the description of your intent, you will probably take into account the expertise of the person or team, the stability of the situation, and your ability to imagine what the outcome might look like.

With more experienced team members, you can concentrate on higher-level goals. If they are less experienced, you have to specify more of the small steps in the plan. In a fluid and unstable situation, you might not want to state any antigoals because things might shift around, and you might change your mind. When your goals are ill defined (you are not clear what outcome you seek), you might give more attention to the key decision points because your image of the outcome might change depending on how the plan goes.

In teams that work together well, the people carrying out the assignments seem to be able to imagine what the leaders and planners were thinking. The people in the field can carry out the plan without needing continual direction from the higher authorities. The better they can do this, the more decisively they can act. It also helps to have common experience, to have worked with the leader enough to anticipate his or her reactions.

The concept of intent can be applied to equipment as well as to people. Particularly in working with sophisticated computer equipment, we struggle to figure out what the machine is trying to do. For example, as commercial airliners become more technologically sophisticated, they include a range of decision support systems. One of these is the flight management system, which helps track the course that an airplane takes from the time it takes off until it lands. This replaces the autopilot and adds to the computerized capability of keeping the plane on course at the correct speed, vectored in the right direction. George Kaempf managed a project funded by NASA in which we studied Flight Management Systems (Kaempf, Klein, & Thordsen, 1991). We found that computer systems also need to communicate intent.

Example 13.7
The Flight Mismanagement System

An airplane is on a routine flight from the West Coast to the East Coast. It is a red eye special and is flying above 30,000 feet. It is 3:30 A.M.

A company employee riding in the jumpseat of the cockpit kicks the rudder control blade by mistake, so that the rudder deflects to an extreme position. At the time of this incident, the switch was located close to the floor, behind a pedestal and thereby shielded from view. No one sees that the control has been displaced, and the flight management system does not notify the crew.

Up to this point, the flight is routine. When the rudder control blade is kicked, the flight management system responds by compensating with other flight controls to keep the aircraft in straight and level flight. The crew notices no change, and the flight management system does not signal to the crew that anything unusual has happened. Because the rudder control blade has been left at an inappropriate setting, the flight management system continues to compensate.

When the flight management system reaches its limit, it gives up. It turns off, handing the controls back to the unsuspecting pilots, with the aircraft in an out-of-tolerance condition. Without warning, the aircraft stalls and begins to plummet. The crew first believes it has an engine problem. To regain control, the crew takes a number of ineffective actions that only make the problem worse. The airplane is falling and increasing in speed.

The story has a happy ending. The pilots are able to wrestle the plane back under control, pulling it out of the steep dive. They eventually figure out what has gone wrong and reset the rudder. But after that, it is hard for the pilots to trust the flight management system fully again.

One problem with the flight management system was that the pilots could not anticipate what the system was going to do. According to Earl Wiener (1989), the questions regarding automated systems most often heard during nonroutine events are: "What is it doing? Why is it doing that? What is it going to do next?" The system was doing a poor job of describing what it was trying to do. The challenge for designers is to figure out how to let systems like these signal their intent. We do not want them spewing forth endless data about every goal and subgoal. These systems have to be able to identify the appropriate times to convey intent and the appropriate level and format for doing it. Only then will the human team members feel that they can read the "minds" of their computer colleagues and feel comfortable working with them.

Applications

There are several possible ways to use what we know about describing intent. One is to prepare training so that people who regularly need to direct others can improve their skills. It may only take a few minutes at the beginning of a project to describe the intent clearly. The benefits of providing a clear description of intent—mistakes that are not committed, requests for help that are not made—are not easy to see.

Once we carefully watched an U. S. Army officer lay out his intent at the beginning of an exercise at the Army War College. We were impressed by his thoroughness, but we grew bored watching his team in action. They were not making interesting mistakes. Unlike the other teams, his team was not going off in wrong directions or getting into conflicts. Everyone knew what to do, and the assignment went off uneventfully. That is what seems to happen when intent is clear from the beginning.

To improve the ability to communicate intent, we cannot try to teach a checklist or set of procedures. A more valuable approach is to set up exercises to provide feedback to leaders about how well their intent is understood. Our training is based on the work of Lieutenant Colonel Larry Shattuck. We arrange for team leaders to describe their intent. Then the person running the exercise identifies an unexpected event that might occur. The leader writes down how he or she expects the subordinates to react, and at the same time the subordinates write down how they think they are supposed to react. Then we compare notes. Obviously, there are going to be mismatches and surprises, and we use those to figure out how the intent should have been phrased to provide guidance that would be more robust. We have applied this training with U.S. Marine Corps squad leaders, who felt that it was very helpful in preparing for field exercises.

Key Points

- Communicating intent helps a team member to read the mind of the person requesting an action.

- The communication of intent is critical for teamwork. No one can anticipate every contingency. Therefore intent is used to improvise and adjust.

- We can identify seven facets for communicating intent.

- The description of intent has to reflect the expertise of the team members, the stability of the situation, and the degree to which the goal is well defined.

- The ability to read a person's mind depends on familiarity with that person and the clarity with which his or her intent is described.

14

The Power of the Team Mind

Team decision making includes properties that we might never predict if we study only individuals—for example, the ability of a team to come up with ideas that are beyond the skills of any single team member.[1] This chapter examines the concept of the team mind to explain how teams can think.[2] The purpose of using this concept is to force us to consider a team as an intelligent entity and to center our attention on the way the team thinks rather than on the individual members.

The Concept of Team Mind

Usually we try to use metaphors based on phenomena that we understand well in order to help make sense of fuzzy phenomena. Computers make good metaphors. So do biological processes. But the concept of mind is a terrible metaphor, and thus a poor candidate to help us study anything. We do not know what it is, or where it is, or even if it is.

And yet the mind of a team can be easier to study than the mind of an individual. Consider the types of information used to make inferences about what is going on in a person's mind.

First, we infer mental activities from behavior. You can study the behavior of a team as easily as that of an individual. For example, aircrews are emitting behaviors, the behaviors of their airplane. The changes in flaps, the radio calls, and the engine adjustments are all observable behaviors emitted by aircrews. The first officer might change the flaps and the captain might make the radio call, but the behaviors are the actions of the crew.

Second, we infer mental processes from our own conscious experience. We see and feel things, and the contents of awareness fill and occupy our minds. This is murky and hard to bring to the surface when studying individual consciousness. Yet there is no difficulty in studying the consciousness of a team; you just watch and listen. The matters the team talks about, even the gestures that team members make to each other, are the contents of the team's consciousness. We can call this the collective consciousness of the team.[3] An outside observer who is familiar with the task can have as clear an understanding of the collective consciousness as any of the team members.

Third, we infer mental processes from activities of which a person is not aware—perhaps physiological or electrical events in the brain, or part of the person's unconscious, to be ferreted out by interpreting dreams and Freudian slips. They can be indicated by brief facial gestures or other nonverbal signs. We have trouble making sense of these in trying to understand an individual's thinking. For the team, it is as easy as interviewing the team members separately to see what they knew that they did not share with the others. We can uncover the ideas that never made it into the collective consciousness. This is the preconscious level of the team mind.[4]

Example 14.1 presents another simulated malfunction from a study we did for NASA.

Example 14.1
The Case of the De-Generators

The B-727 has three generators; it needs at least two generators to fly normally and at least one to fly safely. Each of the three engines on the 727 has its own generator.

A malfunction begins early in the flight when one of the generators fails. This is not unusual or even cause for concern. But as the airplane is making its initial descent prior to landing, the oil pressure on a second engine drops down to 35 psi (pounds per square inch), the borderline value for either operating the engine or shutting it down. The malfunction lets us see how the aircrews would make the decision.

The argument in favor of leaving the engine on is that the more engines that are available, the more power is available. The argument for shutting it down is that the engine can be damaged if used without enough oil. And if the oil pressure decreases more, the crew will have to go through the procedure for shutting it down. If that happens during the landing when everyone is already busy, it will add to the confusion and stress and reduce the margin for error.

> **Example 14.1** (continued)
>
> One of the aircrews we observed hits on a compromise solution: leaving the troublesome engine on standby so it is not being used but is available in case they need the extra power. The decision is reached only after a lot of discussion, and as an observer, I am not sure of the status of all the engines upon landing. Afterward, when we gather the aircrew for the post-flight interview, I remind them of this malfunction and ask them how many generators they had when they landed. "Two," says the copilot, who was flying the plane when they landed. His expression shows that he is not too confident of that answer.
>
> "One and a half," says the captain, meaning the one good engine plus the other on standby; the copilot did not realize it was on standby.
>
> "One," says the flight engineer, reminding the captain that it takes a minute or two to bring an engine back from standby, so the generator was not available when they were landing.
>
> This story seems amusing—that the three have different answers—except that the person with the worst answer was flying the airplane. If he had needed extra power, it would not have been available.

There was disagreement between the contents of the team's preconscious and its collective consciousness. The team had failed to clarify critical information about the status of the machine and at the conscious level had never realized there were such different interpretations.

The Functions of a Team Mind

A team mind has the following functions:

- Working memory. This is the ability to hold information such as telephone numbers for brief periods of time. Applied to a team mind, information is presented and gets some discussion; then the team moves on to another topic and forgets the first one.

- Long-term memory. This ability to store information permanently applies to teams as well as individuals (Wegner, 1987). Teams have to store information to retrieve later. If a team member has particular information and drops out of the team, the information is lost. According to Wegner, teams find it helpful to store the information redundantly, so more than one person knows it.

- Limited attention. We can attend to only one thing at a time. Teams also can discuss only one thing at a time. They have to be careful in directing their attention to make sure that what gets the spotlight is worthwhile.

- Perceptual filters. We experience the world through the sensory mechanisms that convert mechanical energy into patterns of neural activity. Similarly, teams do not have direct experience but must depend on secondhand reports, which can introduce inaccuracies.

- Learning. Teams need to learn in many ways, such as acquiring new procedures, discarding inefficient behaviors, and figuring out how to become more effective.

There are many other correspondences between a team mind and an individual one, and there are dissimilarities as well, since no metaphor can be an exact match. The value of a metaphor is to help illuminate a phenomenon of interest; the value of the team mind metaphor is to put some structure on our understanding of teams to see how far we can use the findings of cognitive psychology.

How a Team Mind Develops

To learn how a team mind increases in ability, Marvin Thordsen and I have compared some of the teams we had studied. We contrasted the best and the worst teams.

Example 14.2
The Best Teams: Wildland Firefighters

The U.S. Forest Service is responsible for handling forest fires. It uses an incident command structure that is similar to the one used by the military. The incident commander is supported by a staff of specialists in planning, operations, logistics, personnel, and so forth.

Marvin Thordsen was on location during a forest fire in Idaho, a large one that covered six mountains. He watched the command staff assemble a team of 4,000 firefighters, drawing them from all over the country. They put together a working organization in only a few days and sent them out to fight the fire. It is hard to manage an intact organization of 4,000 people, to give directions and make policies, even in stable and safe bureaucratic settings. Here, in less than a week, they were building that organization and trusting it enough to risk lives.

Why are they so good?

Example 14.2 (continued)

Experience. They get lots of experience. There are always fires to be fought. We read only about the dramatic ones, but Idaho alone can count on many fires each season. Unlike the military, which does not fight many wars and has to rely on training to keep sharp, the people fighting forest fires have plenty of first-hand experience. Furthermore, they are fighting an adversary that does not change tactics or add new weapons, so the experience gained one year applies the next. The members of the top command and control echelons have decades of experience.

Sharpness. Some members of the strike team fight forest fires twelve months a year. They work the western states during the summer and fall, then travel to Australia and New Zealand to catch the summer and fall fire seasons down there. The rest of the team is engaged in firefighting in the United States for six months each year.

Stability. The members of each core incident command team work side by side every fire season, for decades. This stands in contrast to a military system, where soldiers rotate assignments every few years.

Promotion from within. Everyone starts at the bottom. Everyone has moved up through the ranks. The lowest crew members realize that their leaders have been in their boots and know what it will feel like to carry out the orders they give. This understanding adds to confidence, since the line crews appreciate that their leaders are more skilled and competent than they are.

Networks. This is a closely knit community. Many commanders and their staff members have worked together before—even the ones from different states who may have joined forces on large-scale fires in the past.

Together, these factors resulted in a calm and competent team. Despite the complexity of assembling a large force overnight, the commanders and planners had done it before, even if on a smaller scale. The different team members knew their assignments, and actions were taken smoothly and purposefully. There was not much wasted energy. The tough decisions they had to face were ones they had faced in the past. For example, a common decision was where to set up a firebreak—a bulldozed semicircle in advance of a fire, designed to stop a fire by depriving it of fuel. The temptation is to draw this tightly around the leading edge of the fire because the smaller the firebreak, the faster it can be built. The disadvantage is that the smaller it is, the greater the risk; if the wind shifts, the fire can slide by, and the team has wasted its time. These kinds of decisions are made quickly, using fragmentary information about terrain, weather, characteristics of the wood, extent of underbrush, competence of the bulldozer operators, and so forth.

The command staff met twice a day to make the difficult decisions. After years of working together, the team members knew how to plan together. They did not waste time on politeness, and their egos were strong enough to take criticism without bristling. They were also sensitive to issues of morale. Someone who disagreed with the commander's action would confront

Example 14.2 (continued)

the commander in the meeting only if it was necessary. Otherwise, the disagreement would be expressed in private. They did not want to waste staff time on lower-priority fights or create a feeling of divisiveness.

There was another characteristic that helped their teamwork: their expectation that they would be working together for years to come. In the midst of fighting fires, they were also conducting on-the-job training. They were aware of opportunities for providing new challenges to different people to help them grow in skill. Rather than remove someone doing a poor job, they tried to find an alternate responsibility from which the person could learn. This was part of their culture: ensuring continuity by developing the skills of their successors.[5]

Compare these teams to the worst ones we have observed: crisis management teams. Typically a manufacturing company handling dangerous materials will set up a crisis management team to prepare for emergencies—fires, explosions, and even terrorist attacks. Marvin and I observed several of these teams established by companies manufacturing nuclear weapons (these efforts were sponsored by the Department of Energy). We observed these teams during training exercises, and we were surprised by their incompetence.

One reason that crisis management teams fall apart is that the heads of these teams have to be the corporate executives, because they are the ones who are legally responsible. But these executives have no background in crisis management. They might go through a one- to two-day crisis training exercise a few times a year. During the exercise, they are still learning their basic tasks. The companies do have a director of security, but that person often has low status because the function is a drain on profits. Besides, there are few emergencies. In some industries, the security officer knows that the chance of a single emergency during a twenty-year career is less than 50 percent.

Example 14.3
The Reaction Time of a Crisis Management Team

The training scenario is that some right-wing terrorists have infiltrated a plant that manufactures nuclear materials and are holding some secretaries hostage. The crisis manager is worried that this is a diversion as other ter-

Example 14.3 (continued)

rorists break into sector H, where nuclear materials are stored. Therefore he tells his director of security to make sure the number of guards there is doubled. Later, the crisis management team receives word that the terrorists have just invaded sector H. The crisis manager is furious. He complains that the training exercise is unrealistic. He has just given the order to increase security, and it had no effect.

As I review my notes on the exercise, I see that the crisis manager issued his order thirty-one minutes before receiving the message that sector H had been invaded. I mentally review the chain of events. It begins with the manager issuing the order. Relaying the order to the people at sector H takes maybe ten minutes. The security director has to get through on the busy telephones. The guard on duty has to locate the unit chief and get him to the telephone. The order is communicated, but they may have other things to talk about; for example, the sector H security chief will want a quick briefing on the hostage situation. So it is a minimum of ten minutes before the sector H security chief starts to carry out the order. And how long does that take? He cannot double his force by asking the people to clone themselves. He has to make more telephone calls to line up the extra staff, determine where the low-priority areas are to draw from, call people at their homes. Then he has to arrange the transportation to bring everyone over to sector H. He might even need route planning if he is worried about ambushes by terrorists. It might take two hours to double the staff, and probably more. Finally the terrorists attack sector H. This is a dangerous situation, so only when there is a free moment will anyone pick up the telephone to call headquarters. Now add another five to ten minutes from the start of the terrorist attack in sector H until the phone call is made. What does that add up to? At least a few hours.

Yet the crisis manager is amazed that his orders hadn't been obeyed thirty-one minutes later. He complains that it is a flaw in the exercise. He clearly does not know how long it takes to carry out an order such as the one he gave. He doesn't know the reaction time of his own team.

This incident is reminiscent of an infant who reaches for a slowly bouncing ball. The infant reaches for the ball, but the reaction time is so slow that by the time the child gets to where the ball was, the ball has moved past. So the infant reaches again, aiming directly at the point where he or she sees the ball, again not taking reaction time into account. And again the ball has moved before the infant's hand gets there. This is challenging to infants. It is amusing to their parents. This is not a game of catch but a different game, a precursor that enables the infant to learn his or her own reaction time, to learn how long it takes to get that hand out.

The crisis management team also did not know its own reaction time. Consequently, it was trying to control events inside the time horizon for responding.

We saw other problems with reaction time in this crisis management team. They tried to micromanage events in sector H, relying on photographs showing the terrorists. Again, they ignored the time lag in taking and sending the photographs, and the time lag in deliberating about actions and issuing orders. The team was trying to direct the security forces in sector H using photographs rather than leaving these decisions to the people on the spot. These problems compounded. Before long the crisis management team had done such a poor job that the exercise controller had to replace the crisis manager to prevent the team from becoming totally demoralized.

The Development of Team Decision Making

Building on the metaphor of a team mind, Klein, Zsambok, and Thordsen (1993) identified four features of child development to map onto teams: the development of competencies, identity, cognitive skills, and metacognition. Figure 14.1 presents these four features. It also provides a set of questions that we have found useful in appraising different teams for the degree to which they have matured along these four dimensions. We have found it useful to apply this framework in assessing teams.

Team Competencies

Newborns have few competencies beyond their reflexes. In time, they learn to use their arms and fingers, and all the rest, automatically. They learn how to grasp objects and push other objects away and scoot back in a car seat to let their parents strap them in. Teams too are limited by the competencies of their members. Any evaluation of what to expect from a team must consider the individual levels of skill, particularly if the team members keep changing. Everyone is trying to gauge the level of competency of the other members.

Teams also rely on shared practices and routines. Mature teams are supposed to be automatic in performing their basic procedures.

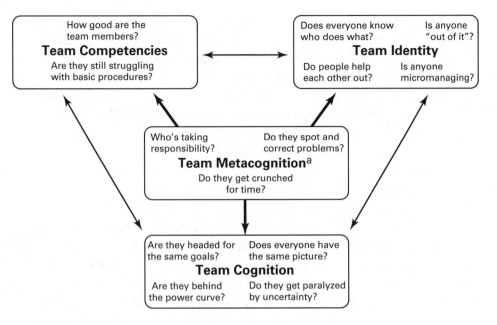

Figure 14.1

Advanced team decision-making model

Team Identity

A newborn does not know where it ends and the rest of the world begins. It does not know it has arms. It sees finger-shaped objects drift in front of its face and does not know that it can take direct control of them. Similarly, the immature teams we have watched lack a sense of what they control. The team members themselves are still learning how to do their individual jobs. The advanced teams have already worked this out. The team members think of the team's requirements as much as their own.

If you try to explain to people on an immature team what the overall goals are, they are likely to respond, "Don't bother me with that. Just tell me what you want me to do and let me do my job." In contrast, the members of experienced teams want to know as much as possible about the overall status of the team. They realize that they may have to compensate for others, ask for help, or pitch in for team goals even if they have to abandon their own tasks temporarily. Experienced teams have integrated identities; the members identify themselves in relationship to the whole team. Inexperienced teams have fragmentary identities and focus on individual assignments more than team requirements.[6]

Identity develops slowly. The team members have to learn their own jobs. Then they have to understand something about the jobs their team-mates are doing. Then they have to develop more automatic ways of coordinating and working together. Finally, when they have the basics down, they can free up attention to see the challenges facing the team as a whole. Even when the team members are experienced and have worked on other teams, it still takes time to learn everyone's characteristics. Team identity continues to grow for a long time.

When teams have not developed sufficient identity, they are confused about roles and functions—about who is responsible for what. Some team members tune out, letting others carry the load. Some may be insensitive to the needs of others, as when one person struggles, with no help from others. In an exercise with a crisis management team, the security director and two assistants were greatly overloaded, trying to make phone calls all over the plant. At the next table, the public relations unit sat without anything to do for several hours until someone realized they could help with the security calls.

When teams have not developed sufficient identity, their leaders can be diverted by low-level tasks without understanding what can happen when they let their responsibilities go. For an illustration of micromanagement, we again turn to the crisis management teams.

Example 14.4
The Crisis Manager Who Became Less Than a Secretary

The company had just installed a new center filled with computers, command desks, and the other paraphernalia. They were conducting their first training exercise in the facility. The crisis manager sat at the head table with four staff members in charge of security, operations, and the like. In the middle of the exercise, he got an idea that he wanted to put into action immediately and dramatically. He made his own phone calls to arrange for support helicopters from a nearby U.S. Air Force base. He didn't tell anyone what he was doing. Instead, he left the head table and went over to where a secretary was sitting and entering messages into the computer system, to notify everyone of key events. He wrote out his own message describing the helicopters and handed it to the secretary. Then he stood behind her, proofreading to catch her typographical mistakes.

The crisis manager wasn't at his post, making himself available to members of his team who needed help. He wasn't even a secretary, entering his own messages. He was a secretary's assistant for the length of time it took to type and revise his message.

Experienced teams have seen instances where roles and functions have broken down, and they know the consequences. One fireground commander working in an urban setting told us about a milk box he brought with him to fires. He explained that when he first became a commander, he was prone to rushing about to offer help, dashing into buildings to assist with rescues, and being an all-around resource. Of course, whenever he left his post, his crew members did not know where to find him if they needed a decision made, and they wasted time searching for him.

Gradually it dawned on him what it meant to be in charge and what his responsibilities were. He knew about his impulsive nature, so he made it a practice to bring the milk box, to serve as his station, and there he stayed. He sat on it, stood on it, kept a foot touching it, remained within sight of it. He had realized the functions he served for his team and where he fit into the jobs of everyone else.

Team Cognition
A few primary questions can be used to distinguish teams with high and low conceptual levels. The first is, How do the teams describe their goals and intents? The answer was covered in chapter 13. Second, to what degree does the team share an understanding of the situation? This can include giving team members a chance to voice divergent views, as well as pulling these ideas together so the members know the assumptions guiding their actions. Some teams take extra steps to keep the members informed as the situation changes.

A third category is the time horizon: How much effort does a team make to look ahead and anticipate problems? Some teams focus on events too close in for them to affect. Example 14.3, on the reaction time of a crisis management team, shows what happens to those who follow events rather than prepare for them.

Fourth, how does the team manage uncertainty, keeping track of gaps and ambiguities? Because the windows of opportunity will close if a team waits to get every last bit of information, good teams must live with uncertainty. At the same time, they have to be sensitive to the assumptions and guesses they have been making in case these turn out to be wrong.

Thus far we have been concentrating on planning teams. When the plans are executed, the team's priorities shift. Now the team needs everyone to have the same overriding goals and to make sure members share the same understanding of the situation.

Recognizing a situation is important, and teams have to work to communicate this recognition, to achieve a shared understanding. Situation awareness incorporates the nature of the goals, and teams have to work to communicate intent. It also highlights critical cues. Teams have to ensure that the right members are searching for these cues and interpreting and communicating them. They also have to make sure some members are looking ahead while others are carrying out the plans. Finally, teams must manage uncertainty and may have to reconcile opposing viewpoints; each member may be certain about what is happening but disagree with other members.

Team Metacognition

Metacognition refers to the concept of thinking about thinking. It emerged from research with children to describe how they learn to take their own thinking strategies into account. They learn the limits of their memory and acquire strategies for working around these limits, such as knowing when to reread something because they are not sure they understood it. Children cannot develop good skills for metacognition until their behaviors become sufficiently stable and predictable for them to anticipate what will happen and take the necessary steps. Metacognition depends on a clear identity.

For teams, as well as individuals, metacognition is an important development. A team can learn its own capabilities and acquire a strong identity and a shared understanding of the situation. Once this awareness is in place, the team can monitor its own performance and select strategies to avoid weaknesses and capitalize on strengths.

One of the pleasures of watching a child grow up is to see the child learn to handle ideas and juggle different concepts. A critical aspect of a child's cognitive development is to manage the flow of ideas.

The same holds for teams. The ability to manage the flow of ideas is one of the central skills that distinguishes immature from experienced teams. Members of an immature team may struggle to come up with any ideas, and often the ideas take the team in all sorts of directions—some useful, some irrelevant. Time winds down, and too quickly the team has to make sense of everything that was said. The team members are so excited to tell everything they know that they do not pay attention to whether their comments fit into their task. Experienced teams are more careful; they try to build on the comments of others and create linkages all along. They bring up new perspectives where appropriate, but are cautious about going off on tangents. During a team decision-making session, the ideas have to be managed. Too few, and the product is disappointing. Too many, and the team is overwhelmed.

This is the power of the team mind: to create new and unexpected solutions, options, and interpretations, drawing on the experience of all the team members to generate products that are beyond the capabilities of any of the individuals.

What makes the process so difficult is that no one knows in advance which ideas will be put forth and how they will coalesce. No one, not even the leader, knows what is in everyone's head. No one can be sure of which suggestions or experiences team members will offer. The team's ideas depend on who shows up that day, who is feeling alert and who is sleepy, who is prepared and who is distracted, which ideas any of the team members articulate, the order of these ideas, and the ways the ideas are combined. Any session could go in different directions if different ideas are voiced, or are joined in different ways. The team can try to manage the flow of ideas, to keep them coherent and linked. But even a good planning team would have some difficulty managing the flow of ideas, since no one knows in advance what is going to come out.

It is not enough to be aware of strengths and weaknesses. A team has to change its approach if it sees itself running into difficulties. Consider the following example, from an interview of the incident commander of a very large forest fire in northern California.

Example 14.5
The Firefighters Who Realized They Weren't Supposed to Fight Fires

The fire, at an order of magnitude greater than anyone had ever seen, is entirely out of control. The commanders pull in all kinds of fire crews, outfitting them and sending them to different parts of the state. Yet the news keeps coming back that they aren't making very much progress.

Example 14.5 (continued)

When the command team meets to figure out what is going wrong, they realize their problem is that they are fighting fires, yet their job is to put fires out. And they simply aren't putting any fires out.

They decide to stop fighting every fire in the state. They list all the fires, and select the one that will be easiest to put out with available resources. Then they move to the next easiest fire, and so on. In this way, they can send their crews where they will have the most impact. For the first time, they start to put fires out.

Their shift in strategy isn't easy. The hardest part is to let some fires go. The crews have been working hard to keep these fires checked. Now they are told that the Forest Service is going to let those fires rage uncontrolled, with the crews transferred elsewhere. It feels like a betrayal. Friendships are broken, some permanently.

A few fires are left burning through the fall, into winter. Some fires, like the one at Klamath, have gotten so hot that when spring arrives, they spontaneously start up again. This time the crews can go after them.

Unlike these wildland firefighters, most teams have trouble correcting their problems. Teams can sometimes go too far in the opposite direction, tying themselves up in an attempt to overcontrol. To illustrate a team that did not know how to manage itself, we turn again to our favorite target, the crisis management teams.

Example 14.6
The Crisis Management Team That Loved to Caucus

The crisis manager has obviously been on teams where things have gotten out of hand and is determined to keep a tight rein. He informs the team that they will caucus regularly so everyone can stay informed. His strategy sounds reasonable—except that he doesn't know what he is doing.

During the first three hours of the scenario, as the crisis swirls around, the crisis manager stands up and loudly announces, "Caucus," interrupting everyone at work. He calls for a caucus every nine minutes, on the average. (I am timing him.) To make matters worse, he lets the caucus ramble on, and then trail off, and usually doesn't announce it is over. People just start to go back to their work.

The unit with the toughest job is the security force. They are constantly on the telephones, trying, with limited success, to talk with the people they want to reach. Just as they are making contact, the leader calls for a caucus, and they have to hang up. Then the leader asks if they have spoken with so-and-so, and they admit they haven't, so the crisis manager berates them and calls more caucuses to check on their progress.

Sometimes leaders become frustrated by the job of managing the team's progress, diagnosing its problems, and taking corrective actions. We have seen leaders disengage in many ways.

Example 14.7
The Leader Who Vanished

The job of the team is to develop a plan over the two and a half days scheduled for the work. The problem is that two or three members insist on dominating the discussion, and the other members are ignored. Worse, the discussions are so chaotic that some members simply leave the room and wander over to another team meeting in parallel. The team leader is frustrated by his inability to create an orderly atmosphere, yet each time the free-for-all starts, he is one of the people fighting hardest to give his own speeches.

On the last day, we are scheduled to work in the morning and give our briefing after lunch. The morning session is more of the same. Around 10:00 we take a break, then reassemble for the final discussion. We wait for the leader, but he doesn't come back. One hypothesis is that he has gone up to his room to take a nap. We call, but he has already checked out. Another hypothesis is that he has taken a walk outside the hotel and has gotten mugged. If that has happened, his luggage will still be in the hotel. We check, but his luggage isn't there. A third hypothesis is that he has been murdered by someone on the team who cannot face yet another session together. This one has some plausibility; the motive is believable, and a murderer might be smart enough to hide the leader's luggage. The fourth hypothesis is that he is fed up and has flown back to California without telling anyone. I call him the following week, and that was the case.

This was a situation where metacognition was needed to change the way the team was doing business, but the leader did not know how to provide the metacognition. The continual interruptions and posturing that made it so hard to work together also prevented us from finding a better way to structure our discussions.

In Figure 14.1, the four features are linked by a set of arrows. One of the central functions of metacognition is to detect strains in the other aspects of teamwork (competencies, identity, and cognition) and make adjustments. Competencies are linked to team identity because until the team develops to a certain level of proficiency, it may have trouble getting the members to identify themselves with the output of the entire team;

as the team develops a stronger identity, the team members will monitor each other and help each other out in ways that improve coordination of basic tasks. Competencies are linked to team cognition because they serve as a limiting factor; as long as the team members are still struggling with basic procedures, they will not be able to pay sufficient attention to larger issues such as situation awareness. As they develop a better sense for time horizons and managing uncertainty, they will find that performance of basic procedures becomes smoother. And team identity is linked to team cognition because a stronger identity helps a team determine if their goals are congruent and if they have a shared situation awareness. As the cognitive processing of the team matures, the individuals gain a stronger sense of identity.

We can use these ideas about a team mind to examine one of the mysteries of the USS *Vincennes* shootdown, described in chapter 6. The captain was monitoring the battle with the surface ships while the Airbus was approaching. At a critical point, the captain asked, "What is 4474 doing?" referring to the original track number used to designate the Airbus, forgetting that it had been changed to 4131. Some crew members punched "4474" into their key pad and found that the airplane currently using that track number was descending. Others used the current number, 4131, and found the airplane was ascending. In the confusion and ambiguity that followed, the captain made the decision to shoot down the unknown airplane.

Something did not happen during this sequence: when the captain asked, "What is 4474 doing?" no one corrected him. Some crew members knew that the track number had been changed but did not remind the captain. If they had, the decision might have been different. As a result, the inconsistent use of track numbers stayed at the preconscious level, where it was inaccessible to scrutiny. There were so many causes contributing to the accident that we cannot single out one and say this was where the team went wrong. But it certainly did not help to have an uncorrected mistake that led half the team to claim the airplane was descending.

There are several possible reasons that no one corrected the captain. Maybe no one realized the mistake. Maybe the crew members who remembered the change did not understand the implications of letting the error stand. Most likely, some did notice the error but adhered to U.S. Navy culture of not correcting a superior officer. Other naval accidents have been documented where crew members failed to inform a captain of an error he was making.

The purpose of the concept of a team mind is to help us see the team and not be distracted by the individuals. A team can have a poor leader, but if others compensate, the job will get done. Or the team may have brilliant individuals who get so caught up in debate that the job does not get done. If we are evaluating a team, we can try to ask how mature it is. If the team was a child, how developed would that child be? Is he or she still clumsy at basic procedures, or has it gotten them down pat? Is the child able to think effectively, or does it get stumped or even overloaded with ideas? Is the child aware of self, or does it have no idea about the way he or she is working? By looking at the team as a thinking organism, we can get a different appreciation of its abilities.

The Chaotic Nature of the Team Mind

The team mind often functions in an "accidental" manner. That is, teams do not reliably follow one idea with its successor, and action-directed teams do not regularly have a clear idea of the reasons for their actions. The word *chaotic* refers to the observation that teams usually do not think in systematic and predictable ways. Their ideas and flow of attention are unpredictable, they have a delusion of controlling their own thoughts and their own actions, and sometimes the ideas control the team.

Unpredictable Ideas
Unless the leaders of a team deliberately stage a meeting, it is virtually impossible to figure out in advance what ideas are going to be brought forward. What gets entered into collective consciousness is only a small part of what all the team members are thinking about. There are many good ideas that never get spoken—and many good ideas that could be combined into real breakthroughs. None of the team members can know what the others have not said, so the team is unaware of what it misses.

Unpredictable Flow of Attention
In most operational settings, teams are exposed to all sorts of interruptions and distractions. In his observations at Fort Hood, Marvin Thordsen made a transcript of the five-hour planning session, then counted

how many times one element, one thought, was followed by a related one. Of the sixty-four segment transitions he identified, only five (8 percent) were categorized as natural transitions. Another twenty-six transitions could be seen as having been within the context of the discussion segment. More than half of the transitions (thirty-three) were unconnected. The most common category, out-of-context questions, accounted for nineteen transitions (30 percent); the planning became diverted to new, unrelated topics for a variety of irrelevant reasons. Someone would receive a phone call, or a messenger would tell them they needed to use transparencies for their briefing and they turned to a discussion of where they were going to make the transparencies. More important, Marvin found that once the interruption was dealt with, the team usually did not return to its original discussion. It moved on to a different topic. The flow of the discussion was driven by random associations people brought up, not by an agenda.

The Delusion of Controlling Their Own Thoughts

After the fact, team members may describe their interactions as consistent and well directed. Once they know what approaches they arrived at, they can trace how those approaches evolved and make the story seem tidy. However, observers watching them struggle to find any approach, decision, or course of action know about the blind alleys, the stumbling, and the confusion.

Interruptions

Even when interruptions do not come from the outside, the team makes its own distractions. One person has just read an interesting article and wants the others to look at it; another person wants to know how to fill out the new time sheets.

The process resembles free association. There is a general expectation that one person's comments will be marginally related to the preceding comments. In the short run, members find or make up connections between their comments and the preceding ones; however, these connections can be varied and tenuous. The members will often wonder how they got on the topic. In immature teams, even an agenda may not be sufficient to keep the discussion on track.

The Delusion of Controlling Their Actions

Often in our observations of a team, a meeting would be ending and someone, usually the leader, would say something like, "Okay. I think we've talked that over long enough. Now let's go out and do it." These comments struck us as odd in cases where no one had defined what the team was supposed to do. Nevertheless, the team members were satisfied to pack up their pads and materials and prepare to swing into action. When asked later, they had trouble describing their goals. Once the action started, the team members took their cues from what others were doing, adjusting and coordinating on the spot. Afterward, when the team leaders see what they have achieved, they can try to weave an explanation showing how their activities were aimed in this direction all the time.

Research in neurophysiology has shown that individuals can have the delusion that they are controlling their own thinking when this is not the case. To illustrate this delusion of controlling the actions taken, consider the following example.

Example 14.8
The Illusion of Rationality

The neuropsychologist Michael Gazzaniga (1985) conducted a study of patients whose uncontrollable epilepsy was so severe that the treatment was to cut the connections between the two hemispheres of the brain so the epileptic seizures would not have a path for spreading throughout the brain.

Working with these patients individually, Gazzaniga presented a written message to the visual field that fed into the right hemisphere, asking the patient to perform some simple act, like standing up and walking around. Next, he presented a written message to the left hemisphere, which controls speech, asking the person why he or she was walking around. Invariably, the person could make up an answer, such as "I just felt like stretching my legs," or "I felt thirsty and wanted to find a Coke." The left hemisphere could not know the true reason for the action, but it showed no hesitation in making up a plausible reason. One speculation is that we have some sort of rational engine whose job it is to observe our behaviors and make inferences about rational causes.

If individuals can form a delusion of rational control over their actions, we should not be surprised to find teams doing the same thing.

Ideas That Control the Team

Skilled rowers refer to a phenomenon they call swing, in which all four or eight rowers catch the water at the same instant, and it feels as if the boat has gone flying out of the water. The rowers stop worrying about their individual actions and try to synchronize their movements, to gain the power of coherent focus like light waves that become lasers when they are brought into coherence.

During a team meeting when individuals are waiting for an opening to speak and preparing what they will say, it sometimes happens that an idea is articulated that captures everyone's attention and refocuses the discussion. We can say that the idea captured the team. It brought the thoughts of the team into coherence. This usually does not last very long, and in most meetings it does not happen at all. When it does occur, it offers a glimpse of the team mind.

The Team Mind as a Metaphor for Thinking

I have been using the concept of an individual's mind to understand team decision making. Now I want to use what we have learned about teams to make more sense of our own individual minds, with team interactions as a metaphor for thinking.

The next time you are in a group or take part in a team discussion, consider the possibility that you may be seeing the way your own mind works from the inside. The chaos, the accidents, the inhibited thoughts, the chance connections, the serendipity: that is what is going on inside your own head. You do not realize it because we cannot bring to consciousness all the fluctuations in our brains. We cannot become aware of the thoughts we suppress. Our thinking usually looks so orderly, so purposive, so clean. Watching a team think is perhaps the closest we will get to being inside a mind.

Each of the "accidental" characteristics of team cognition listed above also seems to describe individual minds, resembling features of our own thinking. Now we have a way of appreciating how accidental the formation of new ideas is. We can be amused at our delusions that we always think clearly, controlling the flow of our thoughts and rationally controlling our actions. We can understand how thoughts can be generated and actions taken without any general awareness of the dynamics of a situation. We can know how different lines of thought can go on in silence and in parallel until one is ready to enter into consciousness. We can see how the other line of thought never gains awareness.

Applications

The impetus for studying teams, and for the team mind concept, was to develop ideas for training. We found an interesting disconnect about training in many organizations we studied, particularly in the Department of Defense. Some high-ranking officers insisted that they already offered team training, while others admitted that this was one of their weak points. In trying to figure out the reason for the disconnect, we found it was based on an ignorance of what team training was.

Team training requires a certain process:

1. Identify a set of functions and processes that teams should master, within a given setting (e.g., how to communicate intent or compensate to help each other out).
2. Evaluate how well the teams in this setting perform those functions and processes.
3. Identify any areas of weakness.
4. Provide specific training in the form of exercises tailored to provide experience or remedy weaknesses.

The officers who were unhappy with team training knew that this type of training never occurred. Yet no one tried to find out why teams went wrong, and then design new scenarios to build the necessary skills.

The officers who were satisfied that they trained teams meant that they trained people in situations where they had to work as teams. If a team fell apart, the observers might comment on the poor outcome but not on what went wrong inside the team. These officers did not know they could do more by examining a team's strategies or its competence. They did not know what they did not know, so they were unaware that they were missing something.

Once at the Army War College I was talking about how the school could adapt its exercises to provide more focused team training. One instructor, a major, took exception to my comments. "How can you claim that we do not already know how to train teams?" he demanded. I replied, then finished my presentation. At the end, he still did not want to make any changes, but for a different reason. "What makes you think we can evaluate these team processes?" he demanded. "We need a lot more preparation than we've been given in this school."

In working in different settings, we realized that lots of training exercises already went on involving teams. It would be easy to add some additional material and make these into directed team training opportunities. We could use the existing exercises for team decision training as well as for familiarity with the tasks themselves.

One of the projects, run by Caroline Zsambok, was to provide team decision training. (This project was sponsored by the Army Research Institute.) Our contract monitor, Owen Jacobs, wanted us to apply the ideas of the team mind to train high-ranking officers, and we worked out arrangements with the Industrial College of the Armed Forces, part of the National Defense University in Washington, D.C. The school trains officers at the rank of lieutenant colonel (U.S. Army or Air Force) or captain (U.S. Navy). Caroline produced a module on advanced team decision making that was adopted by the Industrial College of the Armed Forces. Under her leadership (Zsambok, 1993), we transformed the initial ideas about a team mind into a set of primary dimensions and key behaviors along the lines of the model shown in figure 14.1. This advanced team decision making model has become part of the curriculum of the college's course on strategic decision making. The faculty wanted its students to learn how to observe teams in action and make adjustments on the spot. It also wanted the students to anticipate difficulties and make the necessary changes and preparations in advance.

We have used this team decision-making model in other domains, such as emergency response organizations set up by nuclear power plants. The Nuclear Regulatory Commission (NRC) requires each nuclear power plant to set up an emergency response organization that it evaluates periodically. Members of the emergency response organization have primary jobs in the plant and usually come together only for drills.

In 1995 Duke Power Company hired Klein Associates to study the team decision making in the emergency response organization of one of its nuclear power generating stations. Dave Klinger led the project, which included an independent consultant, Doug Harrington, of Team Formation. They used the advanced team decision-making model as a diagnostic tool. They observed drills and interviewed several people in each of the key positions. (Because the emergency response organization must always be on call to activate, several people fill each position.)

The primary difficulties were that the crews were not clear about their roles and functions, and they were having trouble maintaining a shared situation awareness. Dave and Doug worked with the teams to redefine the roles and functions and to redesign the workspace layout in the emergency response organization. Another change was to conduct after-action reviews to cover team decision making. During the project, more than fifty changes were recommended in organizational structure, processes, and the physical environment of the emergency center.

Over the ten months that this project took, Dave and Doug drastically reduced the number of people in the emergency center. At first, there were more than eighty people crowded into one room. Because the workload was so heavy, Duke Power believed they needed to add even more people, but they weren't sure how to fit them in. Dave and Doug found that the heavy workload was caused, in part, by having too many unnecessary people. They tried cutting out assistants and nonrelevant staff, and performance got better. By the end of the project, the staff was down to thirty-five, and workload had reduced, not increased.

In addition to staff reduction, the station manager and emergency planning director decided to put many of the major recommendations in place shortly before their annual drill with NRC observers—without practice. We were nervous about this. But the previous history of difficulties had raised the possibility that the plant would have to increase the number of practice drills from four a year to six a year (each drill can cost between $250,000 and $500,000) and go from one to two formally evaluated drills a year (each of these can cost between $500,000 and $1 million). The plant personnel were highly motivated to do well.

They decided to institute a new room layout. They placed individuals who must share information next to each other. They moved the status board so that all the major players at the command table could see it. They reorganized the board to show plant status, the status of teams in the plant, the status of equipment, the most recent events, and current priorities. The status board, which had been ignored during previous drills, could now be used during briefings to describe the problems and how they were being addressed. One other major recommendation was the definition of expectations by the team leader. During the drill, but prior to activating the center, the emergency director went around the command table and described to each team member what was expected of him or her and what was not expected. This placed the team in a position to move forward and handle the event without the crippling effects of redundant, ambiguous, and meaningless tasks and information.

Was it worth it? There were several obvious differences. The room was noticeably quieter. There was a shared perception that the problems presented in the drill were easier than in previous drills, whereas in actuality the exercise was more challenging. The improved teamwork just made it seem easier because the team members were no longer getting in their own way. After watching the team in action, the NRC reduced the number of required drills at the plant down to one every two years and wiped the slate clean regarding previous deficiencies. Now the plant was held up as a model of how an emergency response organization should work.

Key Points

- A team is an intelligent entity.
- The cognition of a team can be inferred from three sources: the team's behavior, the contents of the team's collective consciousness, and the team's preconscious.
- The mind of a team shows some familiar features: it has a limited working memory, it has to store some information permanently, it has a limited attention span, it can process information in parallel, and it relies on filtered information.
- The team mind develops basic competencies and routines, forms a clear identity, learns to manage the flow of ideas, and learns to monitor itself to adjust its thinking when necessary.
- The idea of a team mind helps us understand the way individuals think, including the accidental nature of thinking.

15

The Power of Rational Analysis and the Problem of Hyperrationality

Hyperrationality is a mental disturbance in which the victim attempts to handle all decisions and problems on a purely rational basis, relying on only logical and analytical forms of reasoning. In the initial states, this condition can be mistaken for a healthy development of critical thinking. Only later do we observe an unwillingness to act without a sound, empirically or logically supported basis. The final stages degenerate into paralysis by analysis.

To understand the affliction of hyperrationality, other diseases can serve as analogues. Consider two different kinds of diseases that can affect vision. One is macular degeneration, in which the fovea and central zone of the retina is destroyed. The fovea is the center of the retina, packed with cone cells, and is the only part of the eye capable of fine discrimination. When we examine something carefully, we aim our foveas at it. I used to believe this would be about the worst visual impairment I could imagine short of blindness. Every time you tried to see something, you would center it in your visual field, and it would disappear. The second visual disease is retinitis pigmentosa, in which the peripheral vision deteriorates. This never seemed as devastating to me as macular degeneration. Who needs peripheral vision anyway?

I was wrong. Retinitis pigmentosa is the more disorienting condition. To understand why, hold out your arm in front of you as far as it will go. Raise your thumb as if you were hitchhiking. Look at the thumbnail. The area of your thumbnail is the total part of the visual field captured by the fovea. All the rest belongs to peripheral vision. If you lost all your peripheral vision, you would have this tiny searchlight sweeping endlessly back and forth, trying to locate everything and retain orientation. Without peripheral vision, you would even have trouble sitting quietly and reading, since you need peripheral vision to direct your eye movements.

Hyperrationality is like retinitis pigmentosa, in which we try to do all our thinking with just one of our sources of power: the ability to apply rational procedures. In this chapter I examine hyperrationality, but I will not fall into the right brain/left brain, holistic versus linear diatribe. That line usually means the author has dramatically made contact with the right brain and is preaching its virtues while mocking the poor left-brained folks. That's not going to get us anywhere. Besides, this book would never have been written without analyses and even some logical thought.

Kenneth Tynan, the British essayist, producer, and playwright, described some advice he had been given. "Never take the anti-intellectual side in an argument. You'll find that most of the people who applaud you will be people you hate" (Tynan, 1994, p. 88). Rational analysis is a cornerstone of intellectual activities and a very important source of power. We do not want to encourage people to make ill-informed, impulsive decisions.

This chapter compares the experiential sources of power that have been the topic of this book, with analytical sources of power. Our ability to use intuition and pattern matching is based on experience. Our ability to use mental simulation depends on having the knowledge and experience to set up the mental simulations. In contrast, our ability to analyze situations requires rational thought that is independent of experience. Statisticians, logicians, and decision analysts can provide guidance no matter what the domain.

The Role of Rational Analysis

Rational analysis is a specialized and powerful source of power that may play a limited role in many tasks, a dominant role in a few tasks, and sometimes no role at all. Rational thinking is like foveal vision using cone cells, which provides us with the ability to make fine discriminations but is not sufficient to maintain orientation and is irrelevant during nighttime. Analysis lets us make fine discriminations between ideas, and calculations let us find trends in noisy data. We need peripheral vision to detect where to apply the analyses and calculations.

Rational analysis reduces the chance that an important option will be overlooked. It supports the broad search for many options, rather than deep searches of only a few options. It comes closer to error-free decision making than other sources of power. And it allows the decision maker to use declarative knowledge.

Without rational analysis, we would not have the exciting growth of science and technology, the miracles of medicine, and so forth. Decision trees and cost–benefit analyses can help us make sense out of complicated choices, but there are some limitations to rational analysis, and that seems to make some people nervous. If analysis is a source of power, it will have to have some limitations and boundary conditions.[1]

The Nature of Rational Thinking

Rational comes from the Latin root *ratio*, which means "to reckon." To think by reckoning, or calculating, we need to do the following things:

- Decompose. We have to analyze a task—break the task, idea, or argument into small units, basic elements, so we can perform different calculations on them. Seeing how to break something into its components is a source of power in its own right.

- Decontextualize. Since context adds ambiguity, we must try to find units that are independent of context. We want to represent the important parts of context as additional facts and rules and elements. To accomplish this, we try to find a formal way to represent the world, to treat it as a representation, a picture, a model. We try to build theories and maps to substitute for having a sense of the task or the equipment.

- Calculate. We apply a range of formal procedures on the elements, such as deductive rules of logic and statistical analyses.

- Describe. All the analyses and representations should be open to public scrutiny.

Following this agenda often leads to significant accomplishments, particularly in the areas of science and technology. Rational thinking is an important source of power. It provides the benefits of orderly and systematic approaches to complex problems. For a task such as running a complex piece of equipment, perhaps a nuclear power plant, we want the operators to have a theory or mental model of the layout of the plant; we want them to be able to decompose problems to perform troubleshooting when they detect signs of malfunctions; we want them to collect objective data that can be described and checked by others.[2] The goal of making the thinking explicit means that a community can arrive at a common perspective and that teams can be set up to work separately on different parts of a problem with some confidence that their work will fit together at the end.

The Limits of Rational Thinking

Lack of Basic Elements

To perform an analysis means decomposing a situation or problem into its constituents. However, there are not any "primitives" that naturally exist. The components defined are arbitrary and depend on individual goals and methods of calculation. The basic elements of a fire are different to a firefighter, an insurance claims adjuster, and an arson investigator.

Logical atomism, the belief that ideas and concepts can be decomposed into their natural elements, was popular among philosophers in the 1920s and 1930s. It has since been abandoned in philosophy, and in psychology, atomistic schemes have usually proved arbitrary and unworkable. In psychology we usually cannot reduce natural situations to a reliable and valid set of symbolic units that can be treated with logical operators.

There is no "right" way to break down a task. Different people find different schemes. Even the same person might choose different schemes depending on the goals being pursued. If we try to predefine the basic elements, we must either work with an artificial or narrow task, or run the risk of distorting the situation to make it fit into the so-called basic elements.

Alternatively, we can accept the importance of experience in seeking useful ways to decompose a task within a task. Most of the time we blend the analytical and experiential sources of power to get things done. Few of us fall into the trap of hyperrationality.

Ambiguous Rules

Rules and procedures take some sort of the if-then form. They often sound simple, but the hard part is figuring out if the antecedent condition, the "if" part of the rule, has been met.[3] That is why researchers prefer to work on rational inference using context-free artificial problems that leave no ambiguity. Outside the laboratory, we find it difficult to pin down the context so that people can agree that the antecedent conditions were met, and expect that the rule will be carried out. In example 13.1, concerning the *Goeben*, Churchill gave an order that was essentially a rule: if you are faced with a superior force, do not fight it. Can we say that Admiral Troubridge violated the rule? The context of the situation, the ambiguities, make it hard to judge whether the *Goeben* constituted a superior force to Troubridge's twelve ships.

Most people are sensitive to how much judgment and interpretation are needed to carry out a rule or an order. We rarely try to plan out every contingency. Instead, we try to make it easy to understand the intent behind the rule or order.

Difficulty of Setting Up the Calculations

Even when we know which rules apply and which to perform, we still have to initialize the equations or arguments. It is usually difficult to make the estimates called for by calculational methods. When the calculations require people to estimate probabilities or utilities, to estimate their values or to make other unnatural judgments, we are going to have trouble. The experiential sources of power do not appear to be helpful in generating the estimates that would be used in analyses.[4]

Combinatorial Explosions

Formal methods of rational analysis can run into difficulties when they consider a large set of factors (as is found in a natural setting) and try to work out the implications of all the different permutations. As you add more knowledge, the job of searching through the connections will increase exponentially. "The problem with inferences," say Schank and Owens (1987), "is that there are too many of them to make. If, for example, we can make five inferences from a fact, and five more inferences from each of those inferences and so forth, then the combinatorial complexity of trying to investigate inference chains of any length greater than a few steps becomes overwhelming. Processing power is not infinite, either in people or in machines" (p. 12).

In our everyday lives, we do not face combinatorial explosions because we are not relying on calculations. We use experiential sources of power to frame situations and arrive at manageable representations. Then, if necessary, we bring in the analytical methods to add precision.

The analytical methods run into limits when we try to use them without recourse to the experiential sources of power. The problem is not rationality but hyperrationality.

The Hobgoblin

I have always been a fan of consistency. One of my pleasures is detecting inconsistencies in the actions and ideas of other people. My wife has learned to be tolerant when I triumphantly find yet another example of her inconsistencies. She recites the phrase, "A foolish consistency is the hobgoblin of little minds," and turns to more important matters.

We all know that consistency is important because of all the errors that can be traced to inconsistencies. For example, your friend needs to use your car, so you pick the friend up, switch places, get driven to your home and dropped off; you wave goodbye, walk up to your door, and realize that your house key is on the key chain in your car ignition. In one part of your brain, you knew you needed the key chain to get into your house. In another place, maybe just a few neurons away, you knew you had to leave the key chain with your friend. Somehow the two ideas never got connected. If we can detect and eliminate inconsistencies, we can eliminate the errors caused by inconsistencies.

Rational analysis is appealing because it is a strategy for reducing or eliminating inconsistencies. We can try to decompose complex tasks, plans, or beliefs into smaller elements to find any inconsistency. Unhappily, several philosophers have recently questioned our ability to detect inconsistencies reliably (Cherniak, 1981; Harman, 1973, 1986; Stich, 1990).[5] Cherniak (1981) showed that we cannot just use a truth table method to make sure our beliefs are consistent: "Suppose that each line of the truth table for the conjunctions of all beliefs could be checked in the time a light ray takes to traverse the diameter of a proton, an appropriate 'supercycle' time, and suppose that the computer was permitted to run for twenty billion years, the estimated time from the 'bigbang' dawn of the universe to the present. A belief system containing only 138 logically independent propositions would overwhelm the time resources of this supermachine" (p. 93).

In view of this, we cannot expect anyone to maintain a perfectly consistent set of beliefs. It is easy to trace an error backward and find an inconsistency, but that takes advantage of hindsight. We cannot root out the inconsistencies in advance.

Harman examined a type of inconsistency where we continue to hold a belief even when we no longer accept the evidence on which it was based. To stamp out this type of inconsistency, we would have to classify, code, and store in memory all of the evidence on which every belief is based.

Cherniak has presented another type of inconsistency, which he calls memory compartmentalization. Here, a person holds inconsistent beliefs but does not make the connection because the beliefs are stored in different contexts in memory. Cherniak gives these two examples. First, "At least a decade before Fleming's discovery of penicillin, many microbiologists were aware that molds cause clear spots in bacteria cultures, and they knew that such a bare spot indicates no bacterial growth. Yet they did not consider the possibility that molds release an antibacterial agent." The other is that "Smith believes an open flame can ignite gasoline ..., and Smith believes the match he now holds has an open flame ..., and Smith is not suicidal. Yet Smith decides to see whether a gas tank is empty by looking inside while holding the match nearby for illumination" (p. 57).

The Fleming story does not seem like an instance of inconsistency, and the Smith story does. However, both show the same pattern: an inconsistency between the set of beliefs held and the actions taken. Once we see the error or the missed opportunity, we can trace it back to the beliefs that did not get connected. It is too much to expect that every piece of information in memory be continually matched against every other piece to catch these connections and draw their implications. It would take exhaustive memory search to find the interesting connections. We can feel proud when we do discover them, but if the pieces belong to different memory compartments, we cannot expect high levels of success.

These examples indicate that it is impossible to free ourselves from inconsistency, belief perseverance, and memory compartmentalization. Actually, there is one way to ensure that people find inconsistencies and discover connections: by keeping the number of beliefs small. If we could struggle through life with only a few beliefs, perhaps fewer than ten, then we might have a chance to purge inconsistencies.

There is worse news. Consistency may not be as helpful as we imagined. Jonathan Grudin (1989) has questioned the advice given to people who design computer interfaces to eliminate all inconsistencies. He wondered how good this advice was. In his home, he does not keep all his knives in one place. The knives used for eating go in one drawer. The putty knife he uses in his shop goes in a separate room. The set of large carving knives is kept in a wood block on the kitchen counter. The Swiss army knife is with other camping gear. If he stored them together, he would have less trouble trying to find a knife, but many of them would be in inconvenient locations. Grudin is using consistency of *function* as his guiding principle. This takes more effort, judgment, and insight than consistency of *feature*. It is not sufficient to identify something as a knife. You have to understand how it will be used. If you settle for maintaining consistency of feature and expect that this strategy will keep everything well organized, you will be disappointed.

The same problem arises for computer screens. Should a designer adopt only consistent procedures? Consider the rule that if you select an action from a menu, the computer should persevere in that mode. The "last action selected" strategy makes sense for some functions, such as picking a font style. Once I pick a style, the system retains that style until I change it. The "last action selected" rule also makes sense in searching for items. Once I enter a name in the query box and set the computer searching for it, I am likely to want to continue through the document looking for other instances in which the name appears. The search function retains that name until I change it. The "last action selected" rule does not make sense for the cut-and-paste function. When I cut something, the most likely next act will be to paste it somewhere else. My computer anticipates this and makes it easy by switching modes automatically. The designers realized I would not be cutting one sentence or paragraph after another.

The designers would not have done a good job if they insisted on a consistent principle, such as retaining a default option once someone selects it until it is changed. They had to understand how I was going to use the system and design around my needs. They had to preserve the consistency of function rather than consistency of feature.

Therefore, we should be wary of efforts to ensure consistency at the level of features that do not consider the functions we are trying to perform. Rigor is not a substitute for imagination. Consistency is not a replacement for insight. Most of the time we would rather have consistency than leave ourselves open to the problems created by inconsistency. It is a goal worth seeking, but attempts to ensure unrealistic levels of consistency are a symptom of hyperrationality. Our experience helps us anticipate the impacts of inconsistent beliefs and set the level of effort for reducing inconsistencies.

Logic is indifferent to truth. The goal of logic is to root out inconsistent beliefs and generate new beliefs consistent with the original set. Logic does not consider whether our beliefs are true. A logical person can be wrong in everything she or he believes and still be consistent.

Although we cannot always calculate inconsistencies, we are alert for them. We try to perceive inconsistencies in order to detect anomalies; the anomalies trigger our efforts to diagnose situations and initiate problem solving. We try to see the inconsistencies. The following example shows how finding an inconsistency helped someone to see.

Example 15.1
The Case of the Missing Contact Lens

It is Saturday morning. I am lying on the sofa reading a Simenon mystery novel about Inspector Maigret, wandering the streets of Paris with him in search of yet another criminal, when my wife makes an unhappy discovery: one of her contact lenses is missing. Before I start crawling around on the floor, we go over the facts. We had guests for dinner the night before. She removed her contacts after they left. She was seated at the dining room table and carefully removed them over the tablecloth so she could find them easily if they popped out. She thinks something might have distracted her during this time. She put each into its own little cell, screwed the lids on, and carried the case to the bathroom. This morning she picked up the contact lens case, opened up the first compartment, and found that it was empty.

She thinks it is possible that one of the lenses might have stuck to her finger as she attempted to deposit it in the case; this has never happened before, but it is something she worries about.

Example 15.1 (continued)

We deduce that the missing lens could be in one of two places: either it was transferred poorly last night, and should be on the tablecloth or the dining room floor, or it slipped out this morning and is somewhere in the bathroom. A third possibility is that it wound up on the dining room floor and has been crushed or tracked to some unrecoverable place. We choose to repress this third hypothesis.

I spend the next thirty minutes carefully searching the dining room. No luck. The next thirty minutes is devoted to the bathroom. Again, nothing. I am certain that the contact lens is in neither place. The third hypothesis must be true: the lens fell to the dining room floor and has gone to a permanent resting place. I have done all I can and return to my book.

My wife is desperate to find the lens, and she continues her search alone. After an hour she again asks for my help, but we have no new leads, no clues. However, the spirit of the book I am holding steals over me. I quickly review the chronology of events and then lean back on the sofa, puffing an imaginary pipe of the sort Inspector Maigret might smoke. Then a voice disfigured by an attempted French accent tells my wife, "Go into the bedroom, to the clothes hamper, retrieve the tablecloth that is folded there, carefully open up the tablecloth on the floor, and you will find your missing contact lens in the middle."

I settle back into my novel. When I hear my wife's exclamation of triumph, I permit myself a thin, smug smile.

This is one of my most successful cases. (Actually, it is my only successful case, and I am pleased to have this opportunity to get it in print.) What has happened is that the previous night, one contact lens did slip out while my wife transferred it to the case, and it landed on the tablecloth. After bringing the contact lens case to the bathroom, my wife prepared for the next day, as she usually does after a meal, by rolling up the tablecloth to trap all the crumbs and food debris so that they would not fall on the floor. She carried the tablecloth to the hamper, where it would remain until the next washday, when it would be shaken outside. This is her routine. Then we went to sleep. Saturday morning she brought out a fresh tablecloth, performed a number of other tasks, and then went to put in her contact lenses.

The inconsistencies in our beliefs were due to memory compartmentalization. My wife and I knew that Friday night's tablecloth was in the hamper. We knew that the contact lens had been removed Friday night. We searched for it on the clean tablecloth that had been put out Saturday morning. The two tablecloths were even of different colors: yellow (Friday) and blue (Saturday). Yet neither of us noticed the disconnect, until that last-minute mental simulation sorted out the two tablecloths. I am convinced that the credit should go to Inspector Maigret. He and his kind are the only ones who can be relied upon to catch inconsistencies.

Key Points

- Rational analysis is a source of power with strengths and weaknesses.
- Hyperrationality is the attempt to apply deductive and statistical reasoning and analyses to situations where they do not apply.
- Hyperrationality runs into difficulty for a number of reasons:

    There are no basic elements.

    Rules are ambiguous.

    Setting up the calculations requires subjective judgments.

    Formal analyses can degenerate into combinational explosions.

    Trying to conduct a formal analysis can interfere with nonrational forms of thinking.

    The features of natural settings usually prevent formal analysis.

- Consistency is rarely ensured in natural settings.

16
Why Good People Make Poor Decisions

Poor outcomes are different from poor decisions. The best decision possible given the knowledge available can still turn out unhappily. I am interested only in the cases where we regret the way we made the decision, not the outcome. I define a poor decision—where we regret the process we used—in the following way: *A person will consider a decision to be poor if the knowledge gained would lead to a different decision if a similar situation arose.* Simply knowing that the outcome was unfavorable should not matter. Knowing what you failed to consider would matter.

Those who favor analytical approaches to decision making believe poor decisions are caused by biases in the way we think. Naturalistic decision-making researchers disagree. We tend to reject the idea of faulty reasoning and try to show that poor decisions are caused by factors such as lack of experience. The decision bias explanation is the more widespread and popular view so we will examine it first.

Are Poor Decisions Caused by Biased Thinking?

Kahneman, Slovic, and Tversky (1982) present a range of studies showing that decision makers use a variety of heuristics, simple procedures that usually produce an answer but are not foolproof.[1] The studies showed that in making judgments, we rely on information that is more readily available and appears more representative of the situation. We usually start analyses with known facts and make adjustments from these.

Kahneman, Slovic, and Tversky designed their studies so that the heuristics they were trying to demonstrate would lead to worse performance.

The rationale was that the heuristics were so powerful that their subjects would use them even if it meant more errors. The studies used tasks in which probabilities could be calculated in advance, allowing the researchers to set up objective standards for performance. The research strategy was not to demonstrate how poorly we make judgments but to use these findings to uncover the cognitive processes underlying judgments of likelihood.

Because of this strategy, many professionals have interpreted this research as demonstrating biases, not just heuristics. The research strategy has become known as the "heuristics and biases" paradigm. To date, more than two dozen decision biases have been identified. Many researchers interpret this research as showing that people are inherently biased and will misconstrue evidence. Therefore, decision errors must be caused by these biases. Decision training programs, such as the one presented by Jay Russo and Paul Shoemaker in their book *Decision Traps* (1989), were designed to reduce the influence of the decision biases. The heuristics and biases school is active and influential, particularly in the United States and Great Britain, but it is also coming under attack now.

Lola Lopes (1991) has shown that the original studies did not demonstrate biases, in the common use of the term. For example, Kahneman and Tversky (1973) used questions such as this: "Consider the letter *R*. Is *R* more likely to appear in the first position of a word or the third position of a word?" The example taps into our heuristic of availability. We have an easier time recalling words that begin with *R* than words with *R* in the third position. Most people answer that *R* is more likely to occur in the first position. This is incorrect. It shows how we rely on availability.

Lopes points out that examples such as the one using the letter *R* were carefully chosen. Of the twenty possible consonants, twelve are more common in the first position. Kahneman and Tversky (1973) used the eight that are more common in the third position. They used stimuli only where the availability heuristic would result in a wrong answer. Several studies found that decision biases are reduced if the study includes contextual factors and that the heuristics and biases do not occur in experienced decision makers working in natural settings.[2]

There is an irony here. One of the primary "biases" is confirmation bias—the search for information that confirms your hypothesis even though you would learn more by searching for evidence that might disconfirm it. The confirmation bias has been shown in many laboratory studies (and has not been found in a number of studies conducted in natural settings). Yet one of the most common strategies of scientific research is to derive a prediction from a favorite theory and test it to show that it is accurate, thereby strengthening the reputation of that theory. Scientists search for confirmation all the time, even though philosophers of science, such as Karl Popper (1959), have urged scientists to try instead to disconfirm their favorite theories. Researchers working in the heuristics and biases paradigm condemn this sort of bias in their subjects, even as those same researchers perform more laboratory studies confirming their theories.

What Accounts for Errors in Natural Decision Settings?

Naturalistic decision-making researchers are coming to doubt that errors can be neatly identified and attributed to faulty reasoning. Jim Reason, at the University of Manchester, finds that the operator of a system who is blamed for the error is often the victim of a series of problems of faulty design and practice (1990). Reason coined the term *latent pathogens* to refer to all the problems such as poor design, poor training, and poor procedures, that may be undetected until the operator falls into the trap. It is easy to blame the operator for the mistake, yet all of the earlier problems made the mistake virtually inevitable. David Woods and his colleagues at Ohio State University (1993) assert that decision errors do not exist. If we try to understand the information available to a person, the goals the person is pursuing, and the level of experience, we will stop blaming people for making decision errors. No one is arguing that we should not look at poor outcomes. The reverse is true. The discovery of an error is the beginning of the inquiry rather than the end. The real work is to find out the range of factors that resulted in the undesirable outcome.[3]

To get a better sense of what leads to poor decisions, I reviewed the data my colleagues and I had collected in different domains, covering more than six hundred decision points (Klein, 1993).[4] I identified any decision point that resulted in a poor outcome, where the decision maker could have known better. I primarily relied on the comments of the decision makers, for the incidents where they admitted that they had done the wrong thing. I categorized a set of twenty-five decisions as errors. This is a small number so the conclusions are only speculative.

I was able to place the errors into three categories. Of the twenty-five, sixteen were due to lack of experience. For example, a fireground commander failed to call in a second alarm because the fire did not seem large. He did not realize that the balloon construction of the building made it vulnerable to damage to the supporting framework. Now that he knows better, he doubts if he will make the mistake again.

A second cause of poor decisions was lack of information. For example, a flight crew failed to obtain full weather reports prior to takeoff and failed to identify alternate landing sites. When the simulated flight ran into difficulties due to malfunctions thrown at them by the people controlling the exercise, the weather profile was inadequate for selecting an alternate landing site. The third source of poor decisions was due to mental simulation, the *de minimus* error. Decision makers noticed the signs of a problem but explained it away. They found a reason not to take seriously each piece of evidence that warned them of an anomaly. As a result, they did not detect the anomaly in time to prevent a problem.[5]

Example 16.1
The Missed Diagnosis

In the neonatal intensive care unit, the nurse is assigned to a baby who is not in her regular care. She notices that the baby has a distended stomach, blood in the stool, along with a 3 cc aspirate. All these are signs of necrotizing enterocolitis, a condition afflicting premature babies in which the bowel becomes infected. The nurse does nothing, and by the next day the baby is critically ill.

The nurse fails to act because she explains away each symptom. The distended belly reminds her of an earlier case in which the neonatal intensive care unit treated this baby's sister. The sister also had an unusually large belly, so the nurse classifies the feature as a family trait. The blood in the stool is only a small amount and can be related to the baby's nasogastral tube. Finally, the 3 cc aspirate is small enough so that, by itself, it could not be considered unusual.

The weakness is that decision makers can easily dismiss evidence that is inconvenient, explaining away the early warning signs. These limitations could prevent decision makers from detecting the early signs of a problem because they might not recognize anomalies or sense the urgency of the problem. The limitations could lead decision makers to misrepresent the situation, perhaps by explaining away key pieces of information, failing to consider alternate explanations and diagnoses, or leaving decision makers confused by complexity. Finally, the limitations in experience could make it too hard for decision makers to notice weaknesses in their planned courses of action.

The Effect of Stress on Decision Making

We often blame poor decisions on stress. This is too simplistic. The evidence that supposedly shows that stress results in decision errors is not convincing (Klein, 1996). Reflect back on the fireground commanders, nurses, pilots, and others we have examined who perform so well under extreme time pressure, high stakes, ambiguity, and other features of naturalistic decision making. Remember the study described in chapter 10, showing that chess masters continued to make strong moves even under extreme time pressure, an average of six seconds per move. We should not be so willing to accept the premise that stress results in decision errors.

I am not arguing that stressors do not have an effect. My claim is that stress does affect the way we process information, but it does *not* cause us to make bad decisions based on the information at hand. It does not warp our minds into making poor choices. Stressors such as time pressure, noise, and ambiguity, result in the following effects:

- The stressors do not give us a chance to gather as much information.
- The stressors disrupt our ability to use our working memory to sort things out.
- The stressors distract our attention from the task at hand.

Under time pressure, we obviously will not be able to sample as many cues. But if our decisions get worse, it is not because a state of stress clouded our minds but that we did not have the chance to gather all the facts. Incidentally, the data show that experienced decision makers adapt to time pressure very well by focusing on the most relevant cues and ignoring the others.

Stressors such as noise may interfere with the ability to rehearse things in working memory. This factor might be particularly disruptive for tasks requiring a lot of mental simulation. The concentration needed to construct a mental simulation of how a plan will be carried out may sometimes require inner speech. However, I do not know of any studies showing that noise and other distractors interfere with mental simulation.

A third effect of stressors is to capture our attention. If we have to adapt to noise, pain, or fear, for instance, then we may need to monitor ourselves. We have to manage our reactions (e.g., hyperventilation) to the stressor. Now we have two things to do: make the decision and cope with the stressor. The more tasks we have to juggle, the worse we generally do.

Stressors should disrupt decision making the most if people use strategies such as a rational choice analysis. Time pressure and ambiguity alone would prevent anyone from carrying out that type of strategy. If we believed that people ordinarily generated option sets and contrasted the options, then we would expect stress to degrade decision making. However, if people rely on recognitional decision strategies, then we would not expect to see much disruption, particularly when the decision makers were reasonably experienced.

The Problem of Uncertainty

One definition of uncertainty (paraphrasing Lipshitz and Shaul, 1997) is "doubt that threatens to block action." Key pieces of information are missing, unreliable, ambiguous, inconsistent, or too complex to interpret, and as a result a decision maker will be reluctant to act. In many cases, the action will be delayed or will be overtaken by events as windows of opportunity close. Because it is impossible to achieve 100 percent certainty, decision makers must be able to proceed without having a full understanding of events. Some decision makers may be too impetuous, chasing after rumors. Others may require too much information, and as a result they may wait too long to take action.

Uncertainty is the reverse side of the ability to size up situations quickly. To see how doubt can block action, contrast the RPD model with the model of uncertainty in figure 16.1. Everywhere that experience had generated recognition of familiarity, uncertainty generates confusion and lack of understanding. Where experience enables decision makers to take action rapidly, uncertainty results in doubt.

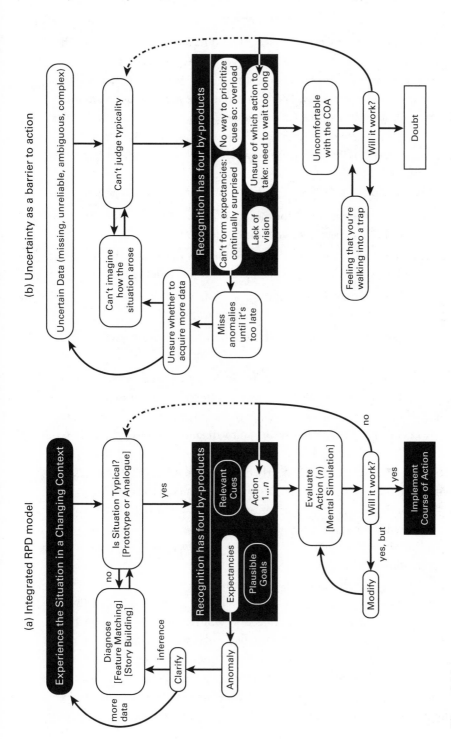

Figure 16.1
How uncertainty leads to doubt

In talking about uncertainty, people tend to mix many things together. A review of the literature shows that people discuss uncertainty in terms of risks, probabilities, confidence, ambiguity, inconsistency, instability, confusions, and complexity. They refer to uncertainty about future states, the nature of the situation, the consequences of actions, and preferences. Because so many concepts are packed into the term *uncertainty*, it is difficult to address how to help people handle uncertainty without becoming more precise.

Schmitt and Klein (1996) identified four sources of uncertainty:

1. Missing information. Information is unavailable. It has not been received or has been received but cannot be located when needed.

2. Unreliable information. The credibility of the source is low, or is perceived to be low even if the information is highly accurate.

3. Ambiguous or conflicting information. There is more than one reasonable way to interpret the information.

4. Complex information. It is difficult to integrate the different facets of the data.

We can also identify several different levels of uncertainty: the level of data; the level of knowledge, in which inferences are drawn about the data; and the level of understanding, in which the inferences are synthesized into projections of the future, into diagnoses and explanations of events.

Is uncertainty inevitable? Clearly the technology available in the future will dramatically increase the information available, yet we cannot be optimistic that increasing information will necessarily reduce uncertainty. It is more likely that the information age will change the challenges posed by uncertainty. For one thing, decision makers will still be plagued with missing information.

Previously, information was missing because no one had collected it; in the future, information will be missing because no one can find it. Moreover, the improved data collection will likely transform into faster decision cycles. By way of analogy, when radar was introduced into commercial shipping, it was for the intent of improving safety so that ships could avoid collisions when visibility was poor. The actual impact was that ships increased their speed, and accident rates stayed constant. On the decision front, we expect to find the same thing. Planning cycles will be expedited, and the plans will be made with the same level of uncertainty as there was before. Moreover, communication technology means that clients expect faster decisions—without the time allowed in the past for thoughtful reflection.

Sometimes it is tempting to believe that we can use information technology to eliminate certain types of uncertainty. For example, an intelligent system could screen all messages to detect inconsistencies and weed these out. This dream is unrealistic. The next generation of computers will not eliminate uncertainty caused by inconsistencies.

Great commanders are able to overcome the problem of uncertainty. Analysis of historical data shows that the effective commanders, such as Grant and Rommel, accepted the inevitability of uncertainty. Rather than being paralyzed, their actions blocked by doubt, they all possessed the ability to shape the battlefield, acting decisively and prudently at the same time. They were able to force the adversary on the defensive, shifting the burden of uncertainty. They were able to maintain flexibility without planning out various contingencies (which were sure to become obsolete). On the battlefield, plans are vulnerable to the cascading probability of disruption. If a plan depends on six steps and each has a 90 percent probability of being carried out successfully, many decision makers will feel confident, whereas the actual probability of carrying out the plan is just over 50 percent since the probabilities multiply. Highly successful commanders seem to appreciate the vagaries of chance and do not waste time worrying about details that will not matter. The inference we draw is that although uncertainty is and will be inevitable, it is possible to maintain effective decision making in the face of it.

Because uncertainty is inevitable, decisions can never be perfect. Often we believe that we can improve the decision by collecting more information, but in the process we lose opportunities. Skilled decision makers appear to know when to wait and when to act. Most important, they accept the need to act despite uncertainty.

Expertise versus Superstition

I have been arguing that expertise can provide important sources of power other than rational analysis. People with greater expertise can see the world differently. They have a larger storehouse of procedures to apply.

They notice problems more quickly. They have richer mental simulations to use in diagnosing problems and in evaluating courses of action. They have more analogies to draw upon.

Expertise can also get us in trouble. It can lead us to view problems in stereotyped ways. The sense of typicality can be so strong that we miss subtle signs of trouble. Or we may know so much that we can explain away those signs, as in the missed diagnosis in example 16.1. In general, these shortcomings seem a small price to pay; however, there may be times when a fresh set of eyes proves helpful.

I am more troubled by the difficulty of learning from experience. We cannot often see a clear link between cause and effect. Too many variables intervene, and time delays create their own complications.[6] If managers find themselves having success—getting projects completed on schedule and under budget—does that success stem from their own skills, the skills of their subordinates, temporary good luck, interventions of higher-level administrators, a blend of these factors, or some other causes altogether? There is no easy way to tell. We can learn the wrong lessons from experience. Each time we compile a story about an experience, we run the risk of getting it wrong and stamping in the wrong strategy.

An analogue here is the way historians debate the causes of famous events—for example, the Great Depression. Franklin Delano Roosevelt was elected president in 1932 to help the nation climb back to prosperity, and he took many strong actions. Some historians and economists argue that these actions did the trick; others claim that they made the problem worse. The Great Depression was an event of major importance in our history that has received enormous scrutiny, and we still do not know if Roosevelt's actions were effective in bringing about economic recovery.

Because of the difficulty of interpreting cause-and-effect relationships, lawmakers cannot achieve high levels of expertise. They can certainly master the procedures of being politicians, for example, getting on the most influential committees, forging ties with lobbyists, doing favors for the right people. Nevertheless, they cannot learn the long-term impacts of the legislation that they consider. They cannot learn the causal dynamics between a piece of legislation and eventual social changes. Their mental models are not flexible or rich. When politicians ask to be reelected because of their experience, they are referring to the efficiency with which they do their job, not their growing wisdom in judging which laws to propose and support.

This brings us to the question of superstition. Many of us consider superstitions as characteristics of primitive cultures that have not been able to figure out cause-and-effect relationships. We hear stories of cultures that never learned the linkage between conception and the birth that occurs nine months later. We hear stories about magical thinking, such as performing rituals to ensure that the crops will be good. Citizens of a rational society should be beyond superstitions.

Yet we follow rituals all the time without any evidence that they work. We pass laws on all sorts of topics without any evidence that they will change behaviors. We encourage unhappy people to seek counseling for a great many problems for which there is no evidence that counseling will provide benefit. Corporations adopt fads to build morale or increase motivation without any evidence that these will work; they reorganize to improve efficiency without any definitive evidence that the new structure will be any better. We read the latest scare reports about foods that are linked to cancers and try to adjust our diets accordingly, even though for most of these reports there is no indication that these linkages will have any practical impacts on life span.

In short, our lives are just as governed by superstitions as those of less advanced cultures. The content of the superstitions has changed but not the degree to which they control us. The reason is that for many important aspects of our lives, we cannot pin down the causal relationships. We must act on faith, rumor, and precedent.

In a domain such as fighting fires, caring for hospitalized infants, or flying an airplane, expertise can be gained. In other domains, such as selecting stocks, making public policy, or raising a child, the time delays are long and the feedback is uncertain. Jim Shanteau (1992) has suggested that we will not build up real expertise when:

- The domain is dynamic.
- We have to predict human behavior.
- We have less chance for feedback.
- The task does not have enough repetition to build a sense of typicality.
- We have fewer trials.

Under these conditions, we should be cautious about assuming that experience translates into expertise. In these sorts of domains, experience would give us smooth routines, showing that we had been doing the job for a while. Yet our expertise might not go much beyond these surface routines; we would not have a chance to develop reliable expertise.

Lia Di Bello has studied the way people in organizations learn different kinds of complex skills.[7] She found that she could distinguish competent workers, who had mastered the routines, from the real experts. If she gave people a task that violated the rules they had been using, the experts would quickly notice the violation and find a way to work around it. They could improvise to achieve the desired goal.

Where does this leave us regarding the growth of expertise? At one extreme is the work of Ericsson and Charness (1994), suggesting almost anyone can become expert at almost anything, given enough practice. At the other extreme is the work of people like Russo and Shoemaker, suggesting that all of us are inherently biased and unreliable as decision makers. And in between is the suggestion by Shanteau that expertise is more easily acquired in some domains than others. In short, we do not have answers, yet we may have a basis for asking better questions about the way expertise develops.

Applications

One way to improve performance is to be more careful in considering alternate explanations and diagnoses for a situation. The *de minimus* error may arise from using mental simulation to explain away cues that are early warnings of a problem. One exercise to correct this tendency is to use the crystal ball technique discussed in chapter 5. The idea is that you can look at the situation, pretend that a crystal ball has shown that your explanation is wrong, and try to come up with a different explanation. Each time you stretch for a new explanation, you are likely to consider more factors, more nuances. This should reduce fixation on a single explanation. The crystal ball method is not well suited for time-pressured conditions. By practicing with it when we have the time, we may learn what it feels like to fixate on a hypothesis. This judgment may help us in situations of time pressure.

A second application is to accept all errors as inevitable. In complex situations, no amount of effort is going to be able to prevent any errors. Jens Rasmussen (1974) came to this conclusion in his work with nuclear power plants, which is one of the industries most preoccupied with safety. He pointed out that the typical method for handling error is to erect defenses that make the errors less and less likely: add warnings, safeguards, automatic shut-offs, and all kinds of other defenses. These do reduce the number of errors, but at a cost, and errors will continue to be made, and accidents will continue to happen. In a massively defended system, if an accident sneaks through all the defenses, the operators will find it far more difficult to diagnose and correct it. That is because they must deal with all of the defenses, along with the accident itself. Recall example 13.7, the flight mismanagement system. A unit designed to reduce small errors helped to create a large one.

Since defenses in depth do not seem to work, Rasmussen suggests a different approach: instead of erecting defenses, accept malfunctions and errors, and make their existence more visible. We can try to design better human-system interfaces that let the system operators quickly notice that something is going wrong and form diagnoses and reactions. Instead of trusting the systems (and, by extension, the cleverness of the design engineers) we can trust the competence of the operators and make sure they have the tools to maintain situation awareness throughout the incident.[8]

Key Points

- Decision biases do not seem to explain poor decisions.
- Stress does not result in faulty decision-making strategies but may limit the information we can consider in making the decisions.
- Most poor decisions may result from having inadequate knowledge and expertise.
- Experience does not translate directly into expertise if the domain is dynamic, feedback is inadequate, and the number and variety of experiences is too small.

17

Conclusions

This book has been an exploration of human strengths and capabilities. Despite the vagaries of experience, we can make reasonable sense of our worlds. Even when we do not achieve high levels of expertise, even when we confront uncertainties and other stressors, we generally find ways to reach and refine our goals.

I have concentrated on the strengths, the sources of power, that are difficult to study and understand. They are the abilities that repeatedly emerge in the study of naturalistic decision making. They are difficult to examine, as we have found, but that should not be grounds for ignoring them.

The sources of power we have been examining are what people do when they are not using deductive logic or probability theory. Work in naturalistic decision making over the past ten to fifteen years has attempted to give these sources a positive definition. We have tried to understand what people were doing and why their strategies might make sense, instead of seeing the lack of rationality as a failure of intellect.

Our efforts were aided by the fact that we were studying highly proficient decision makers. We came to respect and admire them. This admiration may have biased our work, or it may have informed it. When we study naive subjects who are performing unfamiliar tasks, and we know what the right answers are, then the best our subjects can do is not get it wrong. They are not going to surprise us, and it is unlikely that they will impress us. We can use our subjects to learn about our theories, but we will not learn very much from them. The relationship between experimenter and subject is between the one who knows and the one who is ignorant.

In our case, the relationship was reversed. The decision makers we studied were the ones who knew, and we were the ignorant ones, trying to find out. My colleagues and I could not call the people in our studies subjects. We used the terms *participants* or *subject matter experts*. Our motivation was not to test hypotheses, but to follow the lead of curiosity and get insights about the strategies the subject matter experts used.

Do not be misled by the types of experts you have met in this book: firefighters, jet pilots, nurses, and the rest. Each of us has expertise we use to make decisions, in one context or another. How do we decide which line will move faster at the grocery store? Which car will be best to follow through a traffic light? These are trivial examples. Countless others can be found at work, at home, or in school settings.

The sources of power discussed in the previous chapters are going against the general stream of research that emanates from the field of cognitive psychology. As long as the rational and analytical processes were defined as the ideal for reasoning, researchers have filled in more and more parts of the puzzle about how information is received and processed, and stored and retrieved. The computer is taken as a metaphor for the mind so that the challenge of the artificial intelligence framework is to find the right programs or the right architecture. Rational choice strategies offer the same type of general framework, treating decision making as the activity of judging probabilities and utilities. The job of researchers is to understand why people might generate the wrong values or inconsistent values. In both cases, artificial intelligence and rational choice strategies, the research agendas are well established.

In contrast, the processes we have been examining do not fit well into the frameworks of artificial intelligence or rational choice strategies. Rather than helping to tie off loose ends, the sources of power I describe in this book are busily proliferating them. We are finding that it was too early to reach closure about how people make decisions in natural settings. We had not properly understood the phenomena we were trying to model. We need to spend more energy in appreciating how people size up situations, make decisions, and solve problems.

Compiling the Assertions

Experience counts. This sounds so obvious that we should not have to waste time stating it. Yet most studies in decision making use subjects who are inexperienced in the task they are performing, and most advice assumes an inexperienced audience. The different sources of power covered in this book are ways of drawing on experience.

Expertise depends on perceptual skills. You rarely get someone to jump a skill level by teaching more facts and rules. Perhaps in a field such as mathematics, a teacher can move a student rapidly through some concepts. However, in natural settings, perceptual learning takes many cases to develop. Therefore, we cannot expect to grow instant experts by using powerful training methods. We can make training more efficient but cannot radically replace the accumulation of experiences.

The computer metaphor of thinking is incomplete. Mechanistic descriptions of skilled problem solving and decision making emphasize the storage, retrieval, and manipulation of data elements. This is one aspect of expertise, and certainly it is relevant to some tasks. But there are other aspects that are important.

Skilled problem solvers and decision makers are themselves scientists and experimenters. They are actively searching for and using stories and analogues, personal as well as borrowed from others, to learn about the important causal factors in their lives.

Skilled problem solvers and decision makers are chameleons. They can simulate all types of events and processes in their heads. They simulate the thinking of other people with whom they come in contact.

The sources of power described in this book operate in ways that are not analytical.

- They are generative, channeling the decision making from opportunity to opportunity rather than exhaustively filtering through all the permutations.
- They enable the decision maker to redefine goals and also to search for ways to achieve existing goals.
- They trade accuracy for speed and therefore allow errors.

- They are ways of building a person's experience base. Experience can be codified as stories and analogues.
- They can be used in context, with interactive causes.

The sources of power described in this book have limitations as well as strengths. There are additional sources of power, such as analysis and calculation, that break tasks down into abstract elements and perform operations on these elements. In many difficult tasks, we blend the different sources of power and integrate them to fit the needs of the situation. I hope that the crude distinction between analytical and nonanalytical will give way so that we can learn to make more interesting comparisons and connections between the different sources of power.

Connecting the Sources of Power

In the preceding chapters we have examined several different sources of power:

- Intuition (pattern recognition, having the big picture, achieving situation awareness)
- Mental simulation (seeing the past and the future)
- Using leverage points to solve ill-defined problems
- Seeing the invisible (perceptual discriminations and expectancies)
- Storytelling
- Analogical and metaphorical reasoning
- Reading peoples' minds (communicating intent)
- Rational analysis
- Team mind (drawing on the experience base of the team)

We have also encountered a range of other judgments and abilities that could themselves have become the topics of chapters:

- Judging the typicality of a situation
- Judging typical goals
- Recognizing typical courses of action
- Judging the solvability of a problem
- Detecting anomalies
- Judging the urgency of a problem

- Detecting opportunities
- Making fine discriminations
- Detecting gaps in a plan of action
- Detecting barriers that are responsible for gaps in a plan of action

There are many different ways to connect all of these sources of power. Figure 17.1 presents one framework. Here, the two primary sources of power are pattern recognition (the power of intuition) and mental simulation. That is why they are so prominent. Storytelling seems to rely on the same processes as mental simulation, so it is tucked in next to it. The use of metaphors and analogues seems to rely on the same processes as pattern recognition, except that in pattern recognition the specific metaphors and analogues have become merged, so these two are pushed together. These are the four sources of power that refer to processes, to ways of thinking.

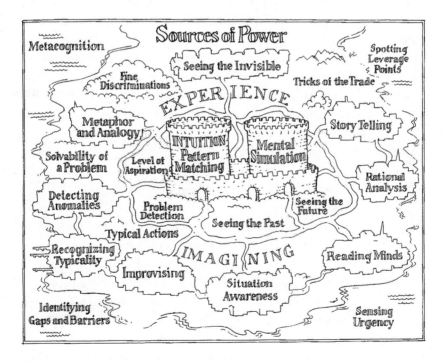

Figure 17.1

Sources of power

The other three sources of power are based on the first four, so they are arranged further into the periphery. These three refer to activities—ways of using the four processes at the base. Expertise (the power to see the invisible) derives from both pattern recognition and mental simulation. The ability to improvise in solving problems also derives from pattern recognition and mental simulation. Our ability to read minds depends on how well we can mentally simulate the thinking of the person. The additional sources of power are arranged according to the same sense of family resemblance. Figure 17.1 is a concept map of the way I am viewing these processes.

Is This Science?

The basic question of the book is, How do people make decisions and solve problems under natural conditions? The book describes the studies and efforts made to provide some answers. We can distinguish between a few different kinds of inquiry. A philosophical inquiry uses rules of logic to draw conclusions. A scientific inquiry uses carefully controlled and repeatable investigations. A pseudo-scientific inquiry pretends to conduct rigorous studies but does not, and it produces findings that are unreliable. What kind of an inquiry has this been? Clearly, it is not philosophical. In some ways it seems scientific, but the studies have weaknesses. That is one reason I spent so much time describing how we ran the studies, to allow you to judge for yourself how much confidence to have in the findings.

The studies I have described are not classical science. We did not calibrate our instruments and present stimuli that were carefully measured to determine their exact visual angle when projected onto the retina. These are the trappings of science but not the central features.

What are the criteria for doing a scientific piece of research? Simply, that the data are collected so that others can repeat the study and that the inquiry depends on evidence and data rather than argument. For work such as ours, replication means that others could collect data the way we have and could also analyze and code the results as we have done. It will be difficult for others to conduct interviews using our methods, but we have published articles describing our methods, so others can learn them. After all, I could not replicate experiments in gene splicing without a considerable amount of training, so the fact that training is needed in data collection to study naturalistic decision making does not present a logical problem. In recent years there have been studies replicating our findings, particularly the findings about the RPD model (Mosier, 1991; Pascual & Henderson, 1997; Randel, Pugh, & Reed, 1996).

Regarding the nature of our data, one weakness of our work is that most of the studies relied on interviews rather than formal experiments to vary one thing at a time and see its effect. There are sciences that do not manipulate variables, such as geology or astronomy or anthropology. Naturalistic decision making research may be closer to anthropology than psychology. Sometimes we observe decision makers in action, but we rely on introspection in nearly all our studies. We ask people to describe what they are thinking, and we analyze their responses. We do not know if the things they are telling us are true, or maybe just some ideas they are making up. We can repeat the studies or, better yet, other investigators can repeat the studies to see if they get the same results. Nevertheless, no one can confidently believe what the decision makers say.

The use of introspection raises questions about how much to trust the findings of studies. However, alternate methods of scientific inquiry have their own problems and limitations. Research on naturalistic decision making collects and reports data, and it can be used as a source of ideas and hypotheses. The think-aloud data are soft, and fuzzy, and they are difficult to interpret. Nevertheless, we can still learn a lot by observing and questioning people as they perform realistic tasks within natural contexts.

The rigorous nature of laboratory research increases our confidence that we can replicate the results, but the rigor does not ensure that we can generalize the results. Orasanu and Connolly (1993) have questioned whether findings that are carefully obtained under laboratory conditions apply outside the laboratory. They cited one study of songbird behavior, showing that the patterns of birdsong found in natural settings varied during the breeding cycle in reaction to courting, nest building, mating, and tending the young. Previously the species had been studied only in the laboratory, and the results had been inconsistent and uninterpretable. A second study they cited found that judges and parole officers made different decisions about criminal sentences when they were in the courtroom than when they were in a laboratory simulation.

Both the laboratory methods and the field studies have to contend with shortcomings in their research programs. People who study naturalistic decision making must worry about their inability to control many of the conditions in their research. People who use well-controlled laboratory paradigms must worry about whether their findings generalize outside the laboratory.

One way to evaluate a naturalistic decision-making approach is by its products: the nature of the ideas and models that it generates and the applications it produces. If **NDM** and the study of different sources of power turn out to make little difference, then we will lose confidence in the approach more surely than any debate over what is science.

Final Thoughts and Final Perceptions

Have you ever noticed, after you have spent an afternoon at an art museum staring hard at paintings and sculpture, that when you walk out, the world looks different from when you entered? Colors become brighter; contrasting shapes are more striking. We go to museums to see objects, but the process of seeing is affected, and that is one of the things we carry away when we are finished walking through the galleries.

One of my goals for this book was to change the way you see the events around you, even if just for a short time. The book has presented many arguments. But arguments can be refuted. I want to have an impact on your perceptions.

When you are with other people, listening to their stories and telling your own stories, you may find yourself listening and speaking differently.

When you give someone instructions or receive instructions for carrying out a task, you may begin appraising whether any important aspects of communicating intent have been left out, or you may appreciate the skillful way some characteristics of intent were described.

When you imagine how something could have occurred or imagine how to make something happen, you may be more aware of how you are building and playing with mental simulations.

When someone uses an example, in an argument or to solve a problem, you may think of it as an informal experiment, an analogue, a carrier of experience.

When you have a chance to work with an expert, you may watch more closely to find out what that person is seeing that you cannot.

When you are a member of a team, you may notice the way the diverse experiences are voiced and blended. You may find yourself watching the way thoughts are created and combined, appreciating the chance to reflect on your own mind and on the sources of power you draw on with so little effort.

Notes

Chapter 1

1. Orasanu and Connolly (1993) and Cannon-Bowers, Salas, and Pruitt (1996) have presented comprehensive sets of criteria for naturalistic decision making research.

2. As far as I know, the term *sources of power* was originated in cognitive science by Doug Lenat (1984), a researcher in the area of artificial intelligence.

Lenat used the term *sources of power* to designate the analytical abilities of breaking a problem down into elements and performing basic operations on these elements as a way of solving a problem. The sources of power discussed in this book go beyond analytical abilities and include abilities that have traditionally been difficult for the field of artificial intelligence to handle. The analytical sources of power that Lenat and other artificial intelligence researchers have emphasized are described in sources such as J. R. Anderson (1983) and Newell (1990). Dreyfus (1972) has presented a critique of conventional artificial intelligence approaches. The work described in this book has been heavily influenced by Dreyfus and the Heideggerian perspective he described.

3. Several books are sympathetic to the analytical approach to decision making (e.g., Baron, 1988; Yates, 1990; and Dawes, 1988). Hastie (1991) has provided a good review of these.

4. Compared to the work in the United States, the European tradition seems to have been more open to field studies, as seen in the research of Rasmussen (1974), Edwards and Lee (1974), and others.

5. Zakay and Wooler (1984) have found that even when subjects are trained to use analytical decision strategies, they do not apply these strategies when they have a minute or less to make a decision.

Chapter 3

1. A great many would argue that we were not studying decision making at all. If you define decision making as deliberately choosing between competing courses of action, this excludes our investigation of how people select courses of action

without making comparisons. This is a valid argument but a dangerous one. It is valid if you insist on defining decision making as a choice between options, and then we just get into a fight about definitions. Researchers such as Berkeley and Humphreys (1982) have argued against such a narrow definition since it threatens to make the study of decision making irrelevant to most everyday activities. A growing body of data suggests that people rarely compare options. The narrow definition of decision making would preserve the traditional approaches to the phenomenon at the cost of reducing the value of studying it.

2. Taynor, Crandall, and Wiggins (1987) performed a study of the reliability of the methods we used and obtained satisfactory data—on the order of 80 to 90 percent agreement among different raters. Kaempf, Wolf, Thordsen, and Klein (1992) also found good reliability for the judgments of decision strategies: inter-rater agreement was higher than 90 percent.

3. Michael Doherty (personal communication, 1996) asserts that "if the cognitive work is done completely intuitively, then I believe it is impossible to make direct comparisons of two complex options in one's head. ... I do not see the alternative that [is dismissed here] as even psychologically possible."

4. Kirlik, Rothrock, Walker, and Fisk (1996) have noted that even in complex situations, decision makers rarely report using complex, enumerative decision strategies. Kirlik et al. performed a set of studies showing that this reported simplicity is not an artifact of recall but an accurate account of how people are able to formulate simple strategies for handling apparent complexity.

5. One area of cognition is the study of how people use categories. In our early interviews with firefighters, we tried to see if they would categorize fires in terms of the structure (e.g., single-family residence, apartment, factory). Instead, we formed the impression that they were categorizing fires in terms of what they had to do (e.g., search and rescue, interior attack, exterior attack, prevention of spread to other structures). In other words, the firefighters seemed to be using functional categories rather than structural categories. They were organizing their world on the basis of the response patterns called for.

6. Vilayanur Ramachandran is a neuroscientist who presented a physiological model of anomaly detection to explain the symptoms of some types of stroke victims. Ramachandran's model is based on the hypothesis that the stroke has impaired these victims' ability to detect anomaly (Shreeve, 1995).

7. The RPD model is one example of how people make decisions in natural settings. There are other models to consider as well, such as the work of Lee Beach and Terry Mitchell on image theory (e.g., Beach, 1990), and the skill-rules-knowledge scheme developed by Jens Rasmussen (1983). P. A. Anderson (1983), Wohl (1981), and Dreyfus and Dreyfus (1986) present ideas similar to the RPD model.

8. Figure 3.1 shows the RPD model in its current form, as it has evolved since 1985. The basic themes are the same, but the model now addresses the function of diagnosis, variation 2, which was not part of the initial account.

9. You could argue that perhaps the decision makers were comparing options but not consciously. We have no way of knowing whether this might be true. Still, you

have to be careful about making that argument because when you do, the burden of proof shifts from me to you. I cannot prove that something is not happening. I can tell you I do not believe decision makers are comparing options since they do not report it, there usually was not enough time for it, and I can explain their actions in other ways. If you want to claim they are subconsciously comparing options, then the burden of proof is on you to provide evidence.

10. Marvin Cohen (personal communication) suggested this criticism: if we do not trust people's ability to make large judgments, we should not trust people to make small judgments. Erev, Bornstein, and Wallsten (1993) have shown another problem with rational choice (e.g., multiattribute utility analyses) strategies, which is that people make worse decisions if they perform analyses first. But we should not be too worried. Jim Shanteau (1992) has noted that when people are dissatisfied with the results of a rational choice exercise, they often change their ratings to make it come out the way they want.

Chapter 4

1. Memory researchers such as Roediger (1990) distinguish implicit memory (memory that is not deliberate or conscious, but is inferred based on the individual's performance on a task that shows the effect of prior experience) from explicit memory (deliberate, conscious recollection). Intuition, and the RPD model, both depend heavily on implicit memory.

2. Much of this progress in understanding intuition is due to studies (e.g., Hammond, Hamm, Grassia, & Pearson, 1987) that contrast analytical and intuitive strategies of highway engineers. Adriaan de Groot (1946), a Dutch psychologist whose early research on chess grand masters has been so influential, has recently written about the nature of intuition (de Groot, 1986; de Groot & Gobet, 1996). Craig McKenzie (1994) has found that intuitive judgment strategies can perform very well and, being simpler than analytical strategies, "may be the most efficient means of ensuring highly accurate judgment." Sloman (1996) has distinguished two processes for generating inferences, one deductive and the other associative, and this may have implications for the phenomenon of intuition.

3. Commanders often check to see if they might be wrong rather than showing confirmation bias (seeking only information that supports their beliefs). Laboratory studies often find that naive subjects show confirmation bias, but Shanteau (1992) has found that experienced decision makers do not fall prey to confirmation bias. Rather, they search for evidence that would be incompatible with their interpretations.

Chapter 5

1. Example 5.2, the Libyan airliner case, was written by Raanan Lipshitz, a psychology professor at the University of Haifa, who interviewed the Israeli generals. I have also used an account by Zvi Lanir (a decision researcher who heads his own company near Tel Aviv), which fills in other parts of the incident.

2. The core of the RPD model is a set of heuristics previously described by Amos Tversky and Daniel Kahneman: the simulation heuristic (1974), used for diagnosis and for evaluation, and the availability and representativeness heuristics (1980), for recognizing situations as typical.

3. Neville Moray (personal communication) has suggested that the term used by Perrow, *de minimus*, is more properly *de minimis*. My knowledge of Latin does not allow an informed judgment of this matter.

4. The *Trademaster/Pisces* example comes from Perrow (1984).

5. The example of "The Disoriented Physicists" is taken from Gell-Mann (1994).

6. The same process occurs in science. Theories are usually not disproved. Even when someone presents evidence that is inconsistent with a theory, others can find a way to patch up the theory. As the inconsistent evidence piles up and the patches get more complicated, scientists lose confidence in the theory and search for simpler alternatives (see Mitroff, 1981).

7. Mitchell, Russo, and Pennington (1989) have discussed this process as "prospective hindsight," which means generating an explanation for an event that will take place in the future, as if that event had already occurred. They found that people generate more reasons for an event if they could frame it as an event that had already occurred. They suggest using this strategy to discover key underlying factors. Their findings and suggestions support the premortem technique.

8. For more information on decision scenarios, see Schwartz (1991).

Chapter 7

1. I thank Len Adelman for this description of example 7.1. For more details, see Hammond and Adelman (1976).

2. Gigerenzer and Goldstein (1996) have recently described a set of algorithms that are both fast and easy to apply, and can perform as well as formal, analytical methods under many conditions. These algorithms take advantage of environmental regularities and constraints.

3. Kaempf, Klein, Thordsen, and Wolf (1996) also found that there were 103 decision points regarding the diagnosis of the situation, in addition to the 78 decisions about courses of action.

4. A large amount of research has been done on the use of prescriptive decision analysis (structured ways of making decisions). See also Baron and Brown (1991) on teaching decision skills to adolescents; Wu, Apostoloakis, and Okrent (1991) on risk assessment for planning for nuclear power plants; and Howard (1992) on the general applications of prescriptive decision analysis. In 1994 the Nobel Prize for economics was given to three researchers who showed the utility of game theory. However, Beyth-Marom, Fischhoff, Quadrel, and Furby (1991) remain skeptical about teaching decision-making skills to adolescents, and Brown (1992) has argued with Howard about how widespread the use of prescriptive decision analysis is.

5. Minsky (1986) has described this as Fredkin's Paradox.

6. John Schmitt pointed out the frequency of this dilemma and contrasted it with the zone of indifference.

7. Ericsson (1996).

8. Shanteau (1992) on ways of achieving expertise.

9. Klein, Kaempf, Thordsen, Wolf, and Miller (1996) have presented more detail in the use of decision requirements.

10. For more details, see Klinger, Andriole, Militello, Adelman, Klein, and Gomes (1993) and Klinger and Gomes (1993).

Chapter 8

1. Zvi Lanir first suggested the phrase "a difference that makes a difference" to explain what an experienced military commander can notice that subordinates would miss.

2. Ecological psychologists would refer to these holds as affordances—the perception of what actions the environment allows.

3. Leverage points are affordances, as discussed in the field of ecological psychology. The primary difference is that I am not viewing problem solving as an entirely perceptual process. The leverage points still need to be elaborated, evaluated, and modified. The concept of leverage points also overlaps with the work of Gestalt psychologists (e.g., Duncker, 1945; Wertheimer, 1959) on insight. The difference is that leverage points do not refer to insights about the stimulus situation but take into account the effects one can achieve through feasible actions.

4. These business examples are from Collins and Porras (1994).

5. I am indebted to Zvi Lanir for example 8.3.

Chapter 9

1. The nonlinear model of problem solving shares a common perspective with the work of Isenberg (1984), Mintzberg, Raisinghani, and Theoret (1976), and Weick (1983).

2. Isenberg (1984), in studying business managers, noted the importance of finding problems (i.e., detecting subtle anomalies that can be early signs of pitfalls).

The ability to find problems, notice anomalies, and identify opportunities, is nontrivial (see also Shulman, 1965; Shulman, Loupe, & Piper, 1968). Failure to detect a problem or opportunity can result from lack of experience in judging a rate of change or in not having a sense of typicality that is sufficiently strong to highlight anomalies when they are just emerging.

A slow problem onset can also result in delayed problem detection. The slow onset is what Xiao, Milgram, and Doyle (1997), in their study of anesthesiologists, refer to as "going sour" incidents. There are no clear markers that the situation is degrading, and by the time the problem solver realizes it, the viable options may have disappeared. De Groot (1946/1965) has referred to the judgment of urgency in chess as the early detection that a threat needs to be taken seriously.

3. Wertheimer (1959), Chi, Feltovich, and Glaser (1981), and others have discussed the importance of problem representation. Problem representation is not simply the number of details noticed. Small differences in the way the problem is categorized can result in large differences in the way it is addressed. A chess player will look at a position very differently if it has arisen in the middle of a game, with the clock running, versus overhearing a spectator comment, "I see a checkmate in three moves." In a manufacturing company, a production problem may turn out to be a morale problem or an employee conflict problem. Adelman,, Gualtieri and Stanford (1995) showed that different problem representations of a parking shortage in a university—that it stemmed from managerial inefficiency or from rapid growth—resulted in the generation and selection of different types of causal hypotheses and the generation and selection of different types of options.

4. The first reference I have found to the judgment of solvability is the work of de Groot (1946). Isenberg (1984) also found that the situation awareness function was important for the managers he studied.

5. Therefore, the function of problem representation includes goal setting because the problem solver must judge whether to try to come up with a solution or turn to other needs. For ill-defined goals, we can expect to see a lot of goal modification during the problem-solving effort. The most obvious modification is to add or subtract goal properties. We can add new properties as we discover them and realize that a course of action without those properties would not be acceptable. We can eliminate restrictions in case of a bottleneck. We can replace one set of properties with another, as in the case of the car rescue.

Goals can also be modified in terms of our level of aspiration. If we find lots of pitfalls in evaluating possible courses of action, we may scale back our hopes. If we notice encouraging possibilities, we may increase our level of aspiration and raise the standard for judging new options. We will need experience to make the judgment, setting an appropriate level of aspiration even before the options are generated and evaluated.

A third way goals can be modified is by moving up and down a goal hierarchy. If we run into a barrier and make its removal the goal, we have moved down the hierarchy as when we might look for a way to cross a rock pile to continue on our original path. If we fail to discover a workable course of action, we may move higher in the goal hierarchy as when we abandon the path and look for a new way to reach the top. A fourth way goals can be modified is to change the relative priorities for different and perhaps competing objectives.

6. See Rasmussen (1993) for a fuller account of the process of diagnosis.

7. The problem of designing a solution to a university's parking shortage was studied by Gettys (1983).

8. Answer to DONALD + GERALD = ROBERT: T = 0, G = 1, O = 2, B = 3, A = 4, D = 5, N = 6, R = 7, L = 8, E = 9.

9. The concept of a problem space can be slippery. For technical uses, a problem space is not simply the way the problem is represented or partitioned for purposes of efficiency. That simply treats problem space as synonymous with problem representation. For a computational model, the problem space refers to the complete set of pathways generated by conducting a permutation of all the possible states of all of the variables.

10. Furthermore, the means-ends heuristic can get us in trouble. The strength of the means-ends analysis is to get closer and closer to the goal by finding the remaining differences and eliminating or reducing those. The advantage is that the problem solver can forget about the previous problem state and concentrate on finding and reducing obstacles. Sweller (1988) pointed out the drawback that you can use means-ends analysis to solve a problem without ever remembering the overall strategy you carried out. As a result, problem solvers may not learn the critical features of the problem that they can apply in the future.

Another limitation of the means-ends analysis is that it can get a problem solver trapped. If the analysis leads to a blind alley, the only way to escape is to increase the distance between what you have and what you want, so you can start down another path. A concrete example would be a situation where a dog attacks a cyclist. If the cyclist interposes the bicycle to block the dog, some dogs do not understand that they need to move farther away, to go around the bicycle, in order to continue the attack. (Unfortunately, some dogs do understand this strategy.) Similarly, a computer program that only tried to reduce differences could become trapped, unable to find a solution path.

11. In the example of the car rescue in which the nature of the goal shifted, one argument is that this is a change in subgoals and that the goal of extricating the motorist from the car remained the same. But the commander's goal of carrying out his responsibilities also remained the same, and so forth. We can play games with what we define as goals and subgoals, but that will not accomplish much. The point is that reformulation can mean a substitution and not necessarily an elimination of goal properties.

12. See Keller and Ho (1988) for a description of option generation strategies such as generating a variety of alternatives for each attribute and elaborating the permutations of these variations.

13. This process involves an appraisal of emotional reactions, comparing the discomfort or worry of the outcome of each option, rather than contrasting the options on the same set of evaluation criteria. De Groot's study of chess players showed the same approach. Moves were evaluated by what they led up to and whether the chess players wanted the projected position or were dismayed by it.

Chapter 10

1. For further reading about the psychology of expertise, see Chi, Glaser, and Farr (1988), Ericsson and Smith (1991), and Ericsson (1996). Another good source is Shanteau (1988), who has studied the psychological characteristics of expert

decision makers. See also Sternberg (1990) on the nature, origins, and development of wisdom.

2. It is easy to toss around concepts such as expertise. How much experience does it take to become an expert? Ericsson and Charness (1994) reviewed studies of expertise in a wide variety of tasks and found that the top performers appeared to practice around four hours a day, six to seven days a week, for approximately a decade. Individual differences in abilities, strength, or other factors did not have the same impact as sheer amount of time spent practicing. You might think that people who were better stayed with the task longer, so the initial skill level was a key to the amount of dedication shown. However, the data do not support this idea. The different studies that Ericsson and Charness reviewed failed to demonstrate that the eventual experts started out as gifted. Rather, it was their dedication that paid off.

One of the keys that Ericsson and Charness identified is the way experts practice. Often they set practice goals for themselves. For example, if a child's mother has insisted she spend an hour practicing the piano, she will be watching the clock the whole time. However, if she marks off an hour to play a certain piece through without any errors and almost has it at the end of the hour, she might consider trying it again—maybe once or twice—until she feels her hands getting too tired. This proactive attitude toward practice is different from simply putting time in. We can see this same difference between children doing spelling drills and children trying to master video games. Work such as the Ericsson and Charness study should open up more research into strategies for gaining expertise.

3. David Noble (personal communication) suggested the term *negative cue*.

4. Endsley (1995) has presented the most influential account of situation awareness. She posits three levels: the data, the inferences, and the projection. The first level, data elements, refers to a skilled decision maker's ability to keep track of all the important details. For example, a skilled pilot will be aware of heading, altitude, fuel level, weather conditions, and on and on, for a great many aspects of the current condition. A novice is less likely to be able to recall these data elements accurately. The second level, inference, refers to the skilled decision maker's ability to draw inferences from these data. The third level, projection, refers to the ability to project the current situation forward in time. A skilled pilot should be able to anticipate what is going to happen to the airplane and to prepare for difficulties. Why didn't the pilot in example 8.4 anticipate difficulties in landing? Several factors may have contributed, such as reluctance to ask the air traffic controller for a change, lack of skill for putting different pieces of the situation together to see their implications, or lack of vigilance in a flight where none of the elements was in itself a warning sign.

We should be careful not to interpret Endsley's model as saying that the inferences are built up from the data elements. There are no basic data elements. The relevant data depend on the decision maker's interpretation. For a pilot flying at 30,000 feet, altitude is not a salient cue, and altitude errors of a few hundred feet usually have no consequences. For a pilot making final approach, altitude becomes much more important. The pilot's goals, and the functions being performed, determine which data elements are relevant.

5. For a fuller discussion of mental models, see Stout, Cannon-Bowers and Salas (1997).

6. Holding and Reynolds (1982) and Charness (1989) have shown that skilled chess players look more moves into the future than less skilled players do. The players do not have better memories, but they can use their knowledge to trace a sequence of moves further ahead.

7. Major John Schmitt, of the U.S. Marine Corps Reserves, has pointed out that the RPD model asserts that people tend to choose the first reasonable action they consider. Yet in dealing with an adversary who might anticipate your tendencies, this strategy can get you in trouble. It leads you to take typical, and therefore predictable, actions. Schmitt recalled one training exercise when he was a platoon leader; he looked over the situation for the following day and immediately recognized how his platoon should make its advance. His next thought was that if it was so obvious to him, it might also be obvious to his opponent. He spent the next three hours crawling through the mud, trying to locate an alternate line of approach. Finally he gave up, even more certain now that his attack would be predictable, but he had to go through with it. The next day, the attack was a convincing success.

After the exercise, Schmitt discussed his tactics with the leader of the defensive forces, an officer for whom Schmitt did not have high regard. The man admitted he had been caught by surprise. He had not even tried to anticipate what Schmitt might do. Apparently Schmitt's strategy was predictable only against an adversary who was actively trying to make predictions, and this adversary was not looking ahead. One of the hallmarks of experts is their ability to project current states into the future.

Schmitt's dilemma is that most officers will not put themselves in the position of their adversary, but if you are unlucky to come across one who does, a Hannibal or a Robert E. Lee, then your recognitional decision making may get you in trouble. In other words, the RPD strategy is still an accurate description of what people do, but it has this drawback in adversarial situations that call for deception and not typical predictable actions. (Schmitt points out that analytical decision making will not do any better.)

My own suspicion is that skilled commanders have developed an ability to recognize when their courses of action are too obvious, just as Schmitt did. During the evaluation of a plan by mental simulation, the skilled commanders will use a sense of predictability to notice that the adversary can easily anticipate their moves, and they will take the necessary precautions.

8. Forrest-Pressley, MacKinnon, and Waller (1985) discuss different aspects of metacognition.

9. This study was funded by the Army Research Institute for the Behavioral and Social Sciences.

10. This is the same experimental method de Groot used in his research, the major difference being that we had objective ratings for all the legal moves.

11. Stokes, Belger, and Zhang (1990) have found that experienced pilots also tend to select the first option they consider even if they have examined others.

12. Marvin Cohen suggested this line of argument to me—that subconscious option comparison runs into logical difficulties because of the impracticability of generating all the possible options.

13. For example, a tennis player might begin by swinging a foreign object, a racket, but after hundreds of hours, that racket will feel like part of his or her arm. The tennis players are not going to swing their rackets at the ball. They are going to feel as if they are hitting the ball themselves. The incorporation of the tool as a body part is like an infant's learning to incorporate an arm so that the strange blob that goes floating by becomes a tool that is used naturally and without any attention.

Radar operators who start learning to operate a complex piece of equipment wind up seeing through the equipment, sensing the objects directly, and adjusting the set as naturally as they squint to look at something in the distance. An instructor pilot once told me that when he started to fly, he was nervous much of the time, afraid that he might make a mistake. After several months, he no longer felt that he was flying the airplane but that he himself was flying. That was the point where flying became enjoyable.

14. Stewart (1994) discusses the importance of intellectual capital.

15. *Knowledge engineering* as a term originated with computer scientists trying to build expert systems. I am appropriating it here to cover the wider process of extracting, processing, and applying expert knowledge.

16. Specialists in the field use many variants of these methods along with additional ones (Crandall, Klein, Militello, & Wolf, 1994; Gordon, 1994; Redding & Seamster, 1994; Woods, 1993).

17. For a good example of cognitive modeling, see Bloom and Broder (1950), who had proficient college students introspect about how they solved multiple-choice problems and then provided these introspections to students who were struggling with test strategies. The intervention worked: the poor students learned more effective strategies, and their performance improved.

18. These studies were sponsored by the Army Research Institute for the Behavioral and Social Sciences.

Chapter 11

1. Many people have speculated about the essential features of a story, and some have argued for the existence of a story grammar (a set of primitive features typical of all stories) to account for the essential features of stories. Other researchers have debated the concept of a story grammar (Wilensky, 1983). Other sources are Pennington and Hastie (1993) and Schank (1990).

2. Lynne Reder (1982; Reder, Wible, & Martin, 1986) has done laboratory research on plausible inference that may be relevant. Adults tend to use plausibility judgments to answer questions about stories they have read.

3. I am indebted to Reid Hastie (personal communication) for clarifying this distinction between mental simulations and stories.

4. Janet Kolodner (1993) has described the features that make cases and stories valuable. According to Kolodner, the stripped-down version of a case would be a description of a problem plus a solution. Next is the problem solution, and success or failure. Then add some additional factors involved. Most useful is a case with a problem, solution, success or failure, factors involved, and the reason the factors resulted in the outcome.

5. I thank Vanessa Polaine for providing me with example 11.3. This is the type of diagnostic problem for which the Kepner-Tregoe method is best suited: mapping out the key difference between the times the problem appears and the times it does not appear.

6. The Critical Decision method was developed and formalized with funding from the U.S. Army Research Institute for the Behavioral and Social Sciences. For more information about the method, see Klein, Calderwood, and MacGregor (1989) and Hoffman, Crandall, and Shadbolt (1998). Benner (1984) has used stories to study the expertise of nurses.

Chapter 12

1. Analogy refers to proportion (e.g., a:b::c:d), and metaphor refers to language. In applying these concepts to naturalistic decision making, I have stretched both definitions, using each to refer to the way we reason from parallel cases.

2. The journal *Metaphor and Symbolic Language* is a good source of current references to metaphor research.

3. This study was funded by the U.S. Air Force's Armstrong Laboratory.

4. Also see Goodman (1972).

5. Our work was sponsored by the Air Force Office of Scientific Research (Klein and Weitzenfeld, 1982).

6. See Klein (1987) for a more detailed discussion of the different ways that analogical reasoning can be used.

7. Kolodner (1993) has written a good summary of the work in the field of case-based reasoning. The case-based reasoning program, *ESTEEM: Enabling Solutions Through Experience Modeling: Introduction Manual* (1992), is available from Esteem Software Inc., Belmont, CA.

Chapter 13

1. This description of the *Goeben* incident is based on Tuchman (1962).

2. Example 13.3 is from Bogner (1997).

3. Our research projects on Commander's Intent statements and scripts were funded by the U.S. Army Research Institute for the Behavioral and Social Sciences.

4. Kahan, Worley, and Stasz (1989) have discussed the issue of describing intent.

5. For a more detailed discussion of meaning as a function of alternative states, see Olson (1970).

Chapter 14

1. Most of the work in this chapter, unless otherwise noted, was funded by the U.S. Army Research Institute for the Behavioral and Social Sciences.

2. Smith (1994) has used a related concept, collective intelligence.

3. I am indebted to Judith Orasanu, now at NASA Ames, for the term *collective consciousness* to refer to this aspect of team interaction. For a definition of *team*, see Orasanu and Salas (1993) and Duffy (1993).

4. Herb Colle suggested the term *preconscious*, using the Freudian framework as an analogue.

5. We have heard suggestions that these factors have been changing in the fire-fighting community as a result of budgetary pressures, downsizing, political factors affecting promotions, and their influences. The sense of community may not be as strong as it was in the past.

6. Jim Banks suggested that we add the category of team identity to the advanced team decision-making model. Driskell and Salas (1993) have empirically demonstrated the gain in performance that occurs when team members abandon their egocentric attitudes.

Chapter 15

1. Perhaps I am misstating the problem. We could just use the term *rational* as a synonym for *reasonable*. Surely we do not want to claim that there is such a thing as being too reasonable.

It is hard to resist a warm appeal to be reasonable. But if we examine the appeal more closely, we find that it is a more extreme position than even I am trying to take. My claim is that we can attach a meaning to the concept of rational analysis. We can treat it as a source of power and try to define its boundary conditions.

William Irving (personal communication, 1994) points out that *reasonable* is different from *rational*. *Reasonable* means "to have reasons." These can be beliefs, logic, tradition, or even superstition, as long as you are prepared to examine the reasons for your actions. An "unreasonable" person is one who refuses to argue, refuses to examine the reasons for beliefs or actions. According to this framework, an intuitive decision, based on pattern matching, may not be easy to describe in terms of reason. Therefore, we may want to contrast *reasonable* and *intuitive* instead of *reasonable* and *irrational*.

2. The Nuclear Regulatory Commission attempts to create procedures for all types of operations and malfunctions, to cut down the room for error and misinterpretation. Emilie Roth (1997) has recently shown that this attempt at decomposition and proceduralization does not always work. Operators still need expertise to handle some difficult malfunctions. During simulations of these

malfunctions, the experienced operators would be explaining "that they were following the procedures," as they took a variety of steps not found in the procedures or even at variance with the procedures.

3. Achinstein (1968) has discussed the difficulty of determining when antecedent conditions are satisfied.

4. People sometimes have trouble blending rational analysis with the other sources of power I have discussed. Once you decompose a problem into elements and shuffle these around, it can be hard to remember your overall impressions. Arthur Reber (1993) showed this. He had subjects perform a complex task, one that had rules they could not identify. Even though the subjects could not figure out the rule, they showed improvement. But when he asked the subjects to try to identify the rules of the task, they had to stop using intuition, and their performance was actually worse. Erev, Bornstein, and Wallster (1993) have reported similar findings. When subjects performed a decision task and had to generate the types of estimates needed to perform a formal analysis, the quality of their decisions declined. See also Wilson and Schooler (1991).

5. Much of the following discussion is based on Stich (1990).

Chapter 16

1. Hubert Dreyfus has noted that in the information science community, heuristics refer to nonexhaustive strategies for searching through a problem space. As such, they are not relevant to decision makers who are not setting up and searching through problem spaces. Decision researchers appear to be using the term *heuristic* to refer to a rule of thumb, or informal reasoning strategy, as opposed to a mathematical formula that can be calculated.

2. Several studies have shown that decision biases are reduced or eliminated if we study people with expertise working in natural settings (Christensen-Szalanski & Beach, 1984; Fraser, Smith, & Smith, 1992; Gigerenzer, 1987; Smith & Kida, 1991; Shanteau, 1992).

3. A number of researchers have been studying naturalistic decision errors. For example, Orasanu and Fischer (1997) collected aviation errors and classed them into the primary categories of failure to detect a problem and failure to perform a worst-case scenario. Mumaw, Roth, and Schoenfeld (1993) have similarly classified the errors found in experienced nuclear power plant operators. Lipshitz and Bar-Ilan (1996) have considered the basis for errors in naturalistic decision making and concluded that the overriding factor was a deficiency in constructing and using mental models that drive the decision making. This claim parallels my own assertion that inadequate experience rather than faulty reasoning is involved.

4. This project was supported by the U.S. Army Institute for the Behavioral and Social Sciences.

5. The *de minimus* explanation is not the same as confirmation bias. With the *de minimus* explanation, the person is aware of disconfirming evidence and may

even seek out such evidence but then explains it away. With the confirmation bias, the person chooses to seek confirming evidence that has little diagnostic value (it does not help distinguish between hypotheses) and does not try to obtain diagnostic evidence that might disconfirm the favored hypothesis.

6. A more formal term for this difficulty is the induction problem—the problem of observing a series of events and inducing rules and relationships.

7. Lia Di Bello, at the Laboratory for Cognitive Studies of Activity, City University of New York Graduate School and University Center in New York, offered these observations during an informal presentation of her research.

8. An additional direction is exemplified by the work of Richard Nisbett (1993). Nisbett has tried to identify and use natural reasoning patterns to teach people to do a better job of representing evidence and considering the implications of their actions.

References

Achinstein, P. (1968). *Concepts of science*. Baltimore: John Hopkins University Press.

Adelman, L. (1992). *Evaluating decision support and expert systems*. New York: Wiley.

Adelman, L., Gualtieri, J., & Stanford, S. (1995). Examining the effect of causal focus on the option generation process: An experiment using protocol analysis. *Organizational Behavior and Human Decision Processes*, *61*, 54–66.

Anderson, J. R. (1983). *The architecture of cognition*. Cambridge, MA: Harvard University Press.

Anderson, J. R. (1993). Problem solving and learning. *American Psychologist*, *48*, 35–44.

Anderson, P. A. (1983). Decision making by objection and the Cuban missile crisis. *Administrative Science Quarterly*, *28*, 201–222.

Baron, J. (1988). *Thinking and deciding*. New York: Cambridge University Press.

Baron, J., & Brown, R. V. (Eds.). (1991). *Teaching decision making to adolescents*. Hillsdale, NJ: Erlbaum.

Beach, L. R. (1990). *Image theory: Decision making in personal and organizational contexts*. West Sussex, England: Wiley.

Beach, L. R., & Mitchell, T. R. (1978). A contingency model for the selection of decision strategies. *Academy of Management Review*, *3*, 439–449.

Bechara, A., Damasio, H., Tranel, D., & Damasio, A. R. (1997). Deciding advantageously before knowing the advantageous strategy. *Science*, *275*, 1293–1295.

Benner, P. (1984). *From novice to expert: Excellence and power in clinical nursing practice*. Menlo Park, CA: Addison-Wesley.

Berkeley, D., & Humphreys, P. (1982). Structuring decision problems and the "bias heuristic.". *Acta Psychologica*, *50*, 201–252.

Berlinger, N. T. (1996). Vital signs: The breath of life. *Discover*, *17*(3), 102–104.

Beyth-Marom, R., Fischhoff, B., Quadrel, M. J., & Furby, L. (1991). Teaching decision making to adolescents: A critical review. In J. Baron & R. V. Brown (Eds.), *Teaching decision making to adolescents* (pp. 19–60). Hillsdale, NJ: Erlbaum.

Bloom, B. S., & Broder, L. J. (1950). *Problem-solving processes of college students: An exploratory investigation*. Chicago: University of Chicago Press.

Bogner, S. (1997). Naturalistic decision making in health care. In C. Zsambok & G. Klein (Eds.), *Naturalistic decision making*. Mahwah, NJ: Erlbaum.

Brown, R. V. (1992). The state of the art of decision analysis: A personal perspective. *Interfaces, 22*, 5–14.

Bruner, J., & Postman, L. (1949). On the perception of incongruity: A paradigm. *Journal of Personality, 18*, 206–233.

Calderwood, R., Klein, G. A., & Crandall, B. W. (1988). Time pressure, skill, and move quality in chess. *American Journal of Psychology, 101*, 481–493.

Cannon-Bowers, J. A., Salas, E., & Pruitt, J. S. (1996). Establishing the boundaries of a paradigm for decision-making research. *Human Factors, 38*(2), 193–205.

Charness, N. (1989). Expertise in chess and bridge. In D. Klahr & K. Kotovsky (Eds.), *Complex information processing: The impact of Herbert A. Simon* (pp. 183–208). Hillsdale, NJ: Erlbaum.

Cherniak, C. (1981). *Minimal rationality*. Cambridge, MA: MIT Press.

Chi, M. T. H., Feltovich, P. J., & Glaser, R. (1981). Categorization and representation of physics problems by experts and novices. *Cognitive Science, 5*, 121–152.

Chi, M. T. H., Glaser, R., & Farr, M. J. (1988). *The nature of expertise*. Hillsdale, NJ: Erlbaum.

Christensen-Szalanski, J. J. J., & Beach, L. R. (1984). The citation bias: Fad and fashion in the judgment and decision literature. *American Psychologist, 39*, 75–78.

Cohen, J. (1992). Yes, Oswald alone killed Kennedy. *Commentary (New York, N.Y.), 93*(6), 32–40.

Cohen, M. (1997). Training the naturalistic decision maker. In C. Zsambok & G. Klein (Eds.), *Naturalistic decision making*. Mahwah, NJ: Erlbaum.

Cohen, M. S., Freeman, J. T., & Thompson, B. (1998). Critical thinking skills in tactical decision making: A model and a training method. In J. Cannon-Bowers & E. Salas (Eds.), *Decision making under stress: Implications for training and simulations* (pp. 155–189). Mahwah, NJ: Erlbaum.

Collins, J. C., & Porras, J. L. (1994). *Built to last: Successful habits of visionary companies*. New York: Harper Business.

Cooper, H. S. F., Jr. (1973). *Thirteen: The flight that failed*. New York: Dial Press.

Crain, W. F. (1990). *The mission: The dilemma of specified task and implied commander's intent*. AD-A225 436. Fort Leavenworth, KS: U.S. Army Command and General Staff College.

Crandall, B., & Getchell-Reiter, K. (1993). Critical decision method: A technique for eliciting concrete assessment indicators from the "intuition" of NICU nurses. *Advances in Nursing Science, 16*(1), 42–51.

Crandall, B., Klein, G., Militello, L., & Wolf, S. (1994). *Tools for applied cognitive task analysis. Contract N66001–94-C-7008.* San Diego, CA: Naval Personnel Research and Development Center.

Crandall, B. W., Kyne, M., Militello, L., & Klein, G. A. (1992). *Describing expertise in one-on-one instruction. Contract MDA903–91-C-0058.* Alexandria, VA: U.S. Army Research Institute.

Dawes, R. M. (1988). *Rational choice in an uncertain world.* San Diego: Harcourt Brace Jovanovich.

de Groot, A. D. (1946). *Thought and choice in chess.* New York: Mouton.

de Groot, A. D. (1986). Intuition in chess. *International Computer Chess Association Journal, 9,* 67–75.

de Groot, A. D., & Gobet, F. (1996). *Perception and memory in chess: Studies in the heuristics of the professional eye.* The Netherlands: Van Gorcum & Co.

Dent-Read, C. H., Klein, G., & Eggleston, R. (1994). Metaphor in visual displays designed to guide action. *Metaphor and Symbolic Activity, 9*(3), 211–232.

Doyle, A. C. (1905). *The complete Sherlock Holmes.* Garden City, NY: Doubleday.

Dreyfus, H. L. (1972). *What computers can't do: A critique of artificial reason.* New York: Harper & Row.

Dreyfus, H. L., & Dreyfus, S. E. (1986). *Mind over machine: The power of human intuitive expertise in the era of the computer.* New York: Free Press.

Driskell, J. E., & Salas, E. (1992). Collective behavior and team performance. *Human Factors, 34*(3), 277–288.

Duffy, L. (1993). Team decision making biases: An information processing perspective. In G. A. Klein, J. Orasanu, R. Calderwood, & C. E. Zsambok (Eds.), *Decision making in action: Models and methods* (pp. 346–359). Norwood, NJ: Ablex.

Duncker, K. (1945). On problem solving. *Psychological Monographs, 58*(5).

Dupuy, T. (1977). *A genius for war: The German army and general staff.* Englewood Cliffs, NJ: Prentice Hall.

Edwards, E., & Lee, F. P. (1974). *The human operator in process control.* London: Taylor & Francis.

Elstein, A. S., Shulman, L. S., & Sprafka, S. A. (1978). *Medical problem solving: An analysis of clinical reasoning.* Cambridge, MA: Harvard University Press.

Endsley, M. R. (1995). Toward a theory of situation awareness in dynamic systems. *Human Factors, 37*(1), 32–64.

Endsley, M. R., & Garland, D. J. (Eds.). (2000). *Situation awareness analysis and measurement.* Mahwah, NJ: Erlbaum.

Erev, L., Bornstein, G., & Wallsten, T. S. (1993). The negative effect of probability assessments on decision quality. *Organizational Behavior and Human Decision Processes, 55*(1), 79–94.

Ericsson, K. A. (1996). The acquisition of expert performance: An introduction to some of the issues. In K. A. Ericsson (Ed.), *The road to excellence*. Mahwah, NJ: Erlbaum.

Ericsson, K. A., & Charness, N. (1994). Expert performance: Its structure and acquisition. *American Psychologist, 49*(8), 725–747.

Ericsson, K. A., & Smith, J. (1991). *Toward a general theory of expertise: Prospects and limits*. Cambridge: Cambridge University Press.

Flin, R. (1996). *Sitting in the hot seat: Leaders and teams for critical incident management*. Chichester: Wiley.

Flin, R., Slaven, G., & Stewart, K. (1996). Emergency decision making in the offshore oil and gas industry. *Human Factors, 38*(2), 262–277.

Forrest-Pressley, D. L., MacKinnon, G. E., & Waller, T. G. (1985). Metacognition, cognition, and human performance (Vol. 2). *Instructional practices*. San Diego: Academic Press.

Foushee, H., Lauber, J. K., Baetge, M. M., & Acomb, D. B. (1986). *Crew performance as a function of exposure to high-density short-haul duty cycles*. NASA Technical Memorandum 99322. Moffett Field, CA: NASA Ames Research Center.

Fraser, J. M., Smith, P. J., & Smith, J. W. (1992). A catalog of errors. *International Journal of Man-Machine Studies, 37*, 265–307.

Gazzaniga, M. (1985). *The social brain: Discovering the networks of the mind*. New York: Basic Books.

Gell-Mann, M. (1994). *The quark and the jaguar: Adventures in the simple and the complex*. New York: Freeman.

Gettys, C. F. (1983). *Research and theory on predecision processes*. Norman, OK: University of Oklahoma, Decision Processes Laboratory.

Gigerenzer, G. (1987). Survival of the fittest probabilist: Brunswik, Thurstone, and the two disciplines of psychology. In L. Kruger, G. Gigerenzer, and M. S. Morgan (Eds.), *A probabilistic revolution: Ideas in the sciences, 2* (pp. 49–72). Cambridge, MA: MIT Press.

Gigerenzer, G., & Goldstein, D. G. (1996). Reasoning the fast and frugal way: Models of bounded rationality. *Psychological Review, 103*(4), 650–669.

Goodman, N. (1972). *Problems and projects*. Indianapolis, IN: Bobbs-Merrill.

Gordon, S. E. (1994). *Systematic training programs: Maximizing effectiveness and minimizing liability*. Englewood Cliffs, NJ: PTR Prentice-Hall.

Greeno, J. G., & Simon, H. A. (1988). Problem solving and reasoning. In R. C. Atkinson, R. J. Herrnstein, G. Lindzey, and R. D. Luce (Eds.), *Stevens' handbook of experimental psychology. Vol. 2: Learning and cognition* (pp. 589–672). New York: Wiley.

Grudin, J. (1989). The case against user interface consistency. *Communications of the ACM, 32*(10), 1164–1173.

Hammond, K. R., & Adelman, L. (1976). Science, values, and human judgment. *Science, 194*, 389–396.

Hammond, K. R., Hamm, R. M., Grassia, J., & Pearson, T. (1987). Direct comparison of the efficacy of intuitive and analytical cognition in expert judgment. *IEEE Transactions on Systems, Man, and Cybernetics, SMC-17*(5), 753–770.

Harman, G. (1973). *Thought.* Princeton, NJ: Princeton University Press.

Harman, G. (1986). *Change in view.* Cambridge, MA: MIT Press.

Hastie, R. (1991). A review from a high place: The field of judgment and decision making as revealed in its current textbooks. *Psychological Science, 2*(3), 135–138.

Hesse, M. (1966). *Models and analogies in science.* Notre Dame: University of Notre Dame Press.

Hirt, E. R., & Sherman, S. J. (1985). The role of prior knowledge in explaining hypothetical events. *Journal of Experimental Social Psychology, 21*, 519–543.

Hoffman, R. R., Crandall, B. E., & Shadbolt, N. R. (1998). A case study in cognitive task analysis methodology: The critical decision method for the elicitation of expert knowledge. *Human Factors, 40*(2), 254–276.

Holding, D. H., & Reynolds, R. I. (1982). Recall or evaluation of chess positions as determinants of chess skill. *Memory & Cognition, 10*, 237–242.

Howard, R. A. (1992). Heathens, heretics, and cults: The religious spectrum of decision aiding. *Interfaces, 22*, 15–27.

Isenberg, D. J. (1984, November–December). How senior managers think. *Harvard Business Review*, 80–90.

Jacobs, E., & Jaques, T. O. (1991). Executive leadership. In R. Gal & D. Mangelsdorff (Eds.), *Handbook of military psychology.* Chichester, England: Wiley.

Janis, I. L., & Mann, L. (1977). *Decision making: A psychological analysis of conflict, choice, and commitment.* New York: Free Press.

Johnson, J., Driskell, J. E., & Salas, E. (1997). Vigilant and hypervigilant decision making. *Journal of Applied Psychology, 82*(4), 614–622.

Kaempf, G. L., Klein, G. A., & Thordsen, M. L. (1991). Applying recognition-primed decision making to man-machine interface design. [Moffett Field, CA: NASA-Ames Research Center.]. *Contract (New York, N.Y.)*, NAS2-NAS13359.

Kaempf, G. L., Klein, G. A., Thordsen, M. L., & Wolf, S. (1996). Decision making in complex command-and-control environments. *Human Factors, 38*(2), 220–231.

Kaempf, G. L., Wolf, S., Thordsen, M. L., & Klein, G. (1992). *Decisionmaking in the AEGIS combat information center. Contract N66001-90-C-6023.* San Diego: Naval Command, Control and Ocean Surveillance Center.

Kahan, J. P., Worley, D. R., & Stasz, C. (1989). *Understanding commanders' information needs. R-3761-A.* Santa Monica, CA: Rand Corporation.

Kahneman, D., & Tversky, A. (1973). On the psychology of prediction. *Psychological Review, 80*, 237–251.

Kahneman, D., & Tversky, A. (1982). On the study of statistical intuitions. *Cognition, 11*, 123–141.

Kahneman, D., Slovic, P., & Tversky, A. (Eds.). (1982). *Judgment under uncertainty: Heuristic and biases.* Cambridge: Cambridge University Press.

Keller, L. R., & Ho, J. L. (1988). Decision problem structuring: Generating options. *IEEE Transactions on Systems, Man, and Cybernetics, 18*(5).

Kepner, C. H., & Tregoe, B. B. (1965). *The rational manager.* New York: McGraw-Hill.

Kepner, C. H., & Tregoe, B. B. (1981). *The new rational manager.* Princeton, NJ: Princeton Research Press.

Kirlik, A., Rothrock, L., Walker, N., & Fisk, A. D. (1996). Simple strategies or simple tasks? Dynamic decision making in "complex" worlds. *Proceedings of the Human Factors and Ergonomics Society 40th Annual meeting,* Philadelphia.

Klein, G. A. (1986). Validity of analogical predictions. *Technological Forecasting and Social Change, 30*, 139–148.

Klein, G. A. (1987). Applications of analogical reasoning. *Metaphor and Symbolic Activity, 2*, 201–218.

Klein, G. A. (1989). Do decision biases explain too much? *Bulletin - Human Factors Society, 23*(5), 1–3.

Klein, G. (1993). Sources of error in naturalistic decision making tasks. In *Proceedings of the Human Factors and Ergonomics Society, 37th Annual Meeting* (pp. 368–371).

Klein, G. (1994). A script for the commander's intent statement. In A. H. Levis & L. S. Levis (Eds.), *Science of command and control: Part III: Coping with change.* Fairfax, VA: AFCEA International Press.

Klein, G. A. (1996). The effect of acute stressors on decision making. In J. E. Driskell & E. Salas (Eds.), *Stress and human performance.* Hillsdale, NJ: Erlbaum.

Klein, G. (1997). Developing expertise in decision making. *Thinking & Reasoning, 3*(4), 337–352.

Klein, G. A., & Brezovic, C. P. (1986). Design engineers and the design process: Decision strategies and human factors literature. In *Proceedings of the 30th Annual Human Factors Society, 2* (pp. 771–775). Dayton, OH: Human Factors Society.

Klein, G. A., Calderwood, R., & MacGregor, D. (1989). Critical decision method for eliciting knowledge. *IEEE Transactions on Systems, Man, and Cybernetics, 19*(3), 462–472.

Klein, G. A., & Crandall, B. (1992). *Recognition-primed decision strategies. Contract MDA903–89-C-0032.* Alexandria, VA: U.S. Army Research Institute.

Klein, G., & Crandall, B. W. (1995). The role of mental simulation in naturalistic decision making. In P. Hancock, J. Flach, J. Caird, & K. Vicente (Eds.), *Local applications of the ecological approach to human-machine systems.* Hillsdale, NJ: Erlbaum.

Klein, G., & Hutton, R. (1995). *The innovators: High-impact researchers at the Armstrong Laboratory Human Engineering Division AL/CF-FR-1995–0027 Wright-Patterson AFB.* OH: Armstrong Laboratory.

Klein, G., Kaempf, G., Thordsen, M., Wolf, S., & Miller, T. (1996). The uses of decision requirements. *International Journal of Human-Computer Studies, 46,* 1–15.

Klein, G., Orasanu, J., Calderwood, R., & Zsambok, C. E. (1993). *Decision making in action: Models and methods.* Norwood, NJ: Ablex.

Klein, G. A., & Weitzenfeld, J. (1978). Improvement of skills for solving illdefined problems. *Educational Psychologist, 13,* 31–41.

Klein, G. A., & Weitzenfeld, J. (1982). The use of analogues in comparability analysis. *Applied Ergonomics, 13,* 99–104.

Klein, G. A., Zsambok, C. E., & Thordsen, M. L. (1993, April). Team decision training: Five myths and a model. *Military Review,* 36–42.

Klein, G., Wolf, S., Militello, L., and Zsambok, C. (1995). Characteristics of skilled option generation in chess. *Organizational Behavior and Human Decision Processes, 61*(3).

Klein, H. A., & Klein, G. A. (1981). Perceptual/cognitive analysis of proficient cardiopulmonary resuscitation (CPR) performance. Paper presented at the Midwestern Psychological Association Meetings, Chicago.

Klinger, D. W., Andriole, S. J., Militello, L. G., Adelman, L., Klein, G., & Gomes, M. E. (1993). *Designing for performance: A cognitive systems engineering approach to modifying an AWACS human-computer interface. AL/CF-TR-1993–0093. Wright-Patterson AFB.* OH: Department of the Air Force, Armstrong Laboratory, Air Force Materiel Command.

Klinger, D. W., & Gomes, M. G. (1993). A cognitive systems engineering application for interface design. In *Proceedings of the Human Factors Ergonomics Society 1993 Annual Meeting* (pp. 16–20). Seattle.

Kolodner, J. (1993). *Case-based reasoning.* San Mateo, CA: Morgan Kaufmann.

Lakoff, G. (1986). A figure of thought. *Metaphor and Symbolic Activity, 1*(3), 215–225.

Lakoff, G., & Johnson, M. (1980). *Metaphors we live by.* Chicago: University of Chicago Press.

Lenat, D. B. (1984). Computer software for intelligent systems. *Scientific American, 251*(3), 204–213.

Lesgold, A., Rubinson, H., Feltovicb, P., Glaser, R., Klopfer, D., & Wang, Y. (1988). Expertise in a complex skill: Diagnosing x-ray pictures. In M. Chi, R. Glaser, & M. J. Farr (Eds.), *The nature of expertise.* Hillsdale, NJ: Erlbaum.

Lipshitz, R., & Bar-Ilan, O. (1996). How problems are solved: Reconsidering the phase theorem. *Organizational Behavior and Human Decision Processes, 65,* 48–60.

Lipshitz, R., & Shaul, O. B. (1997). Schemata and mental models in recognition-primed decision making. In C. Zsambok & G. Klein (Eds.), *Naturalistic decision making* (pp. 293–304). Mahwah, NJ: Erlbaum.

Lopes, L. L. (1991). The rhetoric of irrationality. *Theory & Psychology, 1*(1), 65–82.

Lovell, J., & Kluger, J. (1994). *Apollo 13. New York: Simon & Schuster.* Mager, R. F. *(1972). Goal analysis.* Belmont, CA: Fearon.

McKenzie, C. (1994). The accuracy of intuitive judgment strategies: Covariation assessment and Bayesian inference. *Cognitive Psychology, 26*(3), 209–239.

Means, B., Salas, E., Crandall, B., & Jacobs, O. (1993). Training decision makers for the real world. In G. A. Klein, J. Orasanu, R. Calderwood, & C. E. Zsambok (Eds.), *Decision making in action: Models and methods* (pp. 306–326). Norwood, NJ: Ablex.

Militello, L. G., & Hutton, R. J. B. (1998). Applied cognitive task analysis (ACTA): A practitioner's toolkit for understanding cognitive task demands. *Ergonomics, 41*(11), 1618–1641.

Miller, T. E., Klein, G., & Law, B. A. (1997). Modeling distributed planning teams. *Proceedings of the Third International Command and Control Research and Technology Symposium* (pp. 560–572).

Minsky, M. (1986). *The society of mind.* New York: Simon & Schuster.

Mintzberg, H. (1994). *The rise and fall of strategic planning: Reconceiving roles for planning, plans, planners.* New York: The Free Press.

Mintzberg, H., Raisinghani, D., & Theoret, A. (1976). The structure of unstructured decision processes. *Administrative Science Quarterly, 21,* 246–275.

Mitchell, D. J., Russo, J. E., & Pennington, N. (1989). Back to the future: Temporal perspective in the explanation of events. *Journal of Behavioral Decision Making, 2,* 25–38.

Mitroff, I. I. (1981). Scientists and confirmation bias. In R. D. Tweney, M. D. Doherty, & C. R. Mynatt (Eds.), *On scientific thinking.* New York: Columbia University Press.

Mosier, K. L. (1991). Expert decision making strategies. In P. Jersen (Ed.), *Proceedings of the Sixth International Symposium on Aviation Psychology* (pp. 266–271). Columbus, OH.

Mullen, B., Johnson, C., & Salas, E. (1991). Productivity loss in brainstorming groups: A meta-analytic integration. *Basic and Applied Social Psychology, 12*(1), 3–23.

Mumaw, R. J., Roth, E. M., & Schoenfeld, I. (1993). Analysis of complexity in nuclear accident management. *Proceedings of the Human Factors and Ergonomics Society 37th Annual Meeting,* pp. 377–381.

Newell, A. (1990). *Unified theories of cognition.* Cambridge, MA: Harvard University Press.

Newell, A., & Simon, H. A. (1972). *Human problem solving.* Englewood Cliffs, NJ: Prentice Hall.

Nisbett, R. E. (1993). *Rules for reasoning.* Hillsdale, NJ: Erlbaum.

Olson, D. (1970). Language and thought: Aspects of a cognitive theory of semantics. *Psychological Review, 77*(4), 257–273.

Orasanu, J., & Connolly, T. (1993). The reinvention of decision making. In G. Klein, J. Orasanu, R. Calderwood, & C. E. Zsambok (Eds.), *Decision making in action: Models and methods* (pp. 3–20). Norwood, NJ: Ablex.

Orasanu, J., & Fischer, U. (1997). Finding decisions in natural environments: The view from the cockpit. In C. Zsambok & G. Klein (Eds.), *Naturalistic decision making* (pp. 343–358). Mahwah, NJ: Erlbaum.

Orasanu, J., & Salas, E. (1993). Team decision making in complex environments. In G. A. Klein, J. Orasanu, R. Calderwood, & C. E. Zsambok (Eds.), *Decision making in action: Models and methods* (pp. 327–345). Norwood, NJ: Ablex.

Pascual, R., & Henderson, S. (1997). Evidence of naturalistic decision making in C2. In C. Zsambok & G. Klein (Eds.), *Naturalistic decision making.* Mahwah, NJ: Erlbaum.

Pennington, N., & Hastie, R. (1993). A theory of explanation-based decision making. In G. Klein, J. Orasanu, R. Calderwood, & C. E. Zsambok (Eds.), *Decision making in action: Models and methods* (pp. 188–201). Norwood, NJ: Ablex.

Perrow, C. (1984). *Normal accidents: Living with high-risk technologies.* New York: Basic Books.

Pious, S. (1993). *The psychology of judgment and decision making.* Philadelphia: Temple University Press.

Popper, K. (1959). *The logic of scientific discovery.* New York: Basic Books.

Randel, J. M., Pugh, H., & Reed, S. K. (1996). Methods for analyzing cognitive skills for a technical task. *International Journal of Human-Computer Studies, 45,* 579–597.

Rasmussen, J. (1974). *The human data processor as a system component: Bits and pieces of a model. Riso-M-1722.* Roskilde, Denmark: Danish Atomic Energy Commission, Research Establishment Riso.

Rasmussen, J. (1983). Skill, rules and knowledge: Signals, signs, and symbols, and other distinctions in human performance models. *IEEE Transactions on Systems, Man, and Cybernetics, SMC-13*(3), 257–266.

Rasmussen, J. (1993). Diagnostic reasoning in action. *IEEE Transactions on Systems, Man, and Cybernetics, 23*(4), 981–991.

Reason, J. (1990). *Human error.* Cambridge, MA: Cambridge University Press.

Reber, A. S. (1993). *Implicit learning and tacit knowledge: An essay on the cognitive unconscious.* New York: Oxford University Press.

Redding, R. E., & Seamster, T. L. (1994). Cognitive task analysis in air traffic controller and aviation crew training. In N. Johnston, N. McDonald, & R.

Fuller (Eds.), *Aviation psychology in practice*. Brookfield, VT: Ashgate Publishing Company.

Reder, L. M. (1982). Plausibility judgments vs. fact retrieval: Alternative strategies for sentence verification. *Psychological Review, 89,* 250–280.

Reder, L., Wible, C., & Martin, J. (1986). Differential memory change with age: Exact retrieval versus plausible inference. *Journal of Experimental Psychology: Learning, Memory, and Cognition, 12,* 72–81.

Reitman, W. R. (1965). *Cognition and thought.* New York: Wiley.

Roberts, N. C., & Dotterway, K. A. (1995). The *Vincennes* incident: Another player on the stage? *Defense Analysis, 11,* 31–45.

Roediger, H. L., III. (1990). Implicit memory: Retention without remembering. *American Psychologist, 45,* 1042–1056.

Roth, E. (1997). Analysis of decision making in nuclear power plant emergencies: An investigation of aided decision making. In C. Zsambok & G. Klein (Eds.), *Naturalistic decision making.* Mahwah, NJ: Erlbaum.

Russo, J. E., & Shoemaker, P. J. H. (1989). *Decision traps: Ten barriers to brilliant decision making.* Garden City, NY: Doubleday.

Schank, R. C. (1990). *Tell me a story: A new look at real and artificial memory.* New York: MacMillan.

Schank, R. C., & Owens, C. C. (1987). *Ten problems in artificial intelligence.* New Haven, CT: Yale University, Department of Computer Science.

Schmitt, J. F. (1994). *Masteringtactics.* Quantico, VA: Marine Corps Association.

Schmitt, J. F., & Klein, G. (1996). Fighting in the fog: Dealing with battlefield uncertainty. *Marine Corps Gazette, 80,* 62–69.

Schwartz, P. (1991). *The art of the long view.* Garden City, NY: Doubleday.

Shanteau, J. (1988). Psychological characteristics and strategies of expert decision makers. *Acta Psychologica, 68,* 203–215.

Shanteau, J. (1992). Competence in experts: The role of task characteristics. *Organizational Behavior and Human Decision Processes, 53,* 252–266.

Shattuck, L. (1995). *Communication of intent in distributed supervisory control systems.* Ph.D. dissertation, Ohio State University.

Shreeve, J. (1995). The brain that misplaced its body *Discover, 16*(5).

Shulman, L. S. (1965). Seeking styles and individual differences in patterns of inquiry *School Review, 73,* 258–266.

Shulman, L. S., Loupe, M. J., & Piper, R. M. (1968). *Studies of the process: Inquiry patterns of students in teacher-training programs.* East Lansing: Educational Publications Services, Michigan State University.

Simon, H. A. (1957). *Models of man: Social and rational.* New York: Wiley.

Sloman, S. (1996). The empirical case for two systems of reasoning. *Psychiatric Bulletin, 119*(1), 3–22.

Smith, J. B. (1994). *Collective intelligence in computer-based collaboration.* Hillsdale, NJ: Erlbaum.

Smith, J. F., & Kida, T. (1991). Heuristics and biases: Expertise and task realism in auditing. *Psychological Bulletin, 109*(3), 472–489.

Soelberg, P. O. (1967). Unprogrammed decision making. *Industrial Management Review, 8*, 19–29.

Solomon, A. (1996). Questions of genius. *New Yorker (New York, N.Y.)*, 112–123.

Sternberg, R. (1990). *Wisdom: Its nature, origins, and development.* Cambridge, MA: Harvard University Press.

Sternberg, R. J. (1977). Component processes in analogical reasoning. *Psychological Review, 84*, 353–378.

Stewart, T. A. (1994). Your company's most valuable asset: Intellectual capital. *Fortune*, October 3, 68–74.

Stich, S. P. (1990). *The fragmentation of reason: Preface to a pragmatic theory of cognitive evaluation.* Cambridge, MA: MIT Press.

Stokes, A., Belger, A., & Zhang, K. (1990). *Investigation of factors comprising a model of pilot decision making: Part II. Anxiety and cognitive strategies in expert and novice aviators. ARL-90–8/SCEEE-90–2.* Urbana-Champaign, IL: Institute of Aviation.

Stout, R. J., Cannon-Bowers, J. A., & Salas, E. (1997). The role of shared mental models in developing team situational awareness: Implications for training. *Training Research Journal, 2*, 85–116.

Svenson, O. (1979). Process descriptions of decision making. *Organizational Behavior and Human Performance, 23*, 86–112.

Sweller, J. (1988). Cognitive load during problem solving: Effects on learning. *Cognitive Science, 12*, 257–285.

Taynor, J., Crandall, B., & Wiggins, S. (1987). *The reliability of the critical decision method. Contract MDA903–86-C-0170.* Alexandria, VA: U.S. Army Research Institute Field Unit.

Tuchman, B. W. (1962). *The guns of August.* New York: Bantam Books.

Tversky, A. (1972). Elimination by aspects: A theory of choice. *Psychological Review, 79*(4), 281–299.

Tversky, A. (1977). Features of similarity. *Psychological Review, 84*, 327–352.

Tversky, A., & Kahneman, D. (1974). Judgment under uncertainty: Heuristics and biases. *Science, 185*, 1124–1131.

Tversky, A., & Kahneman, D. (1980). Causal schemas in judgments under uncertainty. In M. Fishbein (Ed.), *Progress in social psychology* (Vol. 1). Hillsdale, NJ: Erlbaum.

Tynan, K. (1994). Life and letters: Between the acts. *New Yorker (New York, N.Y.), 70*(35), 82–89.

Voss, J. F., Greene, T. R., Post, T. A., & Penner, B. C. (1983). Problem solving skill in the social sciences. In G. H. Bower (Ed.), *The psychology of learning and motivation: Advances in research theory, 17.* New York: Academic Press.

Wack, P. (1985a). Scenarios: Uncharted water ahead. *Harvard Business Review*, 63(5), 72–89.

Wack, P. (1985b). Scenarios: Shooting the rapids (part 2). *Harvard Business Review*, 63(6), 139–150.

Wegner, D. (1987). Transactive memory: A contemporary analysis of group mind. In B. Mullen & G. R. Goethals (Eds.), *Theories of group behavior* (pp. 185–208). New York: Springer-Verlag.

Weick, K. E. (1983). Managerial thought in the context of action. In S. Srivastva (Ed.), *The executive mind* (pp. 221–242). San Francisco, CA: Jossey-Bass.

Weitzenfeld, J. (1984). Valid reasoning by analogy: Technological reasoning. *Philosophy of Science, 51*, 137–149.

Wertheimer, M. (1959). *Productive thinking*. New York: Harper & Row.

Wiener, E. L. (1989). *Human factors of advanced technology ("glass cockpit") transport aircraft (NASA Report 177528)*. Moffett Field, CA: Ames Research Center.

Wilensky, R. (1983). Story grammars versus story points. In *Behavioral and Brain Sciences*, 579–623. New York, NY: Cambridge University Press.

Wilson, T. D., & Schooler, J. W. (1991). Thinking too much: Introspection can reduce the quality of preferences and decisions. *Journal of Personality and Social Psychology, 60*, 181–192.

Wohl, J. C. (1981). Force management decision requirements for Air Force tactical command and control. *IEEE Transactions on Systems, Man, and Cybernetics*, 618–639.

Wohlstetter, R. (1962). *Pearl Harbor: Warning and decision*. Stanford, CA: Stanford University Press.

Woods, D. D. (1993). Process-tracing methods for the study of cognition outside of the experimental psychology laboratory. In G. A. Klein, J. Orasanu, R. Calderwood, and C. E. Zsambok (Eds.), *Decision Making in Action: Models and Methods* (pp. 228–251). Norwood, NJ: Ablex.

Woods, D. D., Johannesen, L. J., Cook, R. I., & Sarter, N. B. (1993). *Behind human error: Cognitive systems, computers and hindsight. State-of-the-Art Report*. Dayton, OH: CSERIAC.

Wu, J. S., Apostolakis, G. E., & Okrent, D. (1991). On the inclusion of organizational and managerial influences in probabilistic safety assessments of nuclear power plants. In B. J. Garrick & W. C. Gekler (Eds.), *The analysis, communication, and perception of risk*. New York: Plenum Press.

Xiao, Y., Milgram, P., & Doyle, D. J. (1997). Capturing and modeling planning expertise in anesthesiology: Results of a field study. In C. Zsambok & G. Klein (Eds.), *Naturalistic decision making* (pp. 197–206). Mahwah, NJ: Erlbaum.

Yates, J. F. (1990). *Judgment and decision making*. Englewood Cliffs, NJ: Prentice Hall.

Zakay, D., & Wooler, S. (1984). Time pressure, training, and decision effectiveness. *Ergonomics, 27,* 273–284.

Zsambok, C. E. (1993). Advanced team decision making in C2 settings. In *Proceedings of the 1993 Symposium on Command and Control Research* (pp. 45–52). McLean, VA: Information Systems Division, Science Applications International Corporation.

Zsambok, C., Crandall, B., & Militello, L. (1994). *OJT: Models, programs, and related issues. Prepared under contract MDA903–93-C-0092.* Alexandria, VA: U.S. Army Research Institute for the Behavioral and Social Sciences.

Zsambok, C. E., & Klein, G. (1997). *Naturalistic decision making.* Mahwah, NJ: Erlbaum.

Index